CAMBRIDGE ENGLISH PROSE TEXTS

Critics of Capitalism

CAMBRIDGE ENGLISH PROSE TEXTS

General editor: GRAHAM STOREY

OTHER BOOKS IN THE SERIES
English Science: Bacon to Newton, edited by Brian Vickers
Revolutionary Prose of the English Civil War, edited by
Howard Erskine-Hill and Graham Storey
American Colonial Prose: John Smith to Thomas Jefferson,
edited by Mary Ann Radzinowicz
Burke, Paine, Godwin and the Revolution Controversy, edited by
Marilyn Butler
The Evangelical and Oxford Movements, edited by Elisabeth Jay
Science and Religion in the Nineteenth Century, edited by Tess Cosslett

FORTHCOMING
The English Mystics of the Middle Ages, edited by Barry Windeatt
The Impact of Humanism, 1530–1650, edited by Dominic Baker-Smith
Romantic Critical Essays, edited by David Bromwich

Critics of Capitalism
Victorian Reactions to 'Political Economy'

edited by

ELISABETH JAY

and

RICHARD JAY

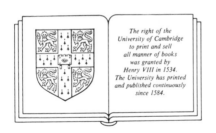

CAMBRIDGE UNIVERSITY PRESS

Cambridge

London   New York   New Rochelle

Melbourne   Sydney

Published by the Press Syndicate of the University of Cambridge
The Pitt Building, Trumpington Street, Cambridge CB2 1RP
32 East 57th Street, New York, NY 10022, USA
10 Stamford Road, Oakleigh, Melbourne, 3166, Australia

First published 1986

Printed in Great Britain at
the University Press Cambridge

British Library cataloguing in publication data

Critics of capitalism: Victorian reactions to
'political economy'. – (Cambridge English prose texts)
1. Economics   2. Social policy
1. Jay, Elisabeth   11. Jay, Richard
330.15′5   HB199

Library of Congress cataloguing in publication data

Critics of capitalism.
(Cambridge English prose texts)
Bibliography
1. English prose literature – 19th century. 2. Criticism – Great Britain.
3. Socialism – Great Britain – History – 19th century – Sources.
4. Capitalism – Great Britain – History – 19th century – Sources.
5. Great Britain – Politics and government – 1837–1901.
6. Great Britain – Economic conditions – 19th century.
1. Jay, Elisabeth. 11. Jay, Richard. 111. Series.
PR1304.C75 1986   828′.808′08   86–9604

ISBN 0 521 26588 6 hard covers
ISBN 0 521 31962 5 paperback

Contents

Editorial note

Where appropriate, the extracts have been taken from the first edition of the particular work. Authorial footnotes, where retained, have been included in the endnotes; editorial footnotes are indicated by letter, and endnotes by number. In bibliographical references, the place of publication is London unless otherwise stated. As a matter of convenience we have used the capitalised phrase Political Economy to refer to the body of economic ideas which the Victorians themselves categorised under this label, though it should be borne in mind that, as the introductory essay points out, it was a label which obscured many differences among the classical economic writers. We are grateful to Professor R. D. C. Black for commenting upon an earlier draft of the introduction, though, of course, the responsibility for any remaining errors lies with us. Laurence and Wishart Ltd have kindly granted permission to reproduce material from their *Marx and Engels Collected Works*.

Introductory essay

Confronted with Ruskin's *Unto This Last*, Shaw's *Fabian Essays*, or Morris's socialist lectures, a student of literature in the late twentieth century is inclined to regard them as aberrant from, or merely marginal to, their more 'imaginative' writings. A cursory glance at their contents appears to confirm a topicality long-outdated, and a subject-matter and terminology now considered to be the province of specialists. Such volumes are once again relegated to the murkier recesses of the college library or second-hand bookshop.

It is the intention behind this volume to rehabilitate the literature of the Victorian debate on Political Economy by suggesting that the individual works selected here are best seen, not as random or eccentric pronouncements, but as central to their authors' respective visions of society. Recognising the extent to which manipulation of the economy was in fact the source of the power to shape society, present and future, the critics of Political Economy regarded the subject as far too important to be abandoned to self-proclaimed specialists. Indeed, the early economists themselves had invariably turned to the subject either as part of some more wide-ranging intellectual inquiry, or as the groundwork for some special study. Adam Smith (1723–90) was a Professor of Moral Philosophy; Thomas Robert Malthus (1766–1834) was an Anglican clergyman, who initially formulated his theory of overpopulation as a challenge to the radical–democratic optimism of Rousseau, Condorcet and Godwin, and went on to hold the first designated chair of Political Economy; David Ricardo (1772–1823) was a successful stockbroker, whose bent towards theoretical analysis was stimulated by disputes over banking policy. A comment made in 1833, that 'whoever will desire to know hereafter the character of our times, must find it in the philosophy of the Economists' (Edward Bulwer, *England and the English*, 2 vols., 1833, II, 160), illustrates the fact that, up until the 1870s, Political Economy was not conceived of merely as a technical mathematical discipline, but as a set of hypotheses and conclusions of analysis derived from a distinct philosophical, political and social perspective. Working on this volume in a year which has seen heightened public debate upon the meaning and contemporary relevance of 'Victorian values', and Bishops of the Church of England seeking to familiarise themselves with 'monetarist' theories in order to offer a convincing challenge to prevailing political viewpoints, has suggested that we may be in a peculiarly favourable position to appreciate the origins of the Victorian debate itself, and the subsequent polarisation of views which took place.

Those whom the Victorians conceived of as 'the' Political Economists are today described as members of the 'classical school'. Adam Smith's *The Wealth of Nations* (1776) was the generally acknowledged masterpiece of the school. Its mode of reasoning and powerful technical apparatus inspired major intellectual advances during the early decades of the nineteenth century as writers like Malthus and Ricardo, together with less original figures such as J. B. Say (1767–1832), James Mill (1773–1836), Nassau Senior (1773–1836), Robert Torrens (1780–1864) and J. R. McCulloch (1789–1864), attempted to develop, correct and update Smith's arguments and conclusions. Like all burgeoning disciplines, economics in these years revealed a great diversity of viewpoints. Malthus and Ricardo, for instance, though friends in constant communication with each other, differed fundamentally over key methodological and substantive issues. In 1821, James Mill instigated the foundation of a Political Economy Club to propagate the new discipline, but it became within a short space of time a forum for acrimonious dispute among the leading practitioners. The scope and power of classical economics is displayed by the fact that Victorian writers like John Bray, J. S. Mill and Karl Marx, represented in this volume, succeeded in using its basic tenets to further profoundly different social and political conclusions. 'Political Economy', however, signified for the Victorian general reading public something rather different from this evolving intellectual discourse. By the early 1830s the concept had, like 'monetarism' in our own day, become something of a catch-phrase, its adherents identified in the popular mind as advocates of materialism, wealth accumulation, free trade and unbridled economic competition, and as exponents of a 'dismal science', in Carlyle's dismissive phrase, of determinate iron laws impervious to the intervention of human agency. In large measure a spurious uniformity was imposed upon the discipline by social critics who lumped together all those whose study was the wealth, rather than the moral and spiritual welfare, of nations, and who erroneously identified economic doctrines as the source of the social ills they condemned. Such critics were aided by the fact that, once the writings of the economists left

2

the study and became popularised, often for ideological purposes, in parliament, journals, pamphlets and the kind of catechism for schools satirised by Dickens in *Hard Times*, they became simplified, distorted and reconstructed as a body of orthodox dogma. A large measure of responsibility for checking the intellectual polarisation, both within and about economics, which had developed by the early Victorian period, falls to J. S. Mill's *Principles of Political Economy* (1848). This classic Victorian text-book ran through seven two-volume editions (together with a single-volume popular edition) in Mill's lifetime, and was read by students, laymen and educated working class alike. Refining Ricardian economics, it appeared to resolve many incongruities in the earlier systems, and to put a very much more humane face upon the 'dismal science' of the previous generation.

The study of economic life as a distinct field of intellectual inquiry had not been Adam Smith's invention. It had emerged in the seventeenth century as thinkers challenged the traditional practice of judging human behaviour according to Christian ethics, and began to search, first, for the foundations of a moral science to match the successes of the burgeoning natural sciences, and secondly, for principles of 'statecraft' appropriate to the growing autonomy of secular political rulers. The moral questions which preoccupied medieval and early Renaissance writers – definition of the 'just price', the relative merits of 'frugality' and 'generosity' as personal or public virtues, the 'rights' of different social strata over God-given natural resources – were not wholly abandoned but became increasingly shaped by a framework of inquiry devoted to studying the sources of national and personal wealth, and the social consequences of men acting according to their 'natural' passions and desires. In this respect, the impact of *The Wealth of Nations* derived, not from its novelty, but from Smith's achievement in organising, and expounding in simple terms, a vast array of economic and political phenomena by means of a few basic principles.

In particular, Smith's work was a reaction to two views of economic life current in the eighteenth century: mercantilism and the physiocratic school. Both systems inquired into the sources of national wealth and economic growth, and the roots of the 'surplus' over a static level of subsistence which any economy had to generate to promote material improvement. Mercantilism reflected the predominant approach of contemporary governments. It tended to contemplate the problem from the point of view of state rulers confronted by an unstable balance of power in international affairs, relating national wealth to the strength and prosperity of the state.

The surplus for economic growth was identified primarily with a favourable balance of overseas trade which would fuel state revenues by means of tariffs and the sale of government franchises to trading companies. Under this system, regulating trade, exploiting colonial possessions, promoting manufactures, and encouraging population growth as the raw material of production and armed might, were all seen as legitimate areas of state activity to enhance its own strength against foreign rivals. The physiocrats, by contrast, had focussed upon agriculture, rather than overseas trade, as the only genuinely 'productive' sector of an economy capable of generating an economic surplus. In agriculture, 'Nature' herself added to the stock of human necessities. Whereas manufacturing and trade merely 'combined' and distributed economic resources without adding to their value, claimed the physiocrats, the application of labour and capital to land directly enhanced the stock of social wealth. Although this school advocated a role for the state in providing a framework of ordered economic life, and in eliminating traditional privileges and practices which militated against economic growth, it popularised the phrase *laissez-faire, laissez-passer* ('let it be, let it go') in opposition to the mercantilist conception of a state actively intervening in the processes of production and exchange. Tariffs, complex systems of taxation, and the direct promotion of manufacturing trade and production, rather than stimulating growth, instead distorted 'natural' agrarian investment opportunities which allowed the productive farming class to create a surplus.

More technically sophisticated than its mercantilist rival, physio-cratic economics was a central inspiration for Smith, and much more attuned to the liberal temper of the whole Anglo-Scottish classical school. Adam Smith's crucial innovation, however, was to shift the emphasis from agriculture to industry as the creator of the economic surplus. The first volume of his masterpiece was a veritable hymn to the 'division of labour' and the specialisation of tasks embodied in new machinery which capital accumulation in the manufacturing sector encouraged. This, for Smith, was the secret of economic progress, a progress whose only natural limitation was the potential size of the market to which finished commodities could be sold.

As with the physiocrats, 'The Natural' was a key concept in Smithian economics. Subscribing to the Enlightenment doctrines of 'natural religion', Smith was concerned to identify the natural order first ordained by a benevolent Prime Mover as a guide to the arrangement of social and political conventions most conducive to human welfare. He belonged to the Scottish 'moral sense' school of philosophy which rejected the orthodox Christian and rationalist ethical view of an antipathy between morality and human desires, and identified moral sentiments as endemic to human nature, positing human happiness as the ultimate goal of both individual and social action. Man, according to Smith, was characterised by three sets of countervailing motives – self-love and sympathy; the desires for freedom and for social approval; the 'habit of labour' and a 'propensity to truck and barter' – and Nature was capable of harmonising these to produce a social order in which individuals, acting out of self-interest automatically promoted the social good. In the pre-Smithian language of Mandeville's *Fable of the Bees* (1714), 'private vices' produced 'public benefits', or, stated in Smith's economic application of the doctrine, the pursuit of self-interest within a system of free labour and exchange tended inherently to promote both social wealth and a natural harmony of interests without the extraneous imposition of binding moral rules or the arm of public authority.

In analysing the operations of what he called a 'natural system of liberty', Smith developed four major themes. First, that behind the apparently random transactions of the market place, there lay a 'hidden hand' which, operating through the interaction of supply and demand and the free movement of prices, automatically directed resources to their most productive use. Secondly, that the components of a market economy were best defined, not as the physiocrats had done by different sectors – trade, agriculture, manufacturing – but by types of income – wages, profit, rents. By dramatic oversimplification, Smith identified these categories with three social classes: wages paid to the labourer for his labour; profit gained, and reinvested for future growth, by the organiser of labour – the capitalist; and rent, appropriated by the landowner for allowing his land to be used for production and extraction. Smith implied that economic freedom would ensure for each class its 'natural' share of national income. Labour, for instance, would normally receive what was necessary for it to live and reproduce at subsistence level; but, in an expanding economy, all classes would find themselves benefiting, though not necessarily equally, from rising production. Thirdly, that the free play of market forces tended, over time, to ensure that the 'market prices' of commodities would fluctuate around their 'natural price', or 'value'. All the classical school felt the need to specify a non-monetary standard embodied in different commodities. This was partly to explain how goods of different kinds could be exchanged for each other at fixed ratios on the market, partly in order to be able to produce an indicator of 'real' as opposed to purely 'monetary' national wealth and growth, partly to differentiate between economic activity which was 'productive' (i.e., capable of adding to the stock of wealth), and 'unproductive' activity which merely appropriated or recirculated that wealth. Despite the fact that the classical economists tended to embrace some version of utilitarian moral philosophy, they did not, as did their late-nineteenth-century successors, posit 'utility' ('usefulness') as the central tool of analysis. Instead, they derived from the seventeenth-century writers, John Locke and William Petty, a view that the 'real' value of commodities was determined by their cost of production, and ultimately the value of labour involved in their creation. The 'labour theory of value' had an inherent plausibility: air and water, Smith argued, commanded no market price despite their enormous utility because they were direct products of nature unmediated by human labour. Yet the theory posed continuous problems. How was the 'value' of labour to be defined? How could the contributions of 'Nature' and machinery to the value of production be measured in terms of it? Were profits and rents rewards for adding to the value of commodities or extractions from value already created by the labourer and, hence, returns for 'unproductive' activity? In the writings of the 'Ricardian socialists' like Bray (extract 1) and of Karl Marx, this last view came to pose a challenge to the role of the profit motive and of the capitalist in the process of wealth creation, and hence to subvert Political Economy itself. Extract 7 from Ruskin, additionally, reveals how slippery such basic concepts as 'wealth', 'value' and 'productive labour' could prove in the hands of an implacable critic of the whole system of thought.

The fourth aspect of Smith's system was its bias towards *laissez-faire*. The title 'Political' Economy connoted a discipline devoted not merely to analysing economic relations, but also to formulating public policy. In his *Principles of Political Economy* (1767), Sir James Steuart (1712–80), the last and perhaps greatest of the mercantilists, had insisted that competitive economic relations rooted in the pursuit of self-interest would necessarily require a constant super-visory role for government; Smith's belief in the automatic operation of the 'hidden hand' allowed him to confine state activity to the role of supplementing a market economy only in three major areas: national defence, 'the exact administration of justice', and the pro-vision of such public utilities as education, roads and bridges. Later popularisers and critics of Smithian economics were largely respon-sible for erroneously equating Political Economy with an unqualified adherence to *laissez-faire* and identifying the Victorian period with the triumph of the doctrine. If, however, it is possible to talk of an 'era of *laissez-faire*', this was a short-lived and pre-Victorian phenomenon. Smith's three qualifications were much more in tune with practical political needs than were the theoretical abstractions of his free-market model, and they opened up a potentially wide area of discretionary government activity. For his intellectual successors, and the Victorian public servants inspired by them, Political Economy was not merely, or even, the science of free markets, but, as the titles of so many of their published works testify, a set of 'principles' which helped in formulating constructive social policies and estimating an equitable distribution of the burdens of public expenditure. In their sweeping condemnations of the age, writers like Carlyle and Ruskin muddied the waters even further by assimilating their attack upon *laissez-faire* with that upon government activity inspired by, as they saw it, such narrowly utilitarian considerations.

In response to the system articulated by Smith and his successors, two major lines of criticism emerged. First, Political Economy had been developed on the presupposition that the moral sciences, including economics, could be studied according to the Newtonian paradigm for the physical sciences of universal mechanical laws. Whether such an abstract deductive system was applicable to the works of human nature was open to question. Did the concept of 'economic man' as an egoistical, rational calculator of material interests not ignore motives of duty and service which lay behind even business transactions? Was labour a necessary evil to be obtained only by the alternate applications of monetary sticks and carrots, or was it, as Romantic critics affirmed, an inherent desire for creativity deformed only by the brutalising process of machine production? Such questions in turn raised others about the historical roots of capitalism and its cultural and institutional framework. *The Wealth of Nations* had been a product of the Franco-Scottish historical school's speculations about the relations between human civilisations and economic systems, and abounded in empirical and quasi-historical observations about the specific factors shaping the modern world of commerce; among Smith's followers, history yielded to an analytical approach which assumed such things as free labour, the profit motive and property relations. Only later in the century did a more historical dimension emphasising the relativity of such concepts re-emerge, as contrasts between the development of British institutions and those of other economies became clearer, and with the increasing popularity of evolutionary theories derived from biology and German historical philosophy.

The second line of criticism was levelled at Political Economy's moral bias towards secular hedonism. Despite the theological under-pinnings of Smith's thinking, or the personal religious faith of Malthus, the close connections between most leading economists and the Bentham–Mill school of utilitarianism appeared to confirm the subject as atheistic and materialist. It could be charged with dissolving the distinction between morality and self-interest, and, in Carlyle's famous phrase, reducing all human life to the 'nexus of cash relations'. Such accusations were often misleading. Hedonism as defined by the early utilitarians was a distinctive ethical system concerned with enhancing human welfare and rationality. Moreover, Political Economy acquired a popular moral legitimacy insofar as the virtues it propounded as integral to the 'spirit of capitalism' corres-ponded with those of the 'protestant ethic': reliance upon individual judgement and effort, and the sacrifice of immediate gratification for future reward.

The fact that such virtues were claimed by the early economists to be particularly the prerogative of the 'middling rank' of society laid them open to the charge that their doctrines were mere ideological weapons in the articulation of selfish class interests, a charge which any examination of Victorian popular propaganda might support, but one not entirely fair in the case of the leading thinkers. J. S. Mill, the leading mid-Victorian exponent of Political Economy, was at pains to distance the subject from identification with any specific class interest, and developed a radical attack upon the restricted quality of life under capitalism. Even Smith, however, had delivered strictures on the morally stultifying consequences of economic specialisation, and the propensity of the capitalist to conspire with others against the interests of the public.

In the event it was neither its intellectual rigour nor its potential class bias that gained an ascendancy for Political Economy in Victorian Britain. England's advanced commercial and political life proved particularly receptive to the ideas formulated initially by eighteenth-century Scottish intellectuals contemplating the tensions between old and new in their relatively backward society, particularly because these ideas were compatible with a variety of political and ideological viewpoints. Radicals from Paine to Cobden, Bright and the Manchester School wielded 'the laws of economics' as a weapon against aristocratic privilege and patronage; Whigs from Burke to the *Edinburgh Review* saw in them the progressive hand of providence working through the spirit of free English institutions; Tories like Huskisson and Peel found them a pragmatic alternative to the mercantile system as a means of enhancing national strength and stability. When Peel abolished the Corn Laws in 1846, the last vestige of the old system fell. There followed soon after twenty years of unparalleled growth and prosperity, shifting Britain from a predominantly agricultural to a predominantly industrial society, and apparently confirming all Smith's prognoses.

Such widespread acceptance, however, necessarily entailed a muddying of Political Economy's theoretical clarity. Mid-nineteenth-century economic conditions led to a popular emphasis upon the Smithian vision of benign economic laws, particularly represented by the naive optimism of the Manchester School which saw 'free trade' allied to political reform as a panacea for political oppression, poverty, ignorance and international war. This simplified version of classical economics ignored the more pessimistic calculations of the Malthus–Ricardo generation, whose thinking about the nature of capitalism had taken place against the turbulent economic background of the Napoleonic Wars and their aftermath. Four areas in particular had elicited less positive predictions from them: the living standards of the working class; the prospects of full employment; the prospects of profits and the rate of growth; and the implications of international free trade.

1. Until J. S. Mill came to argue the contrary, classical economics assumed that the 'laws of political economy' governed, not merely the growth of production, but also the distribution of economic benefits among different classes. A fixed 'wage fund' was presumed to be derived from the sale of previously manufactured products to fund the purchase of raw materials, the payment of interest, wages and investment. Any attempt to push wages beyond their 'natural' (commonly interpreted as subsistence) level would inevitably affect the other factors in the equation and lead to a cut in the demand for labour. Smith, it is true, had implied that an expanding economy might drag wages above subsistence level, but the prospect of ameliorating poverty by collective working-class action or state intervention was denied, both by the wage-fund theory, and by Malthus's theory of population. Malthus's *Essay on Population* (1798) was designed as an attack on works such as William Godwin's *Political Justice* (1793) which had promised progress and prosperity as the fruits of egalitarian political and educational reforms. Egalitarianism, Malthus argued, would universalise rather than resolve the endemic problems of the mass of mankind. Nature, he claimed, had implanted sexual instincts which led to population growth at a geometric rate whilst restricting the increase of food production to

an arithmetical rate, because a growing population would have to resort either to tilling less productive land or overexploiting existing land. As a cleric, Malthus could hardly be expected to advocate birth control (it was for propagating such views, incidentally, that the young J. S. Mill was arrested), and for him famine, war and disease were the major correctives to overpopulation. Only later did he come to place a qualified faith in education and 'moral improvement', that is, the encouragement of sexual self-restraint among the labouring poor, who were always the swiftest to respond to rising living standards by earlier marriage and increased child-bearing. The hated 1834 Poor Law Amendment Act, with its creation of sexually segregated 'Workhouse Bastilles', was in part a practical consequence of Malthusian pessimism reinforcing traditional objections to the disbursement of unregulated charity, which could only redistribute income from productive uses to the 'idle poor' and thus recreate the problem it sought to obviate.

2. The Victorian period saw widespread acceptance of 'Say's Law' (formulated by J. B. Say) which stated that supply created its own demand in a free economy. Since all profits, wages and rents would be either spent or reinvested, no general crises of overpopulation or underconsumption could, it was presumed, occur. So long, therefore, as labour was ready to redeploy itself in a changing economy from declining to expanding industries, unemployment could be only temporary, or a product of irrationality or idleness on the part of the worker. Ricardo and Malthus, had, however, raised serious doubts about aspects of this reasoning. Ricardo, whilst accepting the validity of Say's Law, had, in the third edition of his *Principles of Political Economy* (1817; 3rd edn 1821), raised the spectre of serious structural unemployment emerging as the introduction of new machinery acted, not as a complement to, but as a substitute for, a growing labour force. He was accused of lending theoretical support to the Luddite campaign against new technology, and his idea later found a central place in Marx's theory that technological change had an inherent tendency to cast labour into a permanent pool of the unemployed ('the reserve army of labour') whose competition for jobs was the prime factor in keeping wages at a subsistence level. A second aspect of Marx's view of the dynamics of capitalism, its inherent tendency to generate crises of overproduction, was in part anticipated by Malthus in his *Principles of Political Economy* (1820) and, almost simultaneously, by the Swiss economist, Sismondi (1773–1842). Malthus argued that, in a dynamic economy producing more than bare necessities, markets would quickly become sated if con-

sumer tastes did not shift to purchase novel products, and savings were invested in existing industries rather than in new ones. There were, he argued, two ways of averting the threat of overproduction and consequent unemployment: by public works, and by encouraging the 'conspicuous consumption' of the rentier, landowning classes. However, moral disapprobation of his discovery of a role for 'luxury' consumption and the 'idle rentier' in economic progress, combined with the way that working-class spokesmen of the 1820s seized upon his argument for the state promotion of public works, ensured that Malthus's 'counter-cyclical' views gained little credence in conventional economic circles until the time of J. M. Keynes (1883–1946).

3. Although Smith was popularly read as optimistically forecasting continuous economic growth, his analysis in fact pointed to different conclusions which, in Malthus and Ricardo's generation, were developed to reveal a tendency towards a condition of zero-growth – the 'stationary state' discussed by Mill (extract 6).

Malthus's dystopia of population growth continually pressing upon limited food production became the basis for the development of Ricardo's analytical model of economic development treating the economy as one giant farm. As population grows, the increased labour available will be less economically productive, since food necessary to support it will have to be produced on less fertile, or more intensively cultivated, land. The price of food will thus rise and with it the price of labour if wages are not to fall below the 'natural' subsistence level. As this happens, however, landlords owning less marginal land will experience windfall gains. For, as capitalistic farmers bid for tenancies on land made more profitable by rising food prices, landlords will be able to exploit their monopoly of ownership to extract higher rents. According to Ricardo, there are inexorable consequences: the share of profits will be squeezed between rising rents and rising wage levels, and the profit rate on capital will fall, weakening the key stimulus to investment and hence undermining the source of future economic growth. This prospect of zero-growth was not only developed by Marx to forecast an ultimate 'crisis of capitalism', but underlay many of the proposed reforms of the nineteenth century. The campaign against the Corn Laws, imposed in 1815 to maintain domestic food prices by restricting competitive imports, was fuelled by the Ricardian view that such imports would lower food prices and hence wage levels, erode rents, and hence stimulate both profits and wealth-creation. The moral basis of radical attacks upon an idle rentier class received economic justification in the view that the future of capitalism depended upon curbing the landlords' capacity to exact higher rents. Bray, Mill, Arnold, Green and Shaw, among our authors, all reflected the high priority accorded by 'progressive' thinkers to land reform in Victorian times. Shaw, for instance, was first stimulated into studying economics by Henry George's *Progress and Poverty* (1881), a tract of enormous influence in the last decades of the century, which derived from the Ricardian analysis of rent the case for a 'single tax' upon land values that would stimulate the redistribution of, and ease the tax burden upon, productive wealth.

4. International free trade presented a fourth area of contention. Smith's recognition that 'defence ... is of much more importance than opulence' (*The Wealth of Nations*, 1937, p. 429) made him concede the need to depart from *laissez-faire* principles in guaranteeing defence resources. The assumption of many Enlightenment writers that commercial intercourse was a force which eroded national differences and promoted international amity became one strand in the Manchester School's strident advocacy of free trade. This cosmopolitan internationalism was a far cry from Smith's concession, and anathema to those who held to nationalism whether on moral, political or cultural grounds. Ricardo's theory of 'comparative advantage' held major implications for these contending views, for he argued that free trade would have the consequence of increasing the international specialisation of production and, *pace* Smith, that such a division of labour would increase production overall. For Ricardo and his free-trade followers this conclusion pointed to the great advantages of encouraging international free trade. Yet the immense advantage enjoyed by Britain after the Napoleonic Wars in industrial production alarmed those in Britain who feared that a *laissez-faire* policy would lead to the inevitable swamping of rural by urban industrial life. The abolition of the Corn Laws in 1846 marked the real abandonment of a dual-sector economy, but criticism of the implications of the decision and alternative remedies did not disappear as some extracts (Arnold and Mill) below show. In face of British policy it became apparent to other countries that protectionism would be necessary to foster native infant industries in predominantly agricultural economies. The success of these protectionist policies adopted by countries such as Germany and America made slow inroads on British public opinion, culminating in the challenge to free trade offered by the mercantile imperialism of the Tariff Reform movement of the early 1900s.

Political Economy, then, might be said to have been triumphant in the prosperous 1850s and 1860s, but the changing conditions of the 1870s with their economic instability, rebirth of class politics and nascent socialism marked a crisis point. In the later extracts we have chosen (extract 10ff) the centre of debate seems to have shifted. Political Economy no longer calls the shots in defining the key issues.

Indeed, the notion of Political Economy as a unitary intellectual subject appears to have collapsed, and during the centenary year of Smith's *The Wealth of Nations*, Walter Bagehot felt compelled to state that 'it lies rather dead in the public mind. Not only does it not excite the same interest as formerly but there is not exactly the same confidence in it' (*Economic Studies* (1880), p. 3).

The crucial change was a loss of faith in the existence of immutable laws which determined the production and distribution of national wealth and in the general validity of *laissez-faire* policies. Symbolic of this was a review in 1869 by J. S. Mill of W. T. Thornton's *On Labour*, in which Mill abandoned his life-long commitment to the classical school's shibboleth of the wage-fund theory, opening the way for a recognition that wage levels were a product, not of natural forces, but of human agency, in which trade unions could play a role in determining the real living standards of their members. Even Mill, however, was becoming outmoded. Although he had often acknowledged that policy prescriptions for economic growth in Britain might be inapplicable to 'underdeveloped' economies, he was ill-prepared for the challenge to classical theory posed by emerging historical schools of economics, particularly in Ireland and on the Continent. An article in 1870 by the Irish economist, Cliffe Leslie (1825–82), provided the spearhead for an attack upon Political Economy's neglect of the social and economic preconditions behind its abstract deductions. Such a challenge was, of course, central to Marx and Engels's whole notion of 'bourgeois' economics as an abstraction from specific historical circumstances mediated by the class perceptions of its practitioners (see extract 5), although Leslie's views had a more immediate impact upon mainstream British thought insofar as they were in tune with the evolutionary philosophies which were gaining ascendancy in intellectual life.

Although the writings of Herbert Spencer (1820–1903) reveal how evolutionary ideas derived from biology could be used to reinforce concepts of economic individualism, the division of labour and competitive struggle in a 'free' economy, the main thrust of historical evolutionism tended to challenge the preconceptions of classical theorists. The Oxford philosopher T. H. Green (extract 10) represented a generation which no longer felt hidebound by the 'dismal science' in formulating conceptions of human progress and social policy; and Oxford, particularly, produced figures like Arnold Toynbee (1852–83) and W. J. Ashley (1860–1927) who shifted the emphasis from deductive analysis to studying the development of social and economic institutions as a guide to future trends. Out of such speculations developed both the Fabians' identification of social collectivism as the emerging form of industrial civilization (extract 12), and the 'social imperialism' of Oxford-trained economists like Ashley and W. A. S. Hewins (1865–1921) who provided intellectual support for the Conservative and Unionist party's assault on international free trade during the early 1900s.

In Cambridge, by contrast, Alfred Marshall (1842–1924) established a contending, and ultimately more influential, school of economics which served equally to undermine the old certainties. The year 1871 which had seen Mill's statement in his final edition of the *Principles* that 'there is nothing in the law of value which remains for the present or any future writer to clear up: the theory of the subject is complete', also saw the economist, W. S. Jevons (1835–82), publish an open challenge to the Ricardo–Mill theory of value in his *Theory of Political Economy*. Jevons's views, being formulated simultaneously on the Continent, attacked the classical school's reliance upon theoretical absolutes such as 'natural price' and the 'value' of labour, and tended to disregard their attention to the macro-economic study of economic growth with its effects upon the gross distributions of rent, profit and wages. The emphasis shifted towards analysing the nature of individual rational choice in a free market, constructing models of how relative market prices are determined, and investigating the conditions which maximized the welfare, rather than the wealth, of nations. The 'science' of economics shifted, thereby, from a study of deterministic 'laws' towards a mathematical discipline investigating the interactions of decisions based on subjective judgements of 'utility' made by individuals in the market place.

Adherents of the old school criticized the neglect in this 'neo-classical' economics of such issues as the dynamics of economic growth and wealth distribution, while many socialists believed that its abandonment of the labour theory of value, and emphasis upon the tendency of free markets to optimise welfare, deliberately obscured the subversive and pessimistic implications of the old economics. The new methods developed by Jevons and Marshall also, however, provided reinforcement for the humanitarian reformism expressed by Green and his followers. Armed with more sophisticated techniques of economic analysis, and an increasing body of statistical information, the basis for a practical science of social welfare and social policy-making by legislators appeared to have been laid.

Such a conjunction of challenges, historical and analytical, destroyed the acceptability of classical Political Economy. Only on the extremes of the political spectrum, whether among right-wing diehards or revolutionary Marxists, did it remain imperative to believe in the inexorable operations of iron laws and the essential unchangeability of a capitalist system.

In making our selection of the 'critics of capitalism', we have, in every case, chosen pieces that concentrate upon the issue of Political Economy, whilst also endeavouring to convey the individual angle of vision and unique style of each writer. This has meant that in the case of Ruskin, Arnold, Morris and Shaw we have not taken the easy option of reprinting their best-known and more readily available texts which discuss the role of the artist and prophet in an industrial society, because to do so would both reduce the usefulness of this volume and diminish our appreciation of the seriousness with which they devoted themselves to their role as social critics. They did not see themselves as artists dabbling in a little amateur economics and sociology. Writing on Ruskin, Shaw said that they shared 'the conviction that your art would never come right whilst your economics were wrong' (*Ruskin's Politics* (1921), p. 20). Two further comments need to be made at this stage upon our choice of authors. First, the desire to represent a variety of reactions from articulate and influential thinkers of the period inevitably has led to a concentration on middle-class writing, since literary and intellectual history, together with the conditions of authorship and publication, tended, like the 'laws' of Political Economy itself, to favour the dominance and survival of this class. Secondly, pieces in translation from the works of Engels and Marx may seem inappropriate in the *Cambridge English Prose Text* series, since they are not susceptible to the same kind of stylistic analysis as companion pieces in this volume. Nor are we claiming that their work was widely influential in Britain at the time of publication. But their work was known and revered by at least two of our later contributors, Shaw and Morris. Moreover to omit their thought would involve a kind of historical falsification. Carlyle and Ruskin, in particular, were enormously influential writers in their own day, but their ideas had largely been worked through, assimilated, or discarded, by the early decades of this century, to leave them as towering, but nevertheless 'historic', figures. The nineteenth century contributions of Marx and Engels as critics of capitalism, have, by contrast, only received full attention and made their maximum impact in this century. The loose attribution of the adjective 'Marxist' in our own day seems to make the effort to locate their original ideas within the context of the nineteenth-century debate particularly worthwhile. It is to the origins of this debate that we must now turn.

Marx's *Capital*, in fact, proved to be the last great work to draw upon and adapt the distinctive conceptual apparatus developed by Adam Smith. In retrospect, therefore, what was regarded in the high Victorian period as *the* science of economics proved to be merely a phase in economic thinking, though one lasting for well-nigh a hundred years. During these years, however, what was in reality an evolving field of intellectual inquiry marked by a high level of internal disputation, assumed under the label 'Political Economy' the popular, though never unchallenged, status of a master discipline through which the vast social changes of the age could be comprehended and controlled. As such, it had, as we have seen, appeared compatible with a multiplicity of moral, theological and political positions. On close inspection, the critics of Political Economy emerge as equally diverse in orientation. It has been possible to employ the arbitrary time-span of Victoria's reign for our study precisely because we are not here involved with a coherent linear opposition to Political Economy, but rather with a debate which, at times, was waged as hotly between those who stood outside the tradition as it was within the folds of classical economics. Though Political Economy had become a recognised feature of the intellectual landscape by the time of Victoria's accession, earlier battle lines drawn up in relation to it between rationalism and romanticism, and around French Revolutionary social principles, were, as the career of J. S. Mill best illustrates, increasingly blurred. In the fifty years between Bray's pamphlet and Shaw's lecture, moreover, the battle lines underwent further inevitable change as the 'fixed' concepts were challenged in the way we have outlined. Criticism launched by the Owenite socialists, for instance, did not question the classical school's assumption that maximum productivity was a reasonable goal; indeed Owen's own early experiments with welfare provisions in his New Lanark factory had been parodied as 'philanthropy plus ten percent'. But after the radical critique of economic growth embodied in Mill's *Principles*, a new dimension was added to the conflict. A further trap for the unwary reader lies in the subtle shift in reference behind the same word which might take place over that period. 'Socialism' was a peripheral political phenomenon favoured by such minorities as the Owenites at the beginning of our chosen period. For Marx, Engels and Mill the word relates chiefly to Continental political experiments, whilst for Morris and Shaw, socialism had surfaced again as a small but vociferous native political option.

Although several of the later writers in this volume pay tribute to their predecessors' influence, any imagined meeting of the ten men represented here to organise combined resistance to the forces of Political Economy would almost certainly have proved unworkable. Broadly speaking there were perhaps two issues which might have called forth common assent. All ten would have agreed in pleading for quality rather than quantity as the grounds for assessing human requirements, and in desiring to pursue the question of who could be said to benefit from the workings of a capitalist economy which seemed to operate increasingly inequitably when it came to distributing benefits.

Moving from the realm of moral feeling to planning a campaign strategy would soon have disturbed the consensus. Despite the almost unanimous conviction that the working man suffered most from capitalism's depredations, the extent to which he might be encouraged to contribute towards his own salvation was contentious. Positions, here, ranged from the increasingly authoritarian paternalism of Carlyle, to Marx's faith in the revolutionary potential of the proletariat. The degree and type of engagement in this process envisaged by each writer might have proved equally divisive. Bray's pamphlet emerged directly out of working-class activism as propaganda in the cause, but for members of the intelligentsia there were many options available between Carlyle's prophetic stance beyond the corruption of the world, and Marx's involvement in the first working-men's International after 1864, or Morris's arrest on a mass demonstration in 1887.

Also problematic would have been discussions of the state. Our writers were all united in rejecting the Smithian contention that the 'natural' laws of a capitalist market provided a fully adequate moral and equitable ordering of human affairs, yet all were constrained in resorting to the state as the most obvious corrective to the ills of unbridled economic competition by one or other of three ideas: traditional liberal suspicion of government as essentially a coercive agency; radicalism's identification of the state with privileged ruling classes; or the romantic critique of it as a soul-less, mechanistic instrument of social engineering. Closest to the Smithian tradition were perhaps Bray and Mill, whose visions conceived of free exchange as the basis of social harmony once purged of competitive greed and inequitable property relations. To the extent that Mill, Green and Shaw contemplate intrusions into the *laissez-faire* economy, this is intimately linked to the democratisation of political life and an emphasis upon the role of a decentralised local government system rather than the central state. Marx and Engels, often today identified as the prophets of totalitarianism, looked beyond the inevitable administrative centralisation of economic life under socialism to a future in which the state had 'withered away' because of its irrelevance to a communitarian democracy, a vision given greatest immediacy, perhaps, in Morris's utopian writings. It is significant that of our writers, Carlyle and Ruskin, the closest to the romantic tradition, appeal for strong moral and political leadership while remaining vague and elusive about '*mere political arrangements*' (Carlyle, *Signs of the Times*), while those who speak in the most positive manner of 'the state', Green and Arnold, conceptualised it in idealist terms as an embodiment of the moral will of the community rather than as a system of regulations and institutions. One may also note how policy recommendations made strange bedfellows. The need for better education of the poor united virtually all our critics with the Political Economists themselves, though there were differences over what its precise content should be. The issue of emigration, which many economists by the 1830s had come to advocate as a means of alleviating the Malthusian overpopulation problem, and which in the event proved to be the most persistent working-class response to poverty and unemployment, proved divisive. Bray denounced it as a self-protective device of the idle rich; Mill came to differentiate between its practical contribution to overseas economic development, and its limited part in dealing with domestic overpopulation; Carlyle, however, joined hands with the utilitarian economist, Wakefield, in regarding the colonial resettlement of surplus labour as a central task of government.

Even concepts so apparently simple as 'work' proved to be value-laden, dividing those who saw it as a positive moral force through which men might define themselves and attain dignity, from those who viewed it as, at best, a necessary evil. The former group tended to have individually satisfying work in mind, whilst the latter group tended to be more conscious of the stultifying nature of mass production. At odds, here, were often the influences of a puritanical insistence upon activity, and the classical ideal of *schole*, leisure from mere toil, to cultivate the 'higher' self. This, in turn, affected the response to technological advances brought about by the industrial revolution as either a threat to the organic processes of continuous creation, or as something to be cautiously welcomed insofar as new machines freed men for more satisfying tasks. An underlying, and sometimes secularised, conviction of man's fall from grace seems to have prevented any of these ethically committed writers from wholeheartedly espousing visions of a work-free Paradise or, more importantly, from locating such visions in any previous Golden Age. Even Morris, whose writings of the 1890s sometimes assumed a utopian mould, did not regard these as practical models for the future.

Though many critics, as we have seen, accused Political Economy of inattention to historical and cultural variables, they were once again divided in the use to which they put their historical perceptions and the angle of cultural vision they chose to adopt. Whilst the past did not supply utopias, it could be used as a source for unflattering comparisons which showed the paternalistic qualities of feudalism to be preferable to the mutual indifference of a cash-nexus society. Alternatively, the implications of evolutionary theory could be applied to a reading of the past's power to shape the present; though this process too might result in contradictory conclusions. Just as the scientific evidence for evolution in the animal kingdom could be read either to support a view of slow but invincible adaptation and progress, or to reveal a world of stark immorality in which pain and destruction seemed the only certainties, so the evolutionary process through which human society had moved could be seen as a progressive force to be harnessed and stimulated by the morally educated, or as an ineluctable struggle of which man was merely a more or less conscious witness.

In their concern to repudiate England's insular complacency many of the writers in this volume determined to draw attention to a wider European experience. Some drew on the rich vein of ideas developed in German intellectual life, which had been most fully shaped by reaction to the Enlightenment philosophies that gave rise to Political Economy. Distancing oneself from the British system could also take the straightforward guise of drawing upon Continental countries for alternative political and economic models. Other writers, in particular Carlyle and Arnold, combined this usage with the satirical device of adopting a foreigner's perspective to highlight those incongruities of British economic philosophy which familiarity had rendered invisible to the average native. Alternatively the desire to remind the audience of Britain's European context could stem from a positive espousal of internationalism as a force working against the rigidity of British class divisions.

When we turn from the writings to the personalities behind the extracts in this volume, the possibility of a unified critique of Political Economy seems even more remote. More detailed biographical information will be found, where relevant, in the individual head-notes, but an introductory essay seems the appropriate place to indicate some of the variables influencing these highly individualistic outlooks.

Class, of itself, does not seem to have been an important factor in determining a future position critical of mainstream middle-class philosophy, although it may have played its part in securing Shaw's attachment to the middle-class intelligentsia of Fabianism rather than the working-class movements endorsed by William Morris. A Dublin upbringing of 'genteel' poverty (where his father's drinking had led to the family's social ostracism by their own class although family pride had forbidden easy intercourse with those lower down the social scale), might well have made a London group, to which extensive reading and eagerness for knowledge were the passport, the most attractive option. In several cases 'displacement' from the environment of early life may well have sharpened an awareness of inequitable conditions. Such 'displacement' could take several forms, of which geographical dislocation is the most obvious. Bray, Engels and Marx were forced by economic and political circumstances to undertake the greatest upheaval. Bray, one of seven children born to a Yorkshire singer and comedian who had emigrated to the United States, returned to be left as an orphan living with an aunt in Leeds at the impressionable age of 13. After apprenticeship to a printer he was unable to find work locally and took to the road. He later wrote of this period that 'his tramping experiences were just what he needed to break through the crust of his early prejudices and ideas and show him the world as it is and as it ought to be' (autobiographical sketch). Marx and Engels's early commitments were forged in a mid-century Prussia that had a peculiar capacity to polarise middle-class youth between super-patriotism and political radicalism. However, Marx's first studies of capitalist economics and his conversion to communism in 1844 were the product of exile in the hotbed of Parisian café politics, Engels's the product of his transfer at the age of twenty one to work for the family business in Manchester. Having later fled to London, Marx was to comment that industrially advanced states like Britain only showed to the more backward like Germany 'the face of their future'. Both writers used the unique experience of what became their adoptive country as the laboratory for studies whose results were designed primarily for German audiences. Engels had been sufficiently shocked by conditions in Manchester to devote his first two years there to collecting material published as *The Condition of the Working Class in England* (1845); Marx plundered government Blue Books and the British Museum's resources to develop the theories formulated in Paris.

Carlyle's acquaintance with the literary world in London and his final move there in 1834, after an upbringing in the agricultural Lowlands of Scotland, informs the biting edge of his satire and commentary on the contemporary social malaise. Acceptance of the physical and economic rigours of Scottish peasant life, as experienced in the family home to which he often returned, sharpened the acerbic nature of his observations on the dilettante life of the metropolis and his sense of the squalor, rootlessness and disintegration which characterised much urban industrial life.

Important though these changes of environment were, disruptions to, or a break from, an ideological inheritance were even more decisive in determining a position critical of the accepted social orthodoxies. At first sight this may seem merely to redescribe a necessary disenchantment with the comparative ease of the social background of many of these writers prior to adopting a critical perspective, but it is intended to suggest a more radical philosophical, intellectual and emotional change of heart. In at least three cases (Carlyle, Mill and Ruskin) the crisis provoked assumed the proportions of a breakdown. In the case of Ruskin and Mill only such a tempestuous upheaval could have served to free them from the stranglehold of the claustrophobic intensity of their educations, recorded respectively in *Praeterita* (1889) and *Autobiography* (1873). A life-long agnostic, Mill nevertheless compared his traumatic severance from the strict utilitarian tenets of his father's educational regime in favour of a more humane philosophy, to a religious conversion. Without exception then, the writers featured in this volume seem to have undergone some radical change in their thinking which involved the abandonment of the faith of their childhood in the direction of a less orthodox position. Ruskin, Morris and Green turned away from the Evangelical allegiance of their childhood. Arnold lost the certainty that had marked his father's liberal faith. Shaw's Protestant education never survived the scepticism that family circumstances induced. Marx's own 'alienation' was many-layered. His successful lawyer father had abandoned the family's rabbinical Jewish traditions by expedient conversion to

Lutheranism, and Marx not only turned his own face even more firmly against his Jewish identity, but also rebelled against parental middle-class respectability. Marrying out of his class into the minor Prussian gentry, he ended up living to a large extent off Engels' patrimony, exiled from his homeland on the written authority of his wife's uncle. Engels (extract 3) castigated Carlyle for the persistent transcendentalism of his thinking having but recently fought his own personal struggle against the predestinarian elements of his strict Lutheran upbringing. Not only does he seem unaware of Carlyle's pilgrimage away from dogmatic Calvinism through a period of depressive materialism to a new sense of the mystery of creation (fictionalised in *Sartor Resartus* (1836), bk 2, chs. 6–7), but, many critics would affirm, Engels's later economic determinism suggests that his own predestinarian cast of mind was transposed rather than conquered. It is also perhaps worth remarking that, whilst re-evaluation of the orthodoxies of childhood seems to have been a necessary prelude to questioning the 'fixed' laws of political economy, loss of faith was not always accompanied by loss of dogmatism.

The element of conviction following upon conversion, combined with the moral fervour which followed humanitarian criticism of the classical school's allegedly unrelieved materialism, frequently produced a homiletic style of address. It is part of the business of this series to alert readers to the characteristic devices of the chosen authors, and developing a sensitivity to image and tone can be of particular help in catching the drift of an argument or detecting the writer's bias when the issue under discussion may initially seem remote. Once again the headnotes seem to afford a preferable context for detailed comment on individual texts but some guidelines for comparison can be established here.

Almost all the extracts in this book are 'occasional' in the nature of their composition, written out of a pressing need to react to specific sets of circumstances. This applies just as much to the books of Carlyle, Mill and Marx we have quarried as to the lectures and articles chosen. Mill's *Principles*, for instance, was written in the course of a few months between 1845 and 1847, and was repeatedly revised to take account of contemporary events. The essential ideas of *Capital*, vol. 1 had initially been written-up hastily for publication in 1859 as the *Critique of Political Economy* when Marx interpreted current economic trends as a harbinger of the ultimate crisis of capitalism. It is not so much, then, the form of the publication as the audience to which they were initially addressed which distinguishes the pieces. Engels,

Morris, Shaw and Green could all presuppose a predominantly sympathetic audience who chose to attend their lectures or purchase radical journals. The anticipation of a friendly hearing produces the relaxed assurance of tone, even an occasional conspiratorial intimacy, which marks their works. Mill, Ruskin, Carlyle and Arnold, however, were all forced to strive to create a body of responsive hearers from the inchoate mass of their potential readership. For some, publication over a period of time produced an awareness of hostile as well as friendly reaction to their views. It could be argued that Carlyle's tone is partly determined by a recognition of the reactions to his past publications on this subject. Bray was writing for a radical audience increasingly polarising into different camps over the question of social versus political reform. Like Mill, Marx aimed to educate a popular readership while meeting the highest standards of economic reasoning: in the Preface to *Critique* he had felt it necessary to develop a long self-justification of his credentials to speak on the subject, and, after its publishing failure, Engels prepared seven reviews under different names to announce the rewritten version of *Capital*. Thackeray, as editor of the *Cornhill Magazine*, was forced to terminate Ruskin's series of pieces on Political Economy, just as Leslie Stephen, his son-in-law and editorial successor, found himself compelled to put an abrupt end to Arnold's contributions later published in *Culture and Anarchy* (1932). Certainly Carlyle's and Ruskin's work at times adopts a defensive pugnacity, and both display a penchant for the vocative, lecturing an audience which needs to be prodded into an appropriate response. Even Arnold's celebrated urbanity requires the outlet of a bitter outburst against the culpable blindness of so many commentators in the face of the slum conditions of the East End of London (see extract 9, p. 175). In *Friendship's Garland* Arnold dramatizes his schizophrenia by creating two figures who variously bring into play British complacency, European scepticism, calm discursiveness and boorishly irascible explosions.

The dualism of response indicated in Arnold's fictional dialogue points to a tension which underlies all the ensuing pieces to a greater or lesser extent. On the one hand is the desire to counter the maxims and materialist rationalism of Political Economy by demonstrating its fallacious logic with carefully chosen examples and neatly deployed arguments. On the other hand is the moral *animus* which finds the classical school's utilitarian assumptions sufficiently repulsive to demand the language of strong emotion in which to express the abhorrence. This volume displays an interesting spectrum.

Marx and Bray reveal contrasting, but equally uncomfortable, attempts at a union of analysis and emotion. Elsewhere, the writing ranges from the denunciatory violence of which Carlyle's prose is capable to Mills's discursive analysis, yet each ventures, not always successfully, into the other's more familiar territory in search of a method and language which will convey the totality of their response. Carlyle endeavours to discuss alternative practical strategies, whilst Mill attempts to convey a sense of metaphysical loss and disquiet. At least two of our writers were particularly anxious to achieve a style consonant with the message they wished to convey. Ruskin wrote of the four essays comprising *Unto This Last* as 'the truest, rightest-worded, and most serviceable things I have ever written' (Preface), noting that he had taken especial pains with *Ad Valorem*. Whilst we notice Carlyle's influence in the unorthodox superlative 'rightest', and in the essay itself, Ruskin was later to describe his efforts as devoted to achieving a plainness and transparency of style quite distinct from the word-painting for which he had become famous in *Modern Painters*. Referring to the last paragraph of the essay he remarked, 'there's not any art of an impudently visible kind, and not a word which, as far as I know, you could put another for, without loss to the sense' (*Works*, vol. XXII, p. 514). The Shaw who deployed his oratory to move and manipulate audiences in his plays, is concerned, in his role as Fabian apologist, to stress the reasonableness of the Fabian position and at pains to distance his arguments from contamination by association with the heady emotionalism of revolutionary socialism.

Not surprisingly, given the religious upbringing many of these authors had experienced, their moral indignation sometimes surfaced in Biblical quotation and image, drawing most frequently upon the prophetic books and the gospels. This influence diminishes most markedly in the cases of Mill, Marx and Engels, Morris and Shaw, the first two never having been subjected to systematic Bible-reading, the latter three having found new gospels whose language permeates their thought. Engels came to reveal a devotion to the language of 'science' as a weapon against mysticism reminiscent of the Enlightenment struggle between Reason and Religion. Morris favours the absolutism of revolutionary fervour, and his vocabulary seems to rely more heavily upon the martial and heroic language of epic and saga literature than upon the apocalyptic language of Scripture. Shaw's vocabulary draws upon the new gospel of social evolution, talking of processes of development and extinction, gradual change and transition. Educational background is again responsible for the pronounced influence of classical rhetorical devices in the hands of those subjected to the most rigorous academic training: Carlyle, Marx, Mill, Ruskin, Arnold and Green.

Whether favouring 'right-wing' or 'left-wing' solutions to the menace of looming social disintegration, all our authors, without exception, use anarchy and chaos as their starkest threat, and appeal to an instinct for harmony and community. This instinct for community, or the commonwealth, is most frequently imaged in terms of a healthily functioning organism, threatened by disease or by an alien culture of mechanisation. The machine is seen at best as a neutral force to be harnessed to man's advantage, but at worst as the appropriate symbol of a coldly inhumane world which interests itself more in the composition of abstract statistics than in individual suffering. Equally poignant is the image of human creativity reduced in such a world to purely physical qualities – 'labour', 'hands' – and treated in Political Economy as a thing, a 'commodity', characterised like any other marketable object merely by its price. Those writers most indebted to their romantic predecessors, namely Carlyle, Ruskin and Arnold, can be most clearly observed reacting to the nightmare vision of faceless generality and the operation of 'iron laws' by striving for particularity of image and example. Particularity is employed not in a search for analytical precision, but as part of a creative process which counterposes living images and newly-minted myths to the sterile, life-denying world of the 'dismal science'.

If the views expressed by these critics of Political Economy sometimes seem naive or incoherent to the modern reader, and their terminology and mode of reasoning obscure or idiosyncratic, it is worth remembering the daunting task they faced. On the one hand, they were writing in a well-established tradition of questioning the justice and humanity of commercialised production, economic competition and the private ownership of property. In English prose, this would take us back to Sir Thomas More's *Utopia* (1516), or even the writings associated with the Peasants' Revolt of 1381. On the other hand they were endeavouring to come to grips with that distinctive social transformation brought about by the technological changes of the agricultural and industrial revolutions of the eighteenth century. Few early Victorians entertained any doubts that Political Economy was the model which best explained the workings, and promoted the profitable exploitation of, these new phenomena. Indeed, a leading proponent, Nassau Senior, commenting on the prosperity of the early 1850s, exultantly proclaimed 'It is a triumph of theory. We are governed by philosophers and economists'. Practitioners and critics alike were trapped by the constraints of the technical discipline of Political Economy, and a fresh vocabulary had to be coined as they sought variously to define or break the bonds of this new orthodoxy. Looking back from a debate currently dominated by such concepts as 'Thatcherism', 'monetarism', 'wetness' and 'dryness', it is perhaps both a refreshing and a chastening thought that the neologisms of the early nineteenth century, such as 'capitalism', 'industrialism', 'mechanisation', 'liberalism' and 'socialism', have survived, whilst 'Political Economy' has not.

John Francis Bray

(1809–1897)

At first sight, an obscure Leeds printer may seem oddly out of place amongst the illustrious contributors to the rest of this volume. But *Labour's Wrongs* (1839) may usefully be regarded as the culmination of the first phase of indigenous modern socialism, launched by Robert Owen, and the last, with the exception of Marx's writings, in a series of works which drew upon the classical labour theory of value to attack the foundations of capitalism itself. Of these 'Ricardian Socialists', as they are commonly termed, Marx himself regarded Bray as the best exemplar.

Though a skilled artisan, Bray had early experienced difficulty in finding work, and had been forced to tramp in search of occasional employment on illegally printed periodicals. Such jobs, potentially liable to imprisonment, finally gave way to more secure employment on the *Leeds Mercury* under the editorship of Samuel Smiles, the author of *Self-Help*. Meanwhile Bray had embarked upon an active political life. *Labour's Wrongs* had its origins in a series of letters, initialled 'U.S.', in the *Leeds Times* (19 Dec. 1835; 9, 23, 30 Jan., 13 Feb. 1836). In its present form it was published at Bray's own expense, for the not inconsiderable sum of £70, in weekly parts during 1838, and in book form, price 2s, in 1839. Its second chapter was subsequently released as an Owenite pamphlet in 1842. The evolutionary nature of the text is indicative of Bray's desire to restate the central Owenite message, which had gained so many converts over the previous decade and a half, rather than to offer immediate palliatives for specific ills. Though repetition and the lack of a clear sense of structure occasionally threaten the cogency of its argument, the pamphlet nevertheless successfully combines a powerful denunciation of contemporary injustices with an exposition of the theory of unequal exchange under economic competition, and ingenious proposals for the organisation of a socialist society. Adopting Owen's view that the problems of the age could be solved only by a moral transformation effected by a total transformation of economic life, Bray rejected as insufficient mere legislative and constitutional reforms. This position put him in conflict with fellow-activists in the Leeds Working Men's Association, of which he had become Treasurer in 1837. Accused of utopianism by the Chartists, in 1839 he led a breakaway movement of the Owenite contingent in protest at the limited objectives and growing militancy of the Chartist majority.

Bray's pamphlet appeals beyond the franchise campaign (p. 41) to a recognition of 'first principles' against which to test the injustices arising from the current economic foundations of society, which encourage the propertied classes to live parasitically off the labour of others. He offers the alternative of a system run on co-operativist lines, where all will labour, and all receive rewards commensurate with the value of their labour. Bray's use of 'the political economists' (p. 33ff) to support his case exemplifies the complex relations obtaining at the time among radical critics of the existing order. Like Political Economy itself, Owenism had represented an invasion into England of Scottish Enlightenment rationalism. Owen was friendly with Ricardo, and James Mill had helped, both in preparing Ricardo's *Principles*, and in correcting Owen's *New View of Society* (1813) for publication. William Thompson, who in 1824 had produced the first systematic Ricardian socialist work, was a friend of Bentham, and argued his case on strictly utilitarian grounds. It is perhaps not surprising that Bray's pamphlet, the work of an intelligent, widely read but untutored artisan, betrays signs of ideas being seized upon and moulded to fit his purpose without thorough digestion. The appeals to 'first principles' and to 'Nature' are the language of eighteenth-century rationalism, and sound, in the intellectual climate of the 1830s, peculiarly dated, lacking as they do any substantial philosophical or historical underpinning. There is, too, a tension between the language of 'utility' and that of 'fundamental rights' as a test of contemporary practices. The predominance of the latter reflects the heritage of such men as Paine and Godwin, whose writings formed the staple fare of radical working-class auto-didacts, but also the more class-conscious politics of the 1830s, when Benthamite philosophic radicalism had become associated with the betrayal of working-class interests in the 1832 Reform Act, and with the hated New Poor Law system of 1834.

Like the classical economists, Owen had been firmly committed to economic growth and improvement, but he parted company with the more pessimistic views of Malthus and Ricardo, believing that maldistribution, rather than scarcity, accounted for the major problems of capitalism. We find this same relationship expressed in Bray's pamphlet. It is unafflicted by any nostalgic yearning for the primitive simplicities and spontaneous community of pre-industrial society. Despite the technical innovations which helped to diminish employment in the printing trade, Bray is no Luddite, and looks forward to the time when new machinery can provide equal access for all to the advantages of leisure. He sweeps aside the Malthusian problem of overpopulation, by asserting both the enormous unused productive potential locked up within the existing system, and also the benefits to be harnessed from increasing international trade and specialisation (p. 45ff). Indeed, Bray founds his model for a nationwide collective economic organisation upon the most modern form of capitalist organisation, the joint-stock company. Following Adam Smith in praise of the two great institutions of modern society, market exchange and the division of labour, he super-imposes collectivist and egalitarian principles upon the foundations of an individualist economy from which competition and self-love will have disappeared. Eliminating the capitalists will ensure that commodities are exchanged at their 'real' cost of production, as defined by the value of the labour input, and that the worker receives the full value of his labour less deductions for future investment. It is in this way that the classical economists' conditions for 'equal exchange' and a 'natural harmony of interests' among participants in a market economy can be achieved. Bray is, however, unaware of the problems raised by this line of reasoning. Under the division of labour, the different skills, levels of capitalisation, or conditions of production attached to different kinds of work mean that the productivity of labour will vary. Workers exchanging their products at rates reflecting the different economic value of their labour input will thus be rewarded unequally. Yet the justice of this particular arrangement clashes with Bray's fundamentally egalitarian principle, that 'equal labour of all kinds should be equally remunerated' (p. 35).

Whilst Bray locates the central conflict of interest as that between Labour and Capital, and excuses popular violence employed against injustice, he is no revolutionary. A conviction that the very rationality of his project for transforming human moral life by social engineering, and the coherence of his blueprint for an ideal society, must ensure its success, permeates the work; it ends characteristically, with the assertion that what is 'ushering in the Age of Right' is that 'The light of Mind is beaming through the gloomy boundaries of the Age of Might'. This blend of rationalism and utopianism produces a style where passages of the balanced 'neutral' vocabulary and syntax associated with logic yield to the language of apocalyptic denunciation and prophecy. Give-away words that indicate the strength of emotional commitment occur in ostensibly pragmatic passages. Outlining the workings of his envisaged economy, Bray suddenly refers to 'true value' and 'true remedy' in a manner more appropriate to the visionary than the theorist (p. 45). Likewise on p. 34, he draws from 'the economists' three conditions 'necessary for the production of Utility'. What is then quoted as a means to an end, 'that there shall be labour', is instantly transformed into an absolute moral imperative, THOU SHALT LABOUR, an injunction which has less to do with the requirements of wealth-creation, and more with Bray's hatred of parasitic idleness. The stereotypes of the political platform also make their occasional appearance as brainless aristocrats are paraded before us and capitalists 'traverse the whole earth for customers' in a manner reminiscent of the devil searching for souls. In general, too, the denunciatory passages rely heavily upon clichéd hyperbolic contrasts, for instance the 'pampered aristocrat' and 'the son of labour' (p. 31–2), tyrants and slaves (pp. 38–9).

Biblical echoes, combined with Bray's habit of surveying the world *sub specie aeternitatis*, remind us that he was the inheritor of a rhetorical mode developed in chapel pulpits as well as on political platforms. He rejects orthodox Christianity, while ready to assert the Creator's original intentions for man, faithfully reflecting Owen's own views of himself as the chosen vehicle for a new gospel capable of changing the moral order. Bray reflects, too, the millenarian mood of the 1820s and 1830s, which deeply infected Owenism and increasingly shaped its adherents into a quasi-religious sect.

This is particularly apparent in his choice of introductory quotation: 'And when these things begin to come to pass, then look up, and lift up your heads; for your redemption draweth nigh'. Disillusioned with the progress of British socialism, in 1842 Bray returned to the United States, where he was to display a strong, though critical, interest in spiritualism in the fifties; and, at the height of his renewed involvement with socialist movements in the United States, produced *God and Man: a Unity* (1879), in which he argues that social organisation stemmed from a religious creed, but that Christianity had distorted the relation between man and God.

Nevertheless, the theorising of Bray and the 'Ricardian socialists' had a tendency to look too hard-hearted and rationalist to later generations of British socialists. In the short term they had a limited impact because working-class leaders were preoccupied with the franchise question, various 'causes' like disestablishment formulated by middle-class liberals, and, partly as a consequence of Owenite influence, in building trade unions and co-operative societies to protect their interests within a capitalist society. In the long run, the socialist revival of the 1880s looked to other roots for its ethos, to Ruskin, to renegade 'liberalism' and to the Christian communitarianism preached from Nonconformist pulpits.

1. *Labour's Wrongs and Labour's Remedy; or the Age of Might and the Age of Right* (1839)

pp. 28–31, 41–52 *passim*, 177–92 *passim*

... Past and present events afford ample demonstration that there is something inherently wrong in our social arrangements – something which inevitably tends to generate misery and crime, and to exalt worthlessness at the expense of merit. We are acquainted with justice only by name. Our whole social fabric is one vast Babel of interests, in which true charity, and morality, and brotherly love, have no existence. The hand of every man is more or less raised against every other man – the interest of every class is opposed to the interest of every other class – and all other interests are in opposition and hostility to the interest of the working man. This unnatural state of things was originally induced, and is now maintained, by man's ignorance of, or inattention to, First Principles; and these principles, as promulgated in the great book of Nature, may be thus interpreted: –

1. All men are alike, in regard to their substance, their creation, and their preservation; therefore the nature of all is the same, and the absolute wants of all are the same.

2. The materials requisite for the preservation of life – food,

clothing, and shelter – exist everywhere around us, but they are naturally valueless to man, and cannot be obtained by him, except through the medium of labour; therefore, as the life of no human being can be maintained without a due provision of food, clothing and shelter, and as these cannot be procured without labour, it follows that every human being ought to labour.

3. As the nature and wants of all men are alike, the rights of all must be equal; and as human existence is dependent on the same contingencies, it follows, that the great field for all exertion, and the raw material of all wealth – the earth – is the common property of all its inhabitants.

These simple principles contain within themselves the essence of that fundamental equality of rights which men have for so many ages been endeavouring to establish; and all social and governmental institutions must be in accordance with their dictates, if man would escape from all or any of the evils which he now suffers. Such principles offer the only foundation on which human happiness can be permanently established; and they naturally suggest a mode of action, in respect to social institutions, which will enable man to enjoy all the pleasures and escape from all the ills which his nature can be cognisant of. It is not rational to suppose that the present inequalities in society must always exist, merely because they exist for the time being; nor is it in accordance with experience to infer that, because a mode of action is invariable under certain influences and circumstances, it will continue unalterable under all influences and circumstances. Man is man at the pole as well as at the equator, but the diet and the clothing of the one will never be adopted by the other; nor will the selfish principle exert itself so vilely and so evilly, in a state of society where the rights and the duties of all are equal, as it does under the present social system, where there is no equality either in respect to rights or to duties, to services or to rewards.

That all men are precisely equal in their mental and bodily powers, or that they all require the same quantity of sustenance, no one will attempt to assert; for absolute equality prevails not between any two created beings. But the inequality of powers which at present exists amongst men, has been induced, in a great degree, by the favourable or unfavourable circumstances in which individuals have been placed, in respect to position in society and means of development; and, in most cases, if the circumstances and influences had been reversed, the inequality would also have been reversed.

The proud and pampered aristocrat, who has possessed every advantage which circumstances could afford for the development of his tiny brains, possesses, perhaps, knowledge and acquirements which fall not to the son of labour; but, forgetful of how much circumstances of position have done for him – forgetful that it was the toil and privation of the working man which gave him leisure and means – he tells us, sneeringly and insultingly, that he is a wiser and a higher being than the man whose honest hands procure his bread. But this assumption of superiority has almost had its day, and will soon be neither heeded nor conceded; and the unnatural barriers which ignorance and fraud have reared to separate men into classes and castes, like cattle in a public market, will be broken through and trodden under foot.

As nature has made the preservation of life dependent on the ful-filment of the same conditions, and has given to every human being the powers adequate to maintain existence, strict equity requires not only that these powers should be duly exercised, but likewise that the exertion should be rewarded with success; and that it is not so rewarded, is not the fault of nature, but of man. Nature never commits errors – never inflicts injustice; and when she made man the slave of circumstances, and left him at the mercy of events, she gave him faculties adequate to control the one and direct the other. That he might do this more effectually, and have dominion over most things relating to his existence, man has been taught to institute society; which, if it be wisely regulated, will enable him to accomplish, by a proper union and direction of forces, that which no isolated exertion of human power could ever achieve. This is the intention and end of society; and the first step to the attainment of the wished-for power is the establishment of institutions which will destroy or neutralise the trifling inequalities that nature has created, and at the same time remove all the uncertainty connected with the future welfare of man, and insure him, until death, an abundance of all those things which make life desirable. Society, thus constituted and regulated, will draw the whole human family into one common bond of fellowship and union; for its very principles, by showing to all men their depend-ence on all, prove to them that man has no pre-eminence above his fellow-man; as the wisest and the strongest are but as broken reeds when placed beyond the pale of society, and shut out from the communion and co-operation of their kind.

Thus, from a consideration of the nature of man and the object of society, a principle may be deduced, which, although now unacted upon, and its justice unacknowledged, will ultimately unite the two jagged and far-separated ends of the social chain – forming it into a circle, and putting the last finish upon man and his institutions, namely: –

4. As self-preservation is the end of all labour, and as a general natural equality of powers and wants prevails amongst men, it should follow, that all those who perform *equality of labour* ought likewise to receive *equality of reward*.

However, unpalatable may be these principles, they are not only in strict accordance with justice, but they are the only principles capable of destroying the manifold ills and miseries which a departure from them, in the present constitution of society, necessarily engenders.
. . .

But let not the unjust man and the extortioner, wherever he may be, exult in the immensity of his wealth and the unconquerableness of his power – let not a toil-worn and an impoverished people, wherever they may be, think that their doom is fixed, and that deliverance will never come. That which is true of particular principles under certain influences, is not necessarily true of the same principles under all circumstances; nor is that degradation and poverty, which is the portion of the working man under the present social system, a necessary concomitant of his existence under any and every social system.[1] This shall be proved by the same principles and the same mode of argument by which the political economists, from not going far enough, have proved the contrary. By thus fighting them upon their own ground, and with their own weapons, we shall avoid that senseless clatter respecting 'visionaries' and 'theorists,' with which they are so ready to assail all who dare move one step from that beaten track which, 'by authority,' has been pronounced to be the only right one. Before the conclusions arrived at by such a course of proceeding can be overthrown, the economists must unsay or disprove those established truths and principles on which their own arguments are founded.

'Society,' it has been affirmed by a political economist, 'both in its rudest form, and in its most refined and complicated relations, is nothing but a system of exchanges. An exchange is a transaction in which both the parties who make the exchange are benefited; – and, consequently society is a state presenting an uninterrupted succession of advantages for all its members.'

It has been to make society what it is here represented to be – 'an uninterrupted succession of advantages for ALL its members' – that the efforts of the truly great and good in all ages have been directed. Society *is not* thus universally advantageous to all within its pale, nor has it ever yet been so. Ask the producers of wealth – the despised, the toil-worn, the oppressed working men, of any age or any nation, – if society was ever for them an 'uninterrupted succession of advantages.' Could their voices arise from the grave – could they tell us the sickening tale of their wrongs and their miseries – how wild would be their wailings! – how terrible their imprecations! But even were history silent as to their fate, experience is a perpetual remembrancer to the men of the present day; and they cannot change their situation for a better one, nor will they ever have a proper hold upon society, until First Principles are universally acted upon – until we attend to those conditions which the political economists themselves have confessed to be 'necessary for the production of Utility, or of what is essential to the support, comfort, and pleasure of human life;' – and these conditions are: –

'1. *That there shall be labour.*

'2. *That there shall be accumulations of former labour, or capital.*

'3. *That there shall be exchanges.*'[2]

These three conditions, be it remembered, are those laid down by the economists. There is no reservation made – no distinction of any particular persons or classes with respect to whom these conditions shall or shall not have reference. They are applied to society at large, and, from their nature, cannot exempt any individual or any class from their operation. We must, therefore, take the conditions as they are, and apply them, with their advantages and their disadvantages, to all alike.

Had these conditions been fulfilled by men, as they ought to have been, there would now be no occasion for forming associations to obtain political rights, or trades' unions to protect the employed from the merciless exactions of the employers. But these conditions have been neglected, or only partially observed, and the present condition of the working man and society at large is the consequence. From our habits and prejudices, it is difficult to discover truths or First Principles, but it is still more difficult to apply these principles properly, or even to conceive that they may be acted upon. First Principles are always general in their application – not partial. The ban – 'THOU SHALT LABOUR' – rests alike on all created beings. To this great law, from the minutest animalcule in a drop of water, to the most stupendous whale which dives beneath the waves of ocean, there are naturally, and there should be artificially, no exceptions. Man can only escape this law; and, from its nature, it can be evaded by one man only at the expense of another. The law itself is never destroyed or abrogated – it naturally and perpetually presses equally upon all men – upon the capitalist as well as the working man – and if one man or one class escape its pressure, the sum total of its force will bear up some other man or class. It is an absolute condition of existence 'that there shall be labour.' ...

Labour, like everything else, is good when used legitimately, but becomes prejudicial when abused. It has hitherto been regarded as a curse – and it has to many been an actual curse – only because men have not used it rightly. The great mass of mankind has laboured to excess; and, like every other excess, labour has excited little else than aversion and loathing. ...

Labour is neither more nor less than labour; and one kind of employment is not more honourable or dishonourable than another, although all descriptions of labour may not appear of equal value to society at large. Such inequality of value, however, is no argument for inequality of rewards; and when we have examined the subject in all its bearings and relations, we shall find that it is as just and reasonable that equal labour of all kinds should be equally remunerated, as it is just and reasonable that labour should be universal. Man, properly constituted, requires not the low stimulant of superior pecuniary reward to spur him on to do his duty to his fellow-man.

All kinds of labour are so mixed up together, and so dependent on each other that the institution of inequality of rewards involves more actual pecuniary injustice than can possibly have existence under a system which rewards all men and all trades alike, for a similar application of labour; whilst the moral and physical evils which experience has proved to be inseparable from the present system of inequality – the uncharitableness, the insatiable greediness, the bloodshed, the wrongs of every kind which the records of three thousand years are filled with – can have little or no existence in connection with equality of reward for equal labour.

Not only are the greatest advantages, but strict justice also, on the side of a system of equality. It must be confessed by all men, that the most important discovery or invention, unless labour be applied to bring forth its results, is just as useless to us as the nearest trifle. Thus, although it may be said that he who invents a steam-engine confers a greater benefit upon society than the man who makes it – and that he who makes it does a greater service than he who merely fills it with water and kindles the fire under it, – yet, in reality, the labour of the last man is just as necessary, to produce the effects desired, as the labour of the first. The drawing or model of the inventor is of no value until seconded by the labour of the engine-maker; and the perfected engine, until it be put in motion by fire and water, is as worthless as the mere model. The results to be produced by the instrumentality of the engine are thus dependent, and equally dependent, upon the labour of all the parties concerned. Every man is a link, and an indispensable link, in the chain of effects – the beginning of which is but an idea, and the end, perhaps, the production of a piece of cloth. Thus, although we may entertain different feelings towards the several parties, it does not follow that one should be better paid for his labour than another. The inventor will ever receive, in addition to his just pecuniary reward, that which genius only can obtain from us – the tribute of our admiration.

Under the present social system, with its individualized and opposing interests, and its high and low employments, equal remuneration for equal labour would be both impracticable and unjust. Some professions and trades, to obtain a mastery over them, require quadruple the time and expense which are necessary to be devoted to others. Such time and expense are now borne by isolated individuals; and therefore, as the time and labour attendant on the acquisition of particular employments are so unequal, equal remuneration would involve a positive injustice. But under a rational system of communion and co-operation, where society at large would take upon itself the education and employment of all its members – bear every expense connected with the acquisition of scientific attainments and common trades – and derive, in gross, the peculiar advantages dependent upon the merely momentary unpro-ductiveness of scientific pursuits – equal remuneration for equal labour would be as just towards the inventor of a steam-engine, as towards the maker of the engine, or the man who sets it in motion. Under such a system, containing institutions furnished with every necessary apparatus for investigation and discovery, thousands of persons could easily obtain that scientific knowledge, and enter upon that wide field of experimental research, which it now demands a fortune to acquire and pursue; and equal remuneration for equal labour would be the true and the just recompense for all services.

In the second place, '*There shall be accumulations of former labour, or capital.*'

We all know that accumulations are no more than the unconsumed products of former labour, – whether houses, machinery, ships or anything else that is useful, or that can assist us in creating more wealth. All these things are capital. Had the first and succeeding generations of men consumed all that they produced – had they left their successors neither houses, tools, nor any other kind of wealth – we should now necessarily have been, as they were, half-starved and half-clothed savages. It is in the power of every generation, even under the most unfavourable circumstances, to leave the world richer, in respect to accumulations, than they found it; and it is their duty so to do. The principle of accumulating or saving seems to be instinctive in man, for it has never yet been entirely lost sight of, although it has been acted upon ignorantly, and with little or no knowledge of the important results connected with its fulfilment. We have inherited the greater part of our present accumulation from preceding generations, and merely hold them as it were in trust, for the benefit of ourselves and our successors; for the men of the future have as good a title to them as we have. Every generation thus receives a greater or less amount of accumulated wealth from those which preceded it; therefore, in equity, every generation is bound to provide for its successors in at least the same ratio as itself was provided for; and as population is ever on the increase, so likewise ought accumulations to be always on the increase.

That which applies to a generation, as a whole, applies also to every individual of such generation; and as there ought to be national accumulation, there ought likewise to be individual accumulation, for the first is dependent upon the last. The political economists, with the cold-blooded and calculating voracity induced by the present system, tell the productive classes that they must accumulate – that they must depend upon their own exertions; but however good the advice may be in principle, it is, while the working man is pressed into the earth by existing usages, no more than the addition of an insult to an injury. They *cannot* accumulate; and the reason is, – not because they are idle, not because they are intemperate, not because they are ignorant, – but because those accumulations, which have been handed down for the benefit of the *present generation as a whole*, are usurped, and their advantages exclusively enjoyed, *by particular individuals and classes*.

The third and last condition of the economists is, '*That there shall be exchanges.*'

An exchange is defined to be a transaction between two parties, in which each gives to the other something which he has not so much desire for, as he has for the article which he receives in return. Thus every man who works for hire exchanges his labour for a certain sum of money, because he would rather work, and receive the money, than remain idle, and starve. The capitalist, in like manner, would rather give his money for a certain quantity of labour, than live upon it as long as it should last; for he sells or exchanges the produce of such labour for a greater sum than the labour originally costs him, and by these means is enabled not only to live in idleness, but to increase his store of wealth at the same time. The capitalists, as we have seen, call this species of exchange 'a transaction in which *both* the parties who make the exchange are benefited; consequently, society is a state presenting an uninterrupted succession of advantages for *all* its members'.

The subject of exchanges is one on which too much attention cannot be bestowed by the productive classes; for it is more by the infraction of this third condition by the capitalist, than by all other causes united, that inequality of condition is produced and maintained, and the working man offered up, bound hand and foot, a sacrifice upon the altar of Mammon.

From the very nature of labour and exchange, strict justice not only requires that all exchangers should be *mutually*, but that they should likewise be *equally* benefited. Men have only two things which they can exchange with each other, namely, labour, and the produce of labour; therefore, let them exchange as they will, they merely give, as it were, labour for labour. If a just system of exchanges were acted upon, the value of all articles would be determined by the entire cost of production; *and equal values should always exchange for equal values*. If, for instance, it takes a hatter one day to make a hat, and a shoemaker the same time to make a pair of shoes – supposing the material used by each to be of the same value – and they exchange these articles with each other, they are not only mutually but equally benefited: the advantage derived by either party cannot be a disadvantage to the other, as each has given the same amount of labour, and the materials made use of by each were of equal value. But if the hatter should obtain *two* pairs of shoes for *one* hat – time and value of material being as before – the exchange would clearly be an unjust one. The hatter would defraud the shoemaker of one day's labour; and were the former to act thus in all his exchanges, he would receive, for the labour of *half a year*, the product of some other person's *whole year*; therefore the gain of the first would necessarily be a loss to the last.

We have heretofore acted upon no other than this most unjust system of exchanges – the workmen have given the capitalist the labour of a whole year, in exchange for the value of only half a year – and from this, and not from the assumed inequality of bodily and mental powers in individuals, has arisen the inequality of wealth and power which at present exists around us. It is an inevitable condition of inequality of exchanges – of buying at one price and selling at another – that capitalists shall continue to be capitalists, and working men be working men – the one a class of tyrants and the other a class of slaves – to eternity. By equality of exchanges, however, no able-bodied individual can exist, as thousands now do, unless he fulfil that condition of the economist, 'that there shall be labour;' nor can one class appropriate the produce of the labour of another class, as the capitalists now appropriate and enjoy the wealth which the powers of the working man daily call into existence. It is inequality of exchanges which enables one class to live in luxury and idleness, and dooms another to incessant toil.

By the present unjust and iniquitous system, exchanges are not only *not* mutually beneficial to all parties, as the political economists have asserted, but it is plain, from the very nature of an exchange, that there is, in most transactions between the capitalist and the producer, *after the first remove*, no *exchange* whatever. An exchange implies the giving of one thing for another. But what is it that the capitalist, whether he be manufacturer or landed proprietor, gives in exchange for the labour of the working man? The capitalist gives no labour, for he does not work – he gives no capital, for his store of wealth is being perpetually augmented. It is certain that the capitalist can have only his labour or his capital to exchange against the labour of the working man; and if, as we daily see, the capitalist gives no labour, and his original stock of capital does not decrease, he cannot in the nature of things make an exchange with anything that belongs to himself. The whole transaction, therefore, plainly shews that the capitalists and proprietors do no more than give the working man, for his labour of one week, a part of the wealth which they obtained from him the week before! – which just amounts to giving him *nothing* for *something* – and is a method of doing business which, however consonant with the established usages of the present system, is by no means compatible with a working man's ideas of justice. The wealth which the capitalist appears to give in exchange for the workman's labour was generated neither by the labour nor the riches of the capitalist, but it was originally obtained by the labour of the workman; and it is still daily taken from him, by a fraudulent system of unequal exchanges. The whole transaction, therefore, between the producer and the capitalist, is a palpable deception, a mere farce: it is, in fact, in thousands of instances, no other than a barefaced though legalised robbery, by means of which the capitalists and proprietors contrive to fasten themselves upon the productive classes, and suck from them their whole substance.

Those who assist not in production can never justly be exchangers, for they have nothing on which to draw, and therefore nothing which they can exchange. No man possesses any natural and inherent wealth within himself – he has merely *a capability of labouring*; therefore, if a man possess any created wealth – any capital – and have never made use of this capability, and have never laboured, the wealth which he holds in possession cannot rightly belong to him. It must belong to some persons who have created it by labour; for capital is not self-existent. The vast accumulations now in Great Britain, therefore – as they are neither the production of the labour of the present race of capitalists nor their predecessors, and were never given to them in exchange for any such labour – do not belong to the capitalists either on the principle of creation or the principle of exchange. Nor are they theirs by right of heirship; for having been produced nationally, they can only justly be inherited by the nation as a whole. Thus, view the matter as we will, there is to be seen no towering pile of wealth that has not been scraped together by rapacity – no transaction between the man of labour and the man of money, that is not characterised by fraud and injustice.

Here, then, is demonstration, flowing naturally from facts, that the three great conditions which the economists acknowledge to be 'necessary to the support, comfort, and pleasure of human life,' are almost unheeded, and two of them totally unacted upon, by the capitalists themselves. The law which says 'There shall be labour,' is evaded by them: the law which says 'There shall be accumulations,' is only half fulfilled, and is made to subserve the interests of a particular class, to the detriment of all the rest of the community: the law which says 'There shall be exchanges,' is not and cannot be observed, on the part of the capitalists, so long as they neglect the law of labour; for, unless they themselves labour by assisting in production, they can have nothing to exchange. Thus the infraction of these three conditions, by any one class, renders it morally and physically impossible that society should be what it ought to be – 'an uninterrupted succession of advantages for all its members.' Until these laws are made to operate equally and imperatively upon every part of the community, society must inevitably be what it is now, and what it always has been – an uninterrupted succession of wrongs, and spoilations, and oppressions – a system of perpetual warfare between man and man, under the denomination of employer and employed, in which the last must suffer all the hardship and make good all the damage. The very principles that have been laid down by the political economists incontestibly prove, when we consider the manner in which these principles are acted upon by capitalists and producers, that the interests of the two parties are *not* identified, as those who plunder the working man would have him to believe. The two interests can never be identified – the gain of the employer will never cease to be the loss of the employed – until the exchanges between the parties are equal; and exchanges never can be equal while society is divided into capitalists and producers – the last living upon their labour, and the first bloating upon the profit of that labour. . . .

The great mass of the productive classes look to universal suffrage, or the institution of a republic, as the grand remedy for their wrongs; but it has been shewn that these wrongs arise from a deeper source than form of government, and that they cannot be removed by any mere governmental change. Under the present social system, the whole of the working class are dependent upon the capitalist or employer for the means of labour; and where one class, by its position in society, is thus dependent upon another class for the MEANS OF LABOUR, it is dependent, likewise, for the MEANS OF LIFE; and this is a condition so contrary to the very intention of society – so revolting to reason, to justice, to natural equality of rights – that it cannot for one moment be palliated or defended. It confers on man a power which ought to be vested in nothing mortal. Inequality of possessions give man this dominion over his fellow-man; and therefore inequality of possessions, and not particular forms of government, constitute the great evil: – and inequality of exchanges, as being the cause of inequality of possessions, is the secret enemy that devours us. No simple governmental change can affect the present social system – can alter the relative position of the employer and the employed – can have any influence on inequality of condition; therefore all such changes are illusory, however extensive they may appear; and must, from their nature, be utterly worthless, except in so far as they concern the personal liberty of the governed. Under a state of things like that which now exists, the working classes, no matter what may be their intelligence, or their morality, or their industry, or their political power – are, by the very constitution of society, and their position in it, doomed and damned to hopeless and irremediable slavery until the end of the world! . . .

The present crisis, whatever it may lead to, is no more than a natural movement attending the course of things – it is but one more of that mighty ocean of events, the billows of which have rolled on from eternity, and will progress in unchecked power for ever. It was fulfilling a predestined move at man's creation – it was advancing as civilization succeeded to the primitive condition of man – it was progressing even when polished Greece and Rome degenerated into semi-barbarism – it was coming on when the French Revolution took place, and Kingcraft and Priestcraft soaked the soil of Europe with blood – and it is at this moment passing before our eyes and bearing us along, destroying and reinstituting, as it always has done and ever will do, political and social institutions of every character and kind. The present is not a merely local movement – it is not confined to country, to colour, or to creed – the universe is the sphere in which it acts, and it operates on all creation. In considering social changes, then, men are in no way restricted in their inquiries by existing arrangements and regulations; nor, in carrying forward the changes contemplated, are they in any way bound by the alleged sacredness of particular institutions, whatever may be their character or their object. All such have been established at various times and for various purposes – they have at like times and for the like purposes been modified and amended – and the men of the present day have the same right and power to subvert, as the men of former times had to institute and maintain. All these movements and changes were revolutions; and, as every page of history proves, the greater or less evils which have generally attended such changes, have been produced by the stupid endeavours of rulers and governments to convince nations, by the application of the sabre and the bayonet, that falsehood was truth, that gross wrong was justice, that slavery was liberty.

Thus free to think and to act – having examined and tested the various principles and modes of action which are essential to national prosperity and individual happiness, and beheld some of the innumerable evils which flow from their non-observance – we can at once enter into a more detailed contrast between existing arrangements and the social system of community of possessions under the modifications already briefly considered; and likewise examine a few more of those measures which are contended for by particular sections of the community, as remedies for existing evils.

We have supposed that the present distinctions in society, as relating to rich and poor or employers and employed, are totally subverted – that society is comprised but of one class, labourers mental and manual, who are united together in an indefinite number of communities or joint-stock companies, in which labour is universal and the remuneration in proportion to the time of labour – that these communities hold possession of the land and the productive capital of the nation – that they are likewise possessed of a circulating bank-note or paper medium, amounting to two thousand millions of pounds sterling – and that they mutually and universally produce or distribute wealth, and exchange their labour and their productions on one broad principle of equality. This vast confederation of labour has somewhat the character of a modern joint-stock company, and will bring forth its results by means of similar appliances. The more advanced form of community which has been considered, varies from the movement now under consideration merely in its arrangements. Each movement has the same ultimate end in view; and each will accomplish the object desired by a judicious union and direction of vast powers. . . .

Under the present arrangements of society we place a clog upon production at the very outset; for we compel vast masses of men to exist in idleness, and thus lose all the advantages which might be derived from their labour. This system, then, does not permit us to create and appropriate the greatest amount of wealth, and therefore it is unprofitable. Neither is the present system united in any way with equality of exchanges, and therefore it is unjust. . . .

But under arrangements such as those connected with the system of community, which render it imperative on all able-bodied persons to labour, and which assist such labour by every contrivance which ingenuity can invent, there must be vast production. This universal labour, when united with equal exchanges, will adjust all appropriation on the principles of equity. The system of community, moreover, places the national accumulations of capital at the disposal of the nation as a whole – it allows not one man to be in any way subject to the caprice or the mercy of another – and therefore it must ever equally protect all individuals from every kind of tyranny. Thus, whether in respect to production, or distribution, or appropriation – to the saving of labour or the enjoyment of wealth – to the establishment and maintenance of equal rights and equal laws – to all other things necessary to national greatness and individual happiness, the two systems will admit of no comparison.

The general character of the arrangements necessary to carry forward the joint-stock modification of community would be so similar to those at present existing, that particular enumeration will be unnecessary. There would be general and local accumulations or magazines of food and necessaries; this produce would be distributed by means of large markets or bazaars, instead of through the instrumentality of innumerable petty tradesmen; and every necessary and luxury would be procurable in any part of the country for its cost of production in gross, neither depreciated by abundance nor enhanced by the artifices of speculators. The production and transport of all kinds of commodities would be properly regulated and adjusted, and be limited by no restrictions but those which naturally flow from the gratification of all wants. The affairs of society at large would be regulated and controlled by general and local boards of various kinds, the members of which would be elected by the communities. A national bank would create the circulating medium, and issue it to the managers of the various companies in proportion to the number of members in each company, or the character of their occupation. With this money would all individuals and companies purchase commodities and transact their exchanges, on the present principles of trade; and, either by the imposition of a direct tax on persons, or a percentage on commodities, accumulations would be insured sufficient to provide amply for all exigencies. The money issued would always keep within the limits of the actual effective capital existing; and it would, like blood within the living body, flow equably throughout society at large, and infuse universal health and vigour. The money would always be at hand to pay for the labour – the labour would be ever ready to exert its power for this universal representative – and thus, while the money would insure the labour, the labour itself would insure the creation of the commodities which would be required for the money. There could be no confusion – no gluts – no want of employment – no poverty; but production, and accumulation, and distribution, and consumption, would be naturally adjusted to each other, and would harmoniously work out their common results.

As an example of the working of the system, let it be supposed that that there are five companies – composed of about the same number of men, and making use of the same amount of capital – No. 1 being engaged in the production of food, No. 2 producing woollen cloth, No. 3 being employed in the manufacture of cotton, No. 4 acting as a general home distributor, and No. 5 as a foreign distributor and importer of foreign produce. No. 1 would pay a certain weekly or yearly sum for rent, wages, and other purposes; and the total value of its productions would be equivalent to the gross amount of money or labour which had been expended upon them. The value of the commodities produced by No. 2 and No. 3 would be determined in the same manner; and the distributors, No. 4 and No. 5 would purchase their commodities from the other companies and from other countries, convey them to the general and local markets, and place upon them a per-centage equivalent to the extra labour which had been employed upon their transport and their distribution as a whole. Upon the same principle, and by the same means, would production and distribution be regulated throughout society at large – being alternately increased, or decreased, or turned into new channels, as the exigencies of society might require. Whatever might be the character of the labour of these companies, and wherever they might be situated, every individual member would receive the true value of his labour in wages, and with these wages he would purchase commodities of every kind at their true value – all advantages being equally enjoyed, and neither individuals nor companies deriving gain from the loss of others.

As the payment of every member of these companies will depend upon the condition that he shall labour, it is certain that work will be performed – if labour be employed upon material, it will shew its results in the shape of commodities – and thus, for every hour's labour that is paid for by any community, there will be an equivalent of some kind for the remuneration given, and this equivalent will exchange for another equivalent from some other party. A system like this contains a self-regulating principle such as can never have existence under present arrangements; and, while production and distribution and consumption are linked together, the first and the last are placed in contact, and a circle is thus formed which encloses society at large, and places the welfare of every individual at the disposal of himself.

In every social system, the first and most important arrangements to be considered are those which relate to the production and distribution of food. The defective character of these arrangements in the United Kingdom has long been notorious, and various remedies have been suggested; but there can be no true remedy in connection with the present system. Existing arrangements admit of individual possession of the soil; and such possession, by enabling a particular class to determine upon what terms and to what extent food shall be produced, place the bulk of society at the mercy of this class, and expose them to every species of fraud which avarice can invent. . . .

To remedy this state of things, a repeal of the corn laws is sought for; and it is averred that, if foreign corn be allowed free entrance into the country, home-grown corn must sink in price to the level of the foreign corn – that, as the home-corn is reduced in price, the rents of farms must be reduced – and that, as those rents are brought down, the vast social burthen imposed upon the working class by the proprietors will be reduced; and the greater part of the one hundred millions sterling, now annually lost by them, will be left in the pockets of the producers.

This is a remedy of the same inefficient and fallacious character as those which have been previously examined. It has been again and again proved, that it is the social position of the working class which dooms them to perform a great quantity of labour for a very little

45

reward – that this reward is not measured by the deserts of those who earn it, but by the number of idlers who are to be maintained out of it – and therefore, that any legislative enactment or social regulation which leaves untouched this position and the number of idlers to be supported, must from its nature be useless. That cheap food, in connection with the present system, would produce none of the beneficial effects anticipated, is evident from the condition of the working classes of Europe and of the United States; for they are compelled by the present arrangements of society, in defiance of cheap food, to maintain a trading and commercial aristocracy in full vigour – competition produces among them its common results – they wander about unemployed in thousands, dependent upon the mercy and the caprice of employers – and the greater part of the wealth which they produce is transferred to other classes by means of unequal exchanges. So long as the present social system exists, it will ever be, with the working man, no more than a choice between two means of losing. What is knocked from the hands of the aristocracy of the land, will be instantly snapped up by the aristocracy of the ship, or the mill, or the shop.

The land of the United Kingdom is of various degrees of fertility: some descriptions yield a rich return, and others are not worth cultivating. Under such circumstances it would be the extreme of stupidity to waste labour in producing corn on the unproductive land, when the corn can be procured abroad at one-half the price. . . .

The diversity of soils and products which appertain to various countries, enables men to relieve the wants of each other, and thereby tends to draw them closely together in that bond of fellowship which ever exists, more or less, among all beings of one kind. Under the system of society which has heretofore existed – engendering national as well as individual hostility – it may have been advantageous for nations to be independent of each other in regard to food. Had they not been thus, a whole people might have been starved at the caprice of some neighbouring tyrant. This necessity, however, will cease entirely when nations know and act upon the principles of community and equality.

Although all countries are not equally well adapted for the production of food, there are few which do not furnish a material or commodity of some kind for which food can be obtained in exchange. A nation, when considering what it is in want of, should likewise discover what it has to spare, and what is wanted by the people of other countries. Food, apparel, metals, minerals, and timber, are indispensable commodities; and a nation having a superfluity of any one of these things may be certain of obtaining, in exchange for it, any other article of which it may be in want. There is not a people to be found who are not more or less dependent upon the inhabitants of other countries for certain commodities. ...

Under the social system of community of possessions the principle of free trade could be carried out to its fullest extent, and its vast benefits be universally enjoyed. Under the present system, however, the interests of individuals and nations are so little understood, and are brought into such perpetual collision and hostility, that a really free trade can exist only in name; and the benefits derivable from an interchange of national commodities will be exclusively enjoyed. The existing state of things incontestibly proves that such is and ever will be the case.

It has long been known that the people of the United Kingdom, although destitute of the raw material of many indispensable commodities, possess every requisite for the manufacture of the raw material into the commodities desired. Attention, therefore, has been directed to manufactures; and machinery, as the first step to manufactures, has been of paramount importance, and efforts have been made to apply it to almost every kind of production. As we have already seen, there is now in the United Kingdom machinery adequate to perform the labour of one hundred millions of men. But, under the present system, this vast power neither lightens the labour nor increases the enjoyments of the working class; for it is in the possession, and works for the exclusive advantage, of other classes. The unrestricted machinery remedy contended for by a section of the economists, therefore, is of the same illusory character as all their other remedies. It does not go to the cause, and it cannot do away with the effect. It has been shewn that the present social system, by unequal exchanges places *the commodities created*, or the capital, on the one side, and *the power which creates*, or the labour, on the other. Labour is the only equivalent which a working man has to give for commodities – every invention which lessens the demand for labour takes away a portion of this equivalent – every increase of machinery displaces particular descriptions of labour, and therefore destroys the equivalent of particular workmen, or brings down its value – and thus, under the present system, and in connection with a comparatively limited amount of machinery, thousands are compelled to starve in Britain amidst glutted warehouses, while the capitalists are traversing the whole earth for customers.

Instead of devising and instituting arrangements which will bring into operation the unemployed labour of the destitute workman, and

enable the various sections of the community to produce equivalents
and exchange them with each other, the capitalists seek for a free
trade to foreign countries, that they may get rid of their commodities
among nations who have an equivalent to give for them. An extended
market always leads to the increased introduction of machinery and
the consequent displacement of human labour – and thus what is
called a free trade tends ultimately to lessen the value of the home
workman's equivalent, and to take it from him, and to entail upon
him years of poverty and suffering, although it for a moment imparts
a feverish and unhealthy activity to the body politic. Under the
present social system, as it has been shewn, machinery gradually takes
the labour, and therefore the food resulting from that labour, out of
the hands of the producer, and puts into the pockets of the capitalist
all the wealth which is created. Under these circumstances machinery
is an evil to the workman; and free trade, as it tends to increase
machinery, is likewise an evil; and it is not in the nature of things that
the unlimited extension of two great evils should alter their character
or detract from their potency.

A free trade and unlimited machinery, although thus fatal to the
interest of the producer in connection with the present system,
would, under the system of community, confer upon him incalculable benefits. As it has before been said, men want food, clothing,
shelter, and leisure for mental improvement and recreation – they
want certain *commodities*, and not the *work* which produces them.
Under a system of community of possessions, then, where the
productive forces of society would be common property, and where
all advantages of this kind would be universally and equally enjoyed,
a free trade and unrestricted machinery could be productive only of
good. The machinery would no longer be an antagonist of the
producer – it would no longer work against him, and assist a
capitalist to press him into the earth – but it would be a universal
friend and assistant; and a free trade, while it carried away all the
commodities which he was unable to consume, would bring him, in
exchange, the varied treasures of every corner of the earth. . . .

Intimately connected with the free trade and unrestricted
machinery remedies, and advocated by the same class, is the remedy
of emigration. It has long been seen that there was more labour in the
United Kingdom than could be employed by the capitalists at any
price – it has for years been felt by the workmen engaged in
manufactures, that machinery was slowly but surely taking from
them every thing that can make life desirable, and throwing them
upon the world almost destitute of the power of determining

whether they would live or die. As machinery has superseded the labour of the workmen engaged in particular trades, their wages have come down shilling by shilling and penny by penny, until at length the most incessant labour is scarcely adequate to procure the coarsest food. Large masses of men have been placed in this position; and a great and gradually increasing portion, unable to obtain employment on any terms, have been compelled to fall back upon the slender provision which poor laws yet allow for the relief of the destitute. The remedy which the capitalist has devised for this state of things, does not go to the finding of moderate labour and ample remuneration for the workman – does not go to the equitable division of the wealth which the machinery and the labour call into existence – does not go in any way to alter the cases which have induced the present state of things – but it would expatriate the half-famished workman to some foreign clime, where his murmurings will be unheard, his threats unfeared, and his wants unrelieved by the wretched pittance extorted from capital by means of poor-rates.

In most of the countries to which emigrants are thus despatched, the land is of a barren description and the climate insalubrious. But, were the soil the best that the sun shines upon, and the air the purest that can be breathed – were such a place all that the heart of man can wish for – it could, under the present social system, be productive of no more happiness or morality than is observable here. There would be inequality of possessions, inequality of labour, and inequality of exchanges – there would be superiors and inferiors – there would be discord, and envy, and hatred – there would be tyrants and slaves. That such would be the case, is proved by the records of every colony which Britain or any other nation has yet established; and the reasons why it would be so, and be so necessarily, have already been shown. ...

Among their other speculations, the political economists profess to have discovered that population has a tendency to increase faster than the means of subsistence – which means, in other words, that more children are born into the world than can be properly provided for – and it is from this inferred, that, even if the system of community were securely established, and every person left at liberty to marry, it would in a short time be impossible to provide a sufficiency of subsistence for all; and therefore an immense amount of poverty would be generated, and men would prey upon each other as they do at present.

Whatever may have been the reasons which led to this opinion, and however much or little the doctrine may apply to the present system, is now a matter of no moment. The considerations which have been entered into respecting the nature and origin of wealth, shew that, under the system of community, it will be in the power of society to procure subsistence adequate to meet the wants of all the human beings that may be born for thousands of years. Production is now fettered by innumerable chains – it is not dependent on society at large, but awaits the bidding of particular classes – and instead of breaking the bonds which confine it, and gathering together and uniting its now divided and hostile forces, the economists would restrict population to the capabilities of restricted production.

This remedy is of the same character as those which have been already examined; and it is another blind attempt to relieve a consequence without interfering with its cause. . . .

But it is said that the great principle of equality of rights has been weighed in the balance and found wanting – that its manifestations have been marked by fire, and blood, and desolation – that it levels all that is high and good, and sinks lower still all that was depraved and detestable. The considerations which have been entered into respecting the nature and operation of the principle of equality, so far from bringing into view characteristics such as these, prove most convincingly that such attributes do not belong to equality of rights, and cannot exist in connection with equality. If devastation and slaughter have marked the progress of any social movement – and history tells us that they have hitherto attended every advance of man – it is not the principle of equality of rights which is accountable for them. The principle, from its very nature, can never be productive of such results; and wherever liberty is outraged, and life or property sacrificed, it is the black and bloody spirit of Despotism which is at work, and not the fair and just principle of equality of rights. A principle can never violate itself; and whenever equality of rights is outraged, and wrong and injustice endured, we there behold the operation of a principle which is unconnected with and contrary to equality. . . .

In the common governmental revolutions which occasionally take place in nations, there is much injustice inflicted, and much blood and wealth sacrificed, by both the oppressors and the oppressed. Such movements rarely rest on principles of any kind; but society, split up into factions, and led by men having various and dissimilar objects in view, is more at war with itself than with the enemy which is intended to be overthrown. These changes are never more than a succession of tyrannies; they are generally commenced and carried on for the attainment of exclusive benefits for particular classes; and they often leave the producers of wealth in a worse condition than they were before the change took place. But the present movement is not of this evanescent and exclusive character – it has no leaders, and no class and caste interests to subserve – it is not to be established by a particular party to-day, and subverted by another party to-morrow. Resting on broad principles, having a clear and well-defined object in view, and embracing society at large, it is of a character altogether distinct from the petty movements which have preceded it; and, working out its results by means different to any hitherto made use of, the evils which have existed in connection with previous changes have no necessary connection with the present.

The social system of community of possessions is of such a character, that it contains within itself not only all the requisites desired by the economists, but also all the political equality contended for by the politicians; and it has been proved, from incontrovertible facts, that, under the present system, none of these things can be productive of advantage to the great bulk of society. It has been shewn that existing arrangements tend to create a diversity of interests, and an inequality of condition, and a consequent system of legislation for the exclusive benefit of particular classes; and under such arrangements it is not possible to devise efficient remedies, nor can just laws and regulations be kept sacred. But, under the system of community and equality, the insulting tyrant and the trembling slave – the overgorged capitalist and the famishing producer – every social ill and governmental grievance now endured – will be swept away, and the place which has known them will know them no longer. The present system will then be a memento of the past – a beacon to point out the rocks whereon millions of human barks have been split and stranded – a loathsome shore, covered with broken hearts, and laved by an ocean of human tears!

Thomas Carlyle

(1795–1881)

Few men can have rivalled the hold Carlyle exerted upon successive generations of Victorians, and, like other such magnetic forces, he sustained the
attention of both those who were attracted to and those who were repelled
by his philosophy. Of all the contending voices in this volume only Bray,
who may not have enjoyed access to the expensive periodicals in which
Carlyle was published, fails to acknowledge him as an influence.

Past and Present was written at speed between the autumn of 1842 and the
spring of 1843. The book was sparked off by a visit to East Anglia, undertaken
as part of Carlyle's research for his *Life of Oliver Cromwell*. Whilst there
Carlyle saw, in swift succession, the ruins of an abbey at Bury St Edmunds
and the workhouse at St Ives. In this chance combination Carlyle recognised
the possibility of juxtaposing past and present in such a way as to assuage any
personal anxieties about the escapism implicit in his historical studies. Yet
the book can also be regarded as a natural development of Carlyle's previous
work. A visit to Manchester on 1 May 1842, during a period of factory
closure, must have revealed to him how little impact his diagnosis of
England's plight, published in *Chartism* (1839), had made either in improving
the lot of the working classes or in diminishing the ruling classes' attachment
to the principle of *laissez-faire*. His work as a historian had also left its mark.
Writing from hindsight, as he had done in *The French Revolution* (1837), had
provided Carlyle with a method of revealing the inexorable consequences
which followed from the apparently random nature of events and decisions
taken by the immediate participants. In *Past and Present* he was able to use
his chosen example of medieval monastic order not only as a contrast to the
chaotic anarchy of nineteenth-century society, but also as a substructure to
confirm the inevitability of the predictions he arrived at from his reading of
the contemporary scene.

Divided into four books, the first, *Proem*, deals with the condition of
nineteenth-century England, the second draws upon Jocelin of Brakelond's
Chronicle, a narrative of abbey life in the late twelfth century, which had been
published by the Camden Society in 1840 and read by Carlyle on his return
from Bury St Edmund's: the last two books use the first two as stepping
stones to a vision of the future.

Carlyle does not offer the monastic order as an ideal or an alternative
model for nineteenth-century society, but places both within a far wider
continuum – that of eternity. Poised between heaven and hell each generation can succeed only in as far as it recognises the 'Invisible, Unnameable,

Godlike, present everywhere in all that we see, work and suffer' (p. 64). Two further emphases in Carlyle's argument derive from this perspective. First, Carlyle's political anatomy is offered not as a matter for intellectual controversy, but as an article of faith. The work of regenerating society, therefore, is dependent upon individual conversion rather than state legislation. Furthermore this essentially religious vision of society as a fellowship of souls ensures that Carlyle's analysis derives from a base wholly alien to the Political Economists' appreciation of the competitive notions at the heart of a market economy. Secondly, it enables Carlyle to diagnose a radical disease and to reject analyses which enumerate individual symptoms or cures which are no more than piecemeal panaceas. Society, as he conceives it, plays always for the highest stakes, is never static but forms an arena in which the forces of creativity struggle constantly with the forces of decay and chaos. The opening paragraphs reveal Carlyle reshaping Biblical myth so that his creed can transform work from a primal curse to an organic process having a natural place in a world of continuous creation.

In *Past and Present*, a midway point in Carlyle's thinking, the reader can still see the sensitivity to the dynamics of change at work in his society which formed so prominent a feature of his early work, and detect signs of his increasing fear of irremediable chaos. It was this fear, articulated with greater stridency in later works, that caused him gradually to transfer his emphasis from the people's right to be well-ruled, to open adulation of the strong hero or 'missionary of order'. Although Carlyle's admiration of sprucely attired, well-drilled soldiers is apt to embarrass the modern reader, he is at pains to repudiate any blind worship of force and to offer the army merely as an illustration of the positive action open to a government prepared to discipline the resources available to it. Government intervention is to be applauded in as far as it counteracts the self-interested idleness of the *laissez-faire* philosophy, but can never supersede self-reform.

Since the call to conversion lies close to the heart of Carlyle's message it should not surprise us that he uses the rhetoric of persuasion, relying upon question and assertion, exhortation, reiteration, parable and dramatic allegory rather than the progressions of logical argument. As befitted a contender for the Edinburgh Chair of Rhetoric, behind the artful range of tones and modes Carlyle employs, lies a constant awareness of his audience. Deploying a varied *dramatis personae*, Carlyle produces the illusion of a forum of opinion ranging from corroborative evidence of a picturesque tourist (p. 56) to the puzzled conjures of his German friend, Sauerteig (an allegorical name meaning 'sourdough' or 'leaven'; pp. 62–3). This in turn lends a greater intensity to the convictions that Carlyle voices *in propria persona*. Copious archaisms serve to create a Biblically favoured prophetic register giving Carlyle the foothold outside time that his perspective required. These are counterpointed with the numerous topical allusions which give specificity to Carlyle's panoramic vision.

Carlyle's prose is dense with cumulative images. There are the longer tales such as that of the Irish widow (p. 65) which, when they are first introduced, act as stark examples of the appalling neglect attendant upon a *laissez-faire* policy, but, at each subsequent reference are seen less as atypical horror stories and more as symptomatic of an entire system which discounts individual suffering in pursuit of the abstract rules of political economy. A grim satiric humour is also derived from the absurd collocations which result from the seemingly endless combinations into which these key images are introduced so as to define or morally locate some further episode or agent.

The texture of Carlyle's writing raises a constant protest against jargon and generality. The desire of officialese to abstract and dehumanise is subtly reversed. Take, for example, the passage on the English legislature (pp. 73–4) which begins with a disarming enough tribute to parliament's reverence for tradition. But, as the English legislature begins to take on a distinct identity, achieved by using a technique close to reported speech, a sarcastic tone rings through. We are allowed for a moment to hear the dismissive tones of the self-importantly preoccupied behind 'The English Legislature does not occupy itself with epochs; has indeed other business to do than looking at the Time-Horologe and hearing it tick!' (p. 73). As the inanimate becomes momentarily animate, Carlyle has demonstrated the tendencies of the individual with moral responsibilites to hide behind a corporate abstraction.

The importance of society recognising itself as a living organism constantly being created or destroyed, capable of being mortally injured by the malfunction of any of its parts, receives further emphasis in images derived from Nature (e.g. 'A High Class without duties to do is like a tree planted on precipices; from the roots of which all the earth has been crumbling' p. 66). Only by taking up his inherited place in the order of creation can man fulfil himself, not as a beaver, or a spider, but as a soul conscious of infinity (pp. 62, 68).

Carlyle's habit of reiterating and accumulating images can occasionally seem merely repetitive and, taken as a whole, *Past and Present* does bear the marks of its rapid composition. Sometimes the energy which characterised Carlyle's finest prose does seem to have become a matter of surface achievements rather than inner compulsion as if Carlyle had taken all too literally Browning's apothegm: 'Frothy spume and frequent sputter prove that the soul's depths boil in earnest.' Energy, as Carlyle often argues, needs to be specifically directed to be effective, so that his style, so well adapted to thundering denunciation or withering scorn, can seem peculiarly shapeless and vague when it comes to outlining a positive programme (pp. 70–3). We are left with the impression of an *ad hoc* list (e.g. 'Then again, why should there not be an "Emigration Service" . . . .' p. 72) arrived at in the piecemeal fashion he had castigated in others in the chapter entitled *Morrison's Pill*.

In his best passages it is often this very air of spontaneity, struggling to articulate fresh perception that proves so telling: those irregular comparatives ('doabler', p. 59; 'far fataler', p. 56), or the inverted syntax which serves to place emphasis upon the leading thought, whether by withholding the main verb or the subject. Such a technique also lends syntactic force to

2. *Past and Present*

Carlyle's desire to convince us of the sure determination of events as we are led by curiosity and force by our sense of suspended resolution to follow his curious convolutions. In the following example inversion is reinforced by the hammer beat of the introductory 'there will', whilst monotony is avoided by the variety of the internal play of apposition:

> There will no 'thing' be done that will cure you. There will a radical universal alteration of your regimen and way of life take place; there will a most agonising divorce between you and your chimeras, luxuries and falsities, take place; a most toilsome, all-but 'impossible' return to Nature, and her veracities and her integrities, take place: that so the inner fountains of life may again begin, like eternal Light-fountains, to irradiate and purify your bloated, swollen, foul existence, drawing nigh, as at present, to nameless death! Either death, or else all this will take place (p. 57).

The chaos of detail and movement that always so nearly impends is averted as we emerge into the purposive 'that so' clause. A simple and brief sentence returns us to the dualisms, life and death, heaven and hell, which lie at the root of *Past and Present*.

2. *Past and Present* (1843)

Centenary Edition, ed. H. D. Traill (1879), pp. 1–2, 23–7, 90–2, 144–50, 179, 182–4, 260–7, 271–6, 290–2

Midas (book 1, ch. 1)

The condition of England, on which many pamphlets are now in the course of publication, and many thoughts unpublished are going on in every reflective head, is justly regarded as one of the most ominous, and withal one of the strangest, ever seen in this world. England is full of wealth, of multifarious produce, supply for human want in every kind; yet England is dying of inanition. With unabated bounty the land of England blooms and grows; waving with yellow harvests; thick-studded with workshops, industrial implements, with fifteen millions of workers, understood to be the strongest, the cunningest and the willingest our Earth ever had; these men are here; the work they have done, the fruit they have realised is here, abundant, exuberant on every hand of us: and behold, some baleful fiat as of Enchantment has gone forth, saying, 'Touch it not, ye workers, ye master-workers, ye master-idlers; none of you can touch it, no man of you shall be the better for it; this is enchanted fruit!' On the poor workers such fiat falls first, in its rudest shape; but on the rich master-workers too it falls; neither can the rich master-idlers, nor any richest or highest man escape, but all are like to be brought low with it, and made 'poor' enough, in the money sense or a far fataler one.

Of these successful skilful workers some two millions, it is now counted, sit in Workhouses, Poor-law Prisons; or have 'out-door relief' flung over the wall to them, – the workhouse Bastille being filled to bursting, and the strong Poor-law broken asunder by a stronger.[1] They sit there, these many months now; their hope of deliverance as yet small. In workhouses, pleasantly so-named, because work cannot be done in them. Twelve-hundred-thousand workers in England alone; their cunning right-hand lamed, lying idle in their sorrowful bosom; their hopes, outlooks, share of this fair world, shut-in by narrow walls. They sit there, pent up, as in a kind of horrid enchantment; glad to be imprisoned and enchanted, that they may not perish starved. The picturesque Tourist, in a sunny autumn day, through this bounteous realm of England, describes the Union Workhouse on his path. 'Passing by the Workhouse of St. Ives in Huntingdonshire, on a bright day last autumn,' says the picturesque Tourist, 'I saw sitting on wooden benches, in front of their Bastille and within their ring-wall and its railings, some half-hundred or more of these men. Tall robust figures, young mostly or of middle age; of honest countenance, many of them thoughtful and even intelligent-looking men. They sat there, near by one another; but in a kind of torpor, especially in a silence, which was very striking. In silence: for, alas, what word was to be said? An Earth all lying round, crying, Come and till me, come and reap me; – yet we here sit enchanted! In the eyes and brows of these men hung the gloomiest expression, not of anger, but of grief and shame and manifold inarticulate distress and weariness; they returned my glance with a glance that seemed to say, "Do not look at us. We sit enchanted here, we know not why. The Sun shines and the Earth calls; and, by the governing Powers and Impotences of this England, we are fobidden to obey. It is impossible, they tell us!" There was something that reminded me of Dante's Hell in the look of all this; and I rode swiftly away.' ...

Morrison's Pill[2] (book 1, ch. 4)

What is to be done, what would you have us do? asks many a one with a tone of impatience, almost of reproach; and then, if you mention some one thing, some two things, twenty things that might be done, turns round with a satirical tehee, and 'These are your remedies!' The state of mind indicated by such question, and such rejoinder, is worth reflecting on.

It seems to be taken for granted, by these interrogative philosophers, that there is some 'thing,' or handful of 'things,' which could be done; some Act of Parliament, 'remedial measure' or the like, which could be passed, whereby the social malady were fairly fronted, conquered, put an end to; so that, with your remedial measure in your pocket, you could then go on triumphant, and be troubled no farther. 'You tell us the evil,' cry such persons, as if justly aggrieved, 'and do not tell us how it is to be cured!'

How it is to be cured? Brothers, I am sorry I have got no Morrison's Pill for curing the maladies of Society. It were infinitely handier if we had a Morrison's Pill, Act of Parliament, or remedial measure, which men could swallow, one good time, and then go on in their old courses, cleared from all miseries and mischiefs! Unluckily we have none such; unluckily the Heavens themselves in their rich pharmacopœia, contain none such. There will no 'thing' be done that will cure you. There will a radical universal alteration of your regimen and way of life take place; there will a most agonising divorce between you and your chimeras, luxuries and falsities, take place; a most toilsome, all-but 'impossible' return to Nature, and her veracities and her integrities, take place: that so the inner fountains of life may again begin, like eternal Light-fountains,[a] to irradiate and purify your bloated, swollen, foul existence, drawing nigh, as at present, to nameless death! Either death, or else all this will take place. Judge if, with such diagnosis, any Morrison's Pill is like to be discoverable!

But the Life-fountain within you once again set flowing, what innumerable 'things,' whole sets and classes and continents of 'things,' year after year, and decade after decade, and century after century, will then be doable and done! Not Emigration, Education, Corn-Law Abrogation, Sanitary Regulation, Land Property-Tax; not these alone, nor a thousand times as much as these. Good Heavens, there will then be light in the inner heart of here and there a man, to discern what is just, what is commanded by the Most High God, what *must* be done, were it never so 'impossible.' Vain jargon in favour of the palpably unjust will then abridge itself within limits. Vain jargon, on Hustings, in Parliaments or wherever else, when here and there a man has vision for the essential God's-Truth of the things jargoned of, will become very vain indeed. The silence of here

[a] Victorian sun-lamps.

and there such a man, how eloquent in answer to such jargon! Such jargon, frightened at its own gaunt echo, will unspeakably abate; nay, for a while, may almost in a manner disappear, – the wise answering it in silence, and even the simple taking cue from them to hoot it down wherever heard. It will be a blessed time; and many 'things' will become doable, – and when the brains are out,[a] an absurdity will die! Not easily again shall a Corn-Law argue ten years for itself; and still talk and argue, when impartial persons have to say with a sigh that, for so long back, they have heard no 'argument' advanced for it but such as might make the angels and almost the very jackasses weep! –

Wholly a blessed time: when jargon might abate, and here and there some genuine speech begin. When to the noble opened heart, as to such heart they alone do, all noble things began to grow visible; and the difference between just and unjust, between true and false, between work and sham-work, between speech and jargon, was once more, what to our happier Fathers it used to be, *infinite*, – as between a Heavenly thing and an Infernal: the one a thing which you were *not* to do, which you were wise not to attempt doing; which it were better for you to have a millstone tied round your neck, and be cast into the sea,[b] than concern yourself with doing! – Brothers, it will not be a Morrison's Pill, or remedial measure, that will bring all this about for us.

And yet, very literally, till, in some shape or other, it be brought about, we remain cureless; till it begin to be brought about, the cure does not begin. For Nature and Fact, not Redtape and Semblance, are to this hour the basis of man's life; and on those, through never such strata of these, man and his life and all his interests do, sooner or later, infallibly come to rest, – and to be supported or be swallowed according as they agree with those. The question is asked of them, not, How do you agree with Downing Street and accredited Semblance? but, How do you agree with God's Universe and the actual Reality of things? This Universe *has* its Laws. If we walk according to the Law, the Law-Maker will befriend us; if not, not. Alas, by no Reform Bill, Ballot-box, Five-point Charter,[3] by no boxes or bills or charters, can you perform this alchemy: 'Given a world of Knaves, to produce an Honesty from their united action!' It is a distillation, once for all, not possible. You pass it through alembic after alembic, it comes out still a Dishonesty, with a new dress on it, a new colour to it. 'While we ourselves continue valets, how *can* any hero come to

[a] *Macbeth* 3.iv.79.   [b] Matthew 18.6.

govern us?' We are governed, very infallibly, by the 'sham-hero,' – whose name is Quack, whose work and governance is Plausibility, and also is Falsity and Fatuity; to which Nature says, and must say when it comes to *her* to speak, eternally No! Nations cease to be befriended of the Law-Maker, when they walk *not* according to the Law. The Sphinx-question remains unsolved by them, becomes ever more insoluble.

If thou ask again, therefore, on the Morrison's-Pill hypothesis, What is to be done! allow me to reply: By thee, for the present, almost nothing. Thou there, the thing for thee to do is, if possible, to cease to be a hollow sounding-shell of hearsays, egoisms, purblind dilettantisms; and become, were it on the infinitely small scale, a faithful discerning soul. Thou shalt descend into thy inner man, and see if there be any traces of a *soul* there; till then there can be nothing done! O brother, we must if possible resuscitate some soul and conscience in us, exchange our dilettantisms for sincerities, our dead hearts of stone for living hearts of flesh. Then shall we discern, not one thing, but, in clearer or dimmer sequence, a whole endless host of things that can be done. *Do* the first of these; do it; the second will already have become clearer, doabler; the second, third and three-thousandth will then have begun to be possible for us. Not any universal Morrison's Pill shall we then, either as swallowers or as venders, ask after at all; but a far different sort of remedies: Quacks shall no more have dominion over us, but true Heroes and Healers!

Will not that be a thing worthy of 'doing'; to deliver ourselves from quacks, sham-heroes; to deliver the whole world more and more from such? They are the one bane of the world. Once clear the world of them, it ceases to be a Devil's-world, in all fibres of it wretched, accursed; and begins to be a God's-world, blessed, and working hourly towards blessedness. Thou for one wilt not again vote for any quack, do honour to any edge-gilt vacuity in man's shape: cant shall be known to thee by the sound of it; – thou wilt fly from cant with a shudder never felt before; as from the opened litany of Sorcerers' Sabbaths, and true Devil-worship of this age, more horrible than any other blasphemy, profanity or genuine blackguardism elsewhere audible among men. It is alarming to witness, – in its present completed state! And Quack and Dupe, as we must ever keep in mind, are upper-side and under of the selfsame substance; convertible personages: turn up your dupe into the proper fostering element, and he himself can become a quack; there is in him the due prurient insincerity, open voracity for profit, and closed sense for truth, whereof quacks too, in all the kinds are made.

Alas, it is not to the hero, it is to the sham-hero, that, of right and necessity, the valet-world belongs. 'What is to be done?' The reader sees whether it is like to be the seeking and swallowing of some 'remedial measure'!...

Government (book II, ch. 10)

How Abbot Samson, giving his new subjects seriatim[a] the kiss of fatherhood in the St. Edmundsbury chapterhouse, proceeded with cautious energy to set about reforming their disjointed distracted way of life; how he managed with his Fifty rough *Milites* (Feudal Knights), with his lazy Farmers, remiss refractory Monks, with Pope's Legates, Viscounts, Bishops, Kings; how on all sides he laid about him like a man, and putting consequence on premiss, and everywhere the saddle on the right horse, struggled incessantly to educe organic method out of lazily fermenting wreck, – the careful reader will discern, not without true interest, in these pages of Jocelin Boswell.[4] In most antiquarian quaint costume, not of garments alone, but of thought, word, action, outlook and position, the substantial figure of a man with eminent nose, bushy brows and clear-flashing eyes, his russet beard growing daily grayer, is visible, engaged in true governing of men. It is beautiful how the chrysalis governing-soul, shaking off its dusty slough and prison, starts forth winged, a true royal soul! Our new Abbot has a right honest unconscious feeling, without insolence as without fear or flutter, of what he is and what others are. A courage to quell the proudest, an honest pity to encourage the humblest. Withal there is a noble reticence in this Lord Abbot: much vain unreason he hears; lays up without response. He is not there to expect reason and nobleness of others; he is there to give them of his own reason and nobleness. Is he not their servant, as we said, who can suffer from them, and for them; bear the burden their poor spindle-limbs totter and stagger under; and, in virtue of *being* their servant, govern them, lead them out of weakness into strength, out of defeat into victory!

One of the first Herculean Labours Abbot Samson undertook, or the very first, was to institute a strenuous review and radical reform of his economics. It is the first labour of every governing man, from

[a] In turn.

2. Past and Present

Paterfamilias to *Dominus Rex.ᵃ* To get the rain thatched out from you is the preliminary of whatever farther, in the way of speculation or of action, you may mean to do. Old Abbot Hugo's budget, as we saw, had become empty, filled with deficit and wind. To see his account-books clear, be delivered from those ravening flights of Jew and Christian creditors, pouncing on him like obscene harpies wherever he showed face, was a necessity for Abbot Samson.

On the morrow after his instalment he brings in a load of money-bonds, all duly stamped, sealed with this or the other Convent Seal: frightful, unmanageable, a bottomless confusion of Convent finance. There they are; – but there at least they all are; all that shall be of them. Our Lord Abbot demands that all the official seals in use among us be now produced and delivered to him. Three-and-thirty seals turn up; are straightway broken, and shall seal no more: the Abbot only, and those duly authorised by him shall seal any bond. There are but two ways of paying debt: increase of industry in raising income, increase of thrift in laying it out. With iron energy, in slow but steady undeviating perseverance, Abbot Samson sets to work in both directions. His troubles are manifold: cunning *milites*, unjust bailiffs, lazy sockmen,ᵇ he an inexperienced Abbot; relaxed lazy monks, not disinclined to mutiny in mass: but continued vigilance, rigorous method, what we call 'the eye of the master,' work wonders. The clear-beaming eyesight of Abbot Samson, steadfast, severe, all-penetrating, – it is like *Fiat lux*ᶜ in that inorganic waste whirlpool; penetrates gradually to all nooks, and of the chaos makes a *kosmos* or ordered world!

He arranges everywhere, struggles unweariedly to arrange, and place on some intelligible footing, the 'affairs and dues, *res ac redditus*,' of his dominion. The Lakenheath eels cease to breed squabbles between human beings; the penny of *reap-silver* to explode into the streets of Female Chartism of St. Edmundsbury.[5] These and innumerable greater things. Wheresoever Disorder may stand or lie, let it have a care; here is the man that has declared war with it, that never will make peace with it. Man is the Missionary of Order; he is the servant not of the Devil and Chaos, but of God and the Universe! Let all sluggards, and cowards, remiss, false-spoken, unjust, and otherwise diabolic persons have a care: this is a dangerous man for them. He has a mild grave face; a thoughtful sternness, a sorrowful pity: but there is a terrible flash of anger in him too; lazy monks often

---

ᵃ The head of a household to a king.
ᵇ Those holding tenure of land according to services other than those performed by a knight.
ᶜ The opening words of the Creation: 'Let there be light'.

61

have to murmur, '*Sævit ut lupus*, He rages like a wolf; was not our Dream true!' 'To repress and hold-in such sudden anger he was continually careful,' and succeeded well: – right, Samson; that it may become in thee as noble central heat, fruitful, strong, beneficent; not blaze out, or the seldomest possible blaze out, as wasteful volcanoism to scorch and consume! . . .

Gospel of Mammonism (book III, ch. 2)

Reader, even Christian Reader as thy title goes, hast thou any notion of Heaven and Hell? I rather apprehend, not. Often as the words are on our tongue, they have got a fabulous or semi-fabulous character for most of us, and pass on like a kind of transient similitude, like a sound signifying little.

Yet it is well worth while for us to know, once and always, that they are not a similitude, nor a fable nor semi-fable; that they are an everlasting highest fact! 'No Lake of Sicilian or other sulphur burns now anywhere in these ages,'[6] sayest thou? Well, and if there did not! Believe that there does not; believe it if thou wilt, nay hold by it as a real increase, a rise to higher stages, to wider horizons and empires. All this has vanished, or has not vanished; believe as thou wilt as to all this. But that an Infinite of Practical Importance, speaking with strict arithmetical exactness, an *Infinite*, has vanished or can vanish from the Life of any Man: this thou shalt not believe! O brother, the Infinite of Terror, of Hope, of Pity, did it not at any moment disclose itself to thee, indubitable, unnameable? Came it never, like the gleam of *preter*natural eternal Oceans, like the voice of old Eternities, far-sounding through they heart of hearts? Never? Alas, it was not thy Liberalism, then; it was thy Animalism! The Infinite is more sure than any other fact. But only men can discern it; mere building beavers, spinning arachnes, much more the predatory vulturous and vulpine species, do not discern it well! –

'The word Hell,' says Sauerteig, 'is still frequently in use among the English people: but I could not without difficulty ascertain what they meant by it. Hell generally signifies the Infinite Terror, the thing a man *is* infinitely afraid of, and shudders and shrinks from, struggling with his whole soul to escape from it. There is a Hell therefore, if you will consider, which accompanies man, in all stages of his history, and religious or other development: but the Hells of men and Peoples differ notably. With Christians it is the infinite terror of being found guilty before the Just Judge. With old Romans, I conjecture, it was the terror not of Pluto,[a] for whom probably they cared little, but of doing unworthily, doing unvirtuously, which was their word for un*man*fully. And now what is it, if you pierce through his Cants, his oft-repeated Hearsays, what he calls his Worships and so forth, – what is it that the modern English soul does, in very truth, dread infinitely, and contemplate with entire despair? What *is* his Hell, after all these reputable, oft-repeated Hearsays, what is it? With hesitation, with astonishment, I pronounce it to be: The terror of "Not succeeding"; of not making money, fame, or some other figure in the world, – chiefly of not making money! Is not that a somewhat singular Hell?'

Yes, O Sauerteig, it is very singular. If we do not 'succeed,' where is the use of us? We had better never have been born. 'Tremble intensely,' as our friend the Emperor of China says:[7] *there* is the black Bottomless of Terror; what Sauerteig calls the 'Hell of the English'! – But indeed this Hell belongs naturally to the Gospel of Mammonism, which also has its corresponding Heaven. For there *is* one Reality among so many Phantasms; about one thing we are entirely in earnest: The making of money. Working Mammonism does divide the world with idle game-preserving Dilettantism: – thank Heaven that there is even a Mammonism, *any*thing we are in earnest about! Idleness is worst, Idleness alone is without hope: work earnestly at anything, you will by degrees learn to work at almost all things. There is endless hope in work, were it even work at making money.

True, it must be owned, we for the present, with our Mammon-Gospel, have come to strange conclusions. We call it a Society; and go about professing openly the totalest separation, isolation. Our life is not a mutual helpfulness; but rather, cloaked under due laws-of-war, named 'fair competition' and so forth, it is a mutual hostility. We have profoundly forgotten everywhere that *Cash-payment* is not the sole relation of human beings; we think, nothing doubting, that *it* absolves and liquidates all engagements of man. 'My starving workers?' answers the rich mill-owner: 'Did not I hire them fairly in the market? Did I not pay them, to the last sixpence, the sum covenanted for? What have I to do with them more?' – Verily Mammon worship is a melancholy creed. When Cain, for his own behoof, had killed Abel, and was questioned, 'Where is thy brother?' he too made answer, 'Am I my brother's keeper?'[b] Did I not pay my brother *his* wages, the thing he had merited from me?

O sumptuous Merchant-Prince, illustrious game-preserving Duke, is there no way of 'killing' thy brother but Cain's rude way! 'A good

[a] The mythical king of the underworld.   [b] Genesis 4:9.

man by the very look of him, by his very presence with us as a fellow wayfarer in this Life-pilgrimage, *promises* so much': woe to him if he forget all such promises, if he never knew that they were given! To a deadened soul, seared with the brute Idolatry of Sense, to whom going to Hell is equivalent to not making money, all 'promises,' and moral duties, that cannot be pleaded for in Courts of Requests,*ᵃ* address themselves in vain. Money he can be ordered to pay, but nothing more. I have not heard in all Past History, and expect not to hear in all Future History, of any Society anywhere under God's Heaven supporting itself on such Philosophy. The Universe is not made so; it is made otherwise than so. The man or nation of men that thinks it is made so, marches forward nothing doubting, step after step; but marches – whither we know! In these last two centuries of Atheistic Government (near two centuries now, since the blessed restoration of his Sacred Majesty, and Defender of the Faith, Charles Second), I reckon that we have pretty well exhausted what of 'firm earth' there was for us to march on; – and are now, very ominously, shuddering, reeling, and let us hope trying to recoil, on the cliff's edge! –

For out of this that we call Atheism come so many other *isms* and falsities, each falsity with its misery at its heels! – A SOUL is not like wind (*spiritus*, or breath) contained within a capsule; the ALMIGHTY MAKER is not like a Clockmaker that once, in old immemorial ages, having *made* his Horologe of a Universe, sits ever since and sees it go!⁸ Not at all. Hence comes Atheism; come, as we say, many other *isms*; and as the sum of all, comes Valetism, the *reverse* of Heroism; sad root of all woes whatsover. For indeed, as no man ever saw the above-said wind-element enclosed within its capsule, and finds it at bottom more deniable than conceivable; so too he finds, in spite of Bridgwater Bequests,⁹ your Clockmaker Almighty an entirely questionable affair, a deniable affair; – and accordingly denies it, and along with it so much else. Alas, one knows not what and how much else! For the faith in an Invisible, Unnameable, Godlike, present everywhere in all that we see and work and suffer, is the essence of all faith whatsoever; and that once denied, or still worse, asserted with lips only, and out of bound prayerbooks only, what other thing remains believable? That Cant well-ordered is marketable Cant; that Heroism means gas-lighted Histrionism;*ᵇ* that seen with 'clear eyes' (as they call Valet-eyes) no man is a Hero, or ever was a Hero, but all men are Valets and Varlets. The accursed practical quintessence of all sorts of Unbelief! For if there be now no Hero, and the Histrio

---

ᵃ Small claims courts, abolished in 1846.   *ᵇ* Theatricals.

himself begin to be seen into, what hope is there for the seed of Adam here below? We are the doomed, everlasting prey of the Quack; who now in this guise, now in that, is to filch us, to pluck and eat us, by such modes as are convenient for him. For the modes and guises I care little. The Quack once inevitable, let him come swiftly, let him pluck and eat me; – swiftly, that I may at least have done with him; for in his Quack-world I can have no wish to linger. Though he slay me, yet will I *not* trust in him.*a* Though he conquer nations, and have all the Flunkies of the Universe shouting at his heels, yet will I know well that *he* is an Inanity; that for him and his there is no continuance appointed, save only in Gehenna and the Pool.*b* Alas, the Atheist world, from its utmost summits of Heaven and Westminster-Hall, downwards through poor seven-feet Hats[10] and 'Unveracities fallen hungry,' down to the lowest cellars and neglected hunger-dens of it, is very wretched.

One of Dr. Alison's Scotch facts struck us much.[11] A poor Irish Widow, her husband having died in one of the Lanes of Edinburgh, went forth with her three children, bare of all resource, to solicit help from the Charitable Establishments of that City. At this Charitable Establishment and then at that she was refused; referred from one to the other, helped by none; – till she had exhausted them all; till her strength and heart failed her: she sank down in typhus-fever; died, and infected her Lane with fever, so that 'seventeen other persons' died of fever there in consequence. The humane Physician asks thereupon, as with a heart too full for speaking, Would it not have been *economy* to help this poor Widow? She took typhus-fever, and killed seventeen of you! – Very curious. The forlorn Irish Widow applies to her fellow-creatures, as if saying, 'Behold I am sinking, bare of help: ye must help me! I am your sister, bone of your bone; one God made us: ye must help me!' They answer, 'No, impossible; thou art no sister of ours.' But she proves her sisterhood; her typhus-fever kills *them*: they actually were her brothers, though denying it! Had human creature ever to go lower for a proof?

For, as indeed was very natural in such case, all government of the Poor by the Rich has long ago been given over to Supply-and-demand, Laissez-faire and suchlike, and universally declared to be 'impossible.' 'You are no sister of ours; what shadow of proof is there? Here are our parchments, our padlocks, proving indisputably our money-safes to be *ours*, and you to have no business with them. Depart! It is impossible!' – Nay, what wouldst thou thyself have us do? cry indignant readers. Nothing, my friends, – till you have got a

a Cf. Job 13:15.   *b* Hell.

soul for yourselves again. Till then all things are 'impossible.' Till then I cannot even bid you buy, as the old Spartans[12] would have done, two-pence worth of powder and lead, and compendiously shoot to death this poor Irish Widow: even that is 'impossible' for you. Nothing is left but that she prove her sisterhood by dying, and infecting you with typhus. Seventeen of you lying dead will not deny such proof that she *was* flesh of your flesh; and perhaps some of the living may lay it to heart.

'Impossible': of a certain two-legged animal with feathers it is said, if you draw a distinct chalk-circle round him, he sits imprisoned, as if girt with the iron ring of Fate; and will die there, though within sight of victuals, – or sit in sick misery there, and be fatted to death. The name of this poor two-legged animal is – Goose; and they make him, when well fattened, *Pâté de foie gras*, much prized by some ! . . .

Unworking Aristocracy (book III, ch. 8)

. . . A High Class without duties to do is like a tree planted on precipices; from the roots of which all the earth has been crumbling. Nature owns no man who is not a Martyr withal. Is there a man who pretends to live luxuriously housed up; screened from all work, from want, danger, hardship, the victory over which is what we name work; – he himself to sit serene, amid down-bolsters and appliances, and have all his work and battling done by other men? And such man calls himself a *noble*-man? His fathers worked for him, he says; or successfully gambled for him: here *he* sits; professes, not in sorrow but in pride, that he and his have done no work, time out of mind. It is the law of the land, and is thought to be the law of the Universe, that he, alone of recorded men, shall have no task laid on him, except that of eating his cooked victuals, and not flinging himself out of window. Once more I will say, there was no stranger spectacle ever shown under this Sun. A veritable fact in our England of the Nineteenth Century. His victuals he does eat: but as for keeping in the inside of the window, – have not his friends, like me, enough to do? Truly, looking at his Corn-Laws, Game-Laws, Chandos-Clauses,[13] Bribery-Elections and much else, you do shudder over the tumbling and plunging he makes, held back by the lapels and coat-skirts; only a thin fence of window-glass before him, – and in the street mere horrid iron spikes!

Working Aristocracy (book III, ch. 9)

... The Continental people, it would seem, are 'exporting our machinery, beginning to spin cotton and manufacture for themselves, to cut us out of this market and then out of that!' Sad news indeed; but irremediable; – by no means the saddest news. The saddest news is, that we should find our National Existence, as I sometimes hear it said, depend on selling manufactured cotton at a farthing an ell cheaper than any other People. A most narrow stand for a great Nation to base itself on! A stand which, with all the Corn-Law Abrogations conceivable, I do not think will be capable of enduring.

My friends, suppose we quitted that stand; suppose we came honestly down from it, and said: 'This is our minimum of cotton-prices. We care not, for the present, to make cotton any cheaper. Do you, if it seem so blessed to you, make cotton cheaper. Fill your lungs with cotton-fuzz, your hearts with copperas-fumes,*a* with rage and mutiny; become ye the general gnomes of Europe, slaves of the lamp!' – I admire a Nation which fancies it will die if it do not undersell all other Nations, to the end of the world. Brothers, we will cease to *under*sell them; we will be content to *equal*-sell them; to be happy selling equally with them! I do not see the use of underselling them. Cotton-cloth is already two-pence a yard or lower; and yet bare backs were never more numerous among us. Let inventive men cease to spend their existence incessantly contriving how cotton can be made cheaper; and try to invent, a little, how cotton at its present cheapness could be somewhat justlier divided among us. Let inventive men consider, Whether the Secret of this Universe, and of Man's Life there, does, after all, as we rashly fancy it, consist in making money? There is One God, just, supreme, almighty: but is Mammon the name of him? – With a Hell which means 'Failing to make money,' I do not think there is any Heaven possible that would suit one well; nor so much as an Earth that can be habitable long! In brief, all this Mammon-Gospel, of Supply-and-demand, Competition, Laissez-faire, and Devil take the hindmost, begins to be one of the shabbiest Gospels ever preached; or altogether the shabbiest. Even with Dilettante partridge-nets,[14] and at a horrible expenditure of pain, who shall regret to see the entirely transient, and at best somewhat despicable life strangled out of *it*? At the best, as we say, a somewhat despicable, unvenerable thing, this same 'Laissez-faire'; and now, at the *worst*, fast growing an altogether detestable one!

a Sulphate, used in dyeing, tanning and ink-making.

'But what is to be done with our manufacturing population, with our agricultural, with our ever-increasing population?' cry many – Ay, what? Many things can be done with them, a hundred things, and a thousand things, – had we once got a soul, and begun to try. This one thing, of doing for them by 'underselling all people,' and filling our own bursten pockets and appetites by the road; and turning over all care for any 'population,' or human or divine consideration except cash only, to the winds, with a 'Laissez-faire' and the rest of it: this is evidently not the thing. Farthing cheaper per yard? No great Nation can stand on the apex of such a pyramid; screwing itself higher and higher; balancing itself on its great-toe! Can England not subsist without being *above* all people in working? England never deliberately purposed such a thing. If England work better than all people it shall be well. England, like an honest worker, will work as well as she can; and hope the gods may allow her to live on that basis. Laissez-faire and much else being once well dead, how many 'impossibles' will become possible! They are impossible, as cotton-cloth at two-pence an ell was – till men set about making it. The inventive genius of great England will not forever sit patient with mere wheels and pinions, bobbins, straps and billy-rollers[a] whirring in the head of it. The inventive genius of England is not a Beaver's, or a Spinner's or Spider's genius: it is a *Man's* genius, I hope, with a God over him!

The One Institution (book IV, ch. 3)

... Who can despair of Governments that passes a Soldier's Guard-house, or meets a redcoated man on the streets! That a body of men could be got together to kill other men when you bade them: this, *a priori*, does it not seem one of the impossiblest things? Yet look, behold it: in the stolidest of Donothing Governments, that impossibility is a thing done. See it there, with buff belts, red coats on its back; walking sentry at guard-houses, brushing white breeches in barracks; an indisputable palpable fact. Out of gray Antiquity, amid all finance-difficulties, *scaccarium*-tallies, ship-moneys, coat-and-conduct moneys,[15] and vicissitudes of Chance and Time, there, down to the present blessed hour, it is.

Often, in these painfully decadent and painfully nascent Times, with their distresses, inarticulate gaspings and 'impossibilities';

---

[a] Various tools used in the textile industry.

meeting a tall Lifeguardsman in his snow-white trousers, or seeing those two statuesque Lifeguardsmen in their frowning bearskins, pipe-clayed buckskins, on their coal-black sleek-fiery quadrupeds, riding sentry at the Horse-Guards, – it strikes one with a kind of mournful interest, how, in such universal down-rushing and wrecked impotence of almost all old institutions, this oldest Fighting Institution is still so young! Fresh-complexioned, firm-limbed, six feet by the standard, this fighting man has verily been got up, and can fight. While so much has not yet got into being; while so much has gone gradually out of it, and become an empty Semblance or Clothes-suit; and highest king's-cloaks, mere chimeras parading under them so long, are getting unsightly to the earnest eye, unsightly, almost offensive, like a costlier kind of scarecrow's-blanket, – here still is a reality!

The man in horsehair wig advances, promising that he will get me 'justice': he takes me into Chancery Law-Courts,[16] into decades, half-centuries of hubbub, of distracted jargon; and does *get* me – disappointment, almost desperation; and one refuge: that of dismissing him and his 'justice' altogether out of my head. For I have work to do; I cannot spend my decades in mere arguing with other men about the exact wages of my work: I will work cheerfully with no wages, sooner than with a ten-years gangrene or Chancery Lawsuit in my heart! He of the horsehair wig is a sort of failure; no substance, but a fond imagination of the mind. He of the shovel-hat,[a] again, who comes forward professing that he will save my soul – O ye Eternities, of him in this place be absolute silence! – But he of the red coat, I say, is a success and no failure! He will veritably, if he get orders, draw out a long sword and kill me. No mistake there. He is a fact and not a shadow. Alive in this Year Forty-three, able and willing to do *his* work. In dim old centuries, with William Rufus,[b] William of Ipres,[c] or far earlier, he began; and has come down safe so far. Catapult has given place to cannon, pike has given place to musket, iron mail-shirt to coat of red cloth, saltpetre ropematch to percussion-cap; equipments, circumstances have all changed, and again changed: but the human battle-engine in the inside of any or each of these, ready still to do battle, stands there, six feet in standard size. There are Pay-Offices, Woolwich Arsenals, there is a Horse-Guards, War-Office, Captain-General; persuasive Sergeants, with tap of drum, recruit in market-towns and villages; – and, on the whole, I say, here is your actual drilled fighting-man; here are your actual

---

[a] Clergyman.　　[b] William II (1087–1100).
[c] Commander of Flemish mercenary forces, hired by King Stephen in 1135.

Ninety-thousand of such, ready to go into any quarter of the world and fight!

Strange, interesting, and yet most mournful to reflect on. Was this, then, of all the things mankind had some talent for, the one thing important to learn well, and bring to perfection; this of successfully killing one another? Truly you have learned it well, and carried the business to a high perfection. It is incalculable what, by arranging, commanding and regimenting, you can make of men. These thousand straight-standing firmset individuals, who shoulder arms, who march, wheel, advance, retreat; and are, for your behoof, a magazine charged with fiery death, in the most perfect condition of potential activity: few months ago, till the persuasive sergeant came, what were they? Multiform ragged losels,*a* runaway apprentices, starved weavers, thievish valets; an entirely broken population, fast tending towards the treadmill. But the persuasive sergeant came; by tap of drum enlisted, or formed lists of them, took heartily to drilling them; – and he and you have made them this! Most potent, effectual for all work whatsoever, is wise planning, firm combining and commanding among men. Let no man despair of Governments who looks on these two sentries at the Horse-Guards and our United-Service Clubs!*b* I could conceive an Emigration Service, a Teaching Service, considerable varieties of United and Separate Services, of the due thousands strong, all effective as this Fighting Service is; all doing *their* work, like it; – which work, much more than fighting, is henceforth the necessity of these New Ages we are got into! Much lies among us, convulsively, nigh desperately *struggling to be born* ...

Forty soldiers, I am told, will disperse the largest Spitalfields[17] mob: forty to ten-thousand, that is the proportion between drilled and undrilled. Much there is which cannot yet be organised in this world; but somewhat also which can, somewhat also which must. When one thinks, for example, what Books are become and becoming for us, what Operative Lancashires are become; what a Fourth Estate,*c* and innumerable Virtualities not yet got to be Actualities are become and becoming, – one sees Organisms enough in the dim huge Future; and 'United Services' quite other than the redcoat one; and much, even in these years, struggling to be born!

Of Time-Bill, Factory-Bill[18] and other such Bills the present Editor has no authority to speak. He knows not, it is for others than he to know, in what specific ways it may be feasible to interfere, with Legislation, between the Workers and the Master-Workers; – knows only and sees, what all men are beginning to see, that Legislative

a Wastrels.   *b* Social club for officers.   *c* The Press.

interference, and interferences not a few are indispensable; that as a lawless anarchy of supply-and-demand, on market-wages alone, this province of things cannot longer be left. Nay interference has begun: there are already Factory Inspectors, – who seem to have no *lack* of work. Perhaps there might be Mine-Inspectors too: – might there not be Furrowfield Inspectors withal, and ascertain for us how on seven and sixpence a week a human family does live! Interference has begun; it must continue, must extensively enlarge itself, deepen and sharpen itself. Such things cannot longer be idly lapped in darkness and suffered to go on unseen: the Heavens do see them; the curse, not the blessing of the Heavens is on an Earth that refuses to see them.

Again, are not Sanitary Regulations possible for a Legislature? The old Romans had their Ædiles;[a] who would, I think, in direct contravention to supply-and-demand, have rigorously seen rammed up into total abolition many a foul cellar in our Southwarks, Saint-Gileses,[b] and dark poison-lanes; saying sternly, 'Shall a Roman man dwell there?' The Legislature, at whatever cost of consequences, would have had to answer, 'God forbid! – The Legislature, even as it now is, could order all dingy Manufacturing Towns to cease from their soot and darkness; to let-in the blessed sunlight, the blue of Heaven, and become clear and clean; to burn their coal-smoke, namely, and make flame of it. Baths, free air, a wholesome temperature, ceilings twenty feet high, might be ordained, by Act of Parliament, in all establishments licensed as Mills. There are such Mills already extant; – honour to the builders of them! The Legislature can say to others: Go ye and do likewise,[c] better if you can.

Every toiling Manchester, its smoke and soot all burnt, ought it not, among so many world-wide conquests, to have a hundred acres or so of free greenfield, with trees on it, conquered, for its little children to disport in; for its all-conquering workers to take a breath of twilight air in? You would say so! A willing Legislature could say so with effect. A willing Legislature could say very many things! And to whatsoever 'vested interest,' or suchlike, stood up, gainsaying merely, 'I shall lose profits,' – the willing Legislature would answer, 'Yes, but my sons and daughters will gain health, and life, and a soul.' – 'What is to become of our Cotton-trade?' cried certain Spinners, when the Factory Bill was proposed;[19] 'What is to become of our invaluable Cotton-Trade?' The Humanity of England answered steadfastly: 'Deliver me these rickety perishing souls of infants, and let your Cotton-trade take its chance. God Himself commands the

---

[a] Municipal officers.   [b] Notorious slum areas of London.   [c]Luke 10:37.

one thing; not God especially the other thing. We cannot have prosperous Cotton-trades at the expense of keeping the Devil a partner in them! –

Bills enough, were the Corn-Law Abrogation Bill once passed, and a Legislature willing! Nay this one Bill, which lies yet unenacted, a right Education Bill, is not this of itself the sure parent of innumerable wise Bills, – wise regulations, practical methods and proposals, gradually ripening towards the state of Bills? To irradiate with intelligence, that is to say, with order, arrangement and all blessedness, the Chaotic, Unintelligent: how, except by educating, *can* you accomplish this? That thought, reflection, articulate utterance and understanding be awakened in these individual million heads, which are the atoms of your Chaos: there is no other way of illuminating any Chaos! The sum-total of intelligence that is found in it, determines the extent of order that is possible for your Chaos, – the feasibility and rationality of what your Chaos will dimly demand from you, and will gladly obey when proposed by you! It is an exact equation; the one accurately measures the other. – If the whole English People, during these 'twenty years of respite,' be not educated, with at least schoolmaster's educating, a tremendous responsibility before God and men, will rest somewhere! How dare any man, especially a man calling himself minister of God, stand up in any Parliament or place, under any pretext or delusion, and for a day or an hour forbid God's Light to come into the world, and bid the Devil's Darkness continue in it one hour more! For all light and science, under all shapes, in all degrees of perfection, is of God; all darkness, nescience, is of the Enemy of God. 'The schoolmaster's creed is somewhat awry?' Yes, I have found few creeds entirely correct; few light-beams shining *white*, pure of admixture: but of all creeds and religions now or ever before known, was not that of thoughtless thriftless Animalism, of Distilled Gin, and Stupor and Despair, unspeakably the least orthodox? We will exchange *it* even with Paganism, with Fetishism; and, on the whole, must exchange it with something.

An effective 'Teaching Service' I do consider that there must be; some Education Secretary, Captain-General of Teachers, who will actually contrive to get us *taught*. Then again, why should there not be an 'Emigration Service,' and Secretary, with adjuncts, with funds, forces, idle Navy-ships, and ever-increasing apparatus; in fine an *effective system* of Emigration; so that, at length, before our twenty years of respite ended, every honest willing Workman who found England too strait, and the 'Organisation of Labour' not yet sufficiently advanced, might find likewise a bridge built to carry him into new Western Lands, there to 'organise' with more elbow-room some labour for himself? There to be a real blessing, raising new corn for us, purchasing new webs and hatchets from us; leaving us at least in peace; – instead of staying here to be a Physical-Force Chartist, unblessed and no blessing! Is it not scandalous to consider that a Prime Minister could raise within the year, as I have seen it done, a Hundred and Twenty Millions Sterling to shoot the French;[20] and we are stopt short of want of the hundredth part of that to keep the English living? The bodies of the English living, and the souls of the English living: – these two 'Services,' an Education Service and an Emigration Service, these with others will actually have to be organised! . . .

It is true the English Legislature, like the English People, is of slow temper; essentially conservative. In our wildest periods of reform, in the Long Parliament[a] itself, you notice always the invincible instinct to hold fast by the Old; to admit the *minimum* of New; to expand, if it be possible, some old habit or method, already found fruitful, into new growth for the new need. It is an instinct worthy of all honour; akin to all strength and all wisdom. The Future hereby is not dissevered from the Past, but based continuously on it; grows with all the vitalities of the Past, and is rooted down deep into the beginnings of us. The English Legislature is entirely repugnant to believe in 'new epochs.' The English Legislature does not occupy itself with epochs; has, indeed, other business to do than looking at the Time-Horologe and hearing it tick! Nevertheless new epochs do actually come; and with them new imperious peremptory necessities; so that even an English Legislature has to look up, and admit, though with reluctance, that the hour has struck. The hour having struck, let us not say 'impossible': – it will have to be possible! 'Contrary to the habits of Parliament, the habits of Government?' Yes: but did any Parliament or Government ever sit in a Year Forty-three before? One of the most original, unexampled years and epochs; in several important respects totally unlike any other! For Time, all-edacious and all-feracious, does run on: and the Seven Sleepers,[b] awakening hungry after a hundred years, find that it is not their old nurses who can now give them suck!

For the rest, let not any Parliament, Aristocracy, Millocracy, or Member of the Governing Class, condemn with much triumph this

[a] Summoned by Charles I in 1640, dissolved by Cromwell in 1653.
[b] Third century Christians, of whom it is related that they were walled up in a cave and awoke two hundred years later.

small specimen of 'remedial measures'; or ask again, with the least anger, of this Editor, What is to be done, How that alarming problem of the Working Classes is to be managed? Editors are not here, foremost of all, to say How. A certain Editor thanks the gods that nobody pays him three hundred thousand pounds a year, two hundred thousand, twenty thousand, or any similar sum of cash for saying How; – that his wages are very different, his work somewhat fitter for him. An Editor's stipulated work is to apprise *thee* that it must be done. The 'way to do it,' – is to try it, knowing that thou shalt die if it be not done. There is the bare back, there is the web of cloth; thou shalt cut me a coat to cover the bare back, thou whose trade it is. 'Impossible?' Hapless Fraction, dost thou discern Fate there, half unveiling herself in the gloom of the future, with her gibbet-cords, her steel-whips, and very authentic Tailor's Hell; waiting to see whether it is 'possible'? Out with thy scissors, and cut that cloth or thy own windpipe!

Captains of Industry (book IV, ch. 4)

. . . The Leaders of Industry, if Industry is ever to be led, are virtually the Captains of the World! if there be no nobleness in them, there will never be an Aristocracy more. But let the Captains of Industry consider: once again, are they born of other clay than the old Captains of Slaughter; doomed forever to be no Chivalry, but a mere gold-plated *Doggery*, – what the French well name *Canaille*,[a] 'Doggery' with more or less gold carrion at its disposal? Captains of Industry are the true Fighters, henceforth recognisable as the only true ones: Fighters against Chaos, Necessity and the Devils and Jötuns;[b] and lead on Mankind in that great, and alone true, and universal warfare; the stars in their courses[c] fighting for them, and all Heaven and all Earth saying audibly, Well done! Let the Captains of Industry retire into their own hearts, and ask solemnly, If there is nothing but vulturous hunger, for fine wines, valet reputation and gilt carriages, discoverable there? Of hearts made by the Almighty God I will not believe such a thing. Deep-hidden under wretchedest god-forgetting Cants, Epicurisms[d] Dead-Sea Apisms;[e] forgotten as under foulest fat Lethe mud and weeds, there is yet, in all hearts born into this God's-World, a spark of the Godlike slumbering. Awake, O

---

[a] Rabble.   [b] Giants of Scandinavian mythology.   [c] Judges 5:20.
[d] The pursuit of sensual pleasures.   [e] Lifeless mimicries.

nightmare sleepers; awake, arise, or be forever fallen! This is not playhouse poetry; it is sober fact. Our England, our world cannot live as it is. It will connect itself with a God again, or go down with nameless throes and fire-consummation to the Devils. Thou who feelest aught of such a Godlike stirring in thee, any faintest intimation of it as through heavy-laden dreams, follow *it*, I conjure thee. Arise, save thyself, be one of those that save thy country.

Bucaniers, Chactaw Indians, whose supreme aim in fighting is that they may get the scalps, the money, that they may amass scalps and money: out of such came no Chivalry, and never will! Out of such came only gore and wreck, infernal rage and misery; desperation quenched in annihilation. Behold it, I bid thee, behold there, and consider! What is it that thou have a hundred thousand-pound bills laid-up in thy strong-room, a hundred scalps hung-up in thy wigwam? I value not them or thee. Thy scalps and thy thousand-pound bills are as yet nothing, if no nobleness from within irradiate them; if no Chivalry, in action, or in embryo ever struggling towards birth and action, be there.

Love of men cannot be bought by cash-payment; and without love men cannot endure to be together. You cannot lead a Fighting World without having it regimented, chivalried: the thing, in a day, becomes impossible; all men in it, the highest at first, the very lowest at last, discern consciously, or by a noble instinct, this necessity. And can you any more continue to lead a Working World unregimented, anarchic? I answer, and the Heavens and Earth are now answering, No! The thing becomes not 'in a day' impossible; but in some two generations it does. Yes, when fathers and mothers, in Stockport hunger-cellars, begin to eat their children, and Irish widows have to prove their relationship of dying by typhus-fever; and amid Governing 'Corporations of the Best and Bravest',[a] busy to preserve their game by 'bushing,' dark millions of God's human creatures start up in mad Chartisms, impracticable Sacred-Months,[21] and Manchester Insurrections; – and there is a virtual Industrial Aristocracy as yet only half-alive, spell-bound amid money-bags and ledgers; and an actual Idle Aristocracy seemingly near dead in somnolent delusions, in trespasses and double-barrels; 'sliding,' as on inclined-planes, which every new year they *soap* with new Hansard's-jargon[b] under God's sky, and so are 'sliding,' ever faster, towards a 'scale' and balance-scale whereon is written *Thou art found Wanting*:[c] in such

[a] Cf. *Chartism* ch. 6. 'What is an Aristocracy? A Corporation of the Best, of the Bravest'.
[b] Hansard contains the official report of the proceedings of the Houses of Parliament.
[c] Daniel 5:27.

days, after a generation or two, I say, it does become, even to the low and simple, very palpably impossible! No Working World, any more than a Fighting World, can be led on without a noble Chivalry of Work, and laws and fixed rules which follow out of that, – far nobler than any Chivalry of Fighting was. As an anarchic multitude on mere Supply-and-demand, it is becoming inevitable that we dwindle in horrid suicidal convulsion and self-abrasion, frightful to the imagination, into *Chactaw* Workers. With wigwams and scalps, – with palaces and thousand-pound bills; with savagery, depopulation, chaotic desolation! Good Heavens, will not one French Revolution and Reign of Terror suffice us, but must there be two? There will be two if needed; there will be twenty if needed; there will be precisely as many as are needed. The Laws of Nature will have themselves fulfilled. That is a thing certain to me.

Your gallant battle-hosts and work-hosts, as the others did, will need to be made loyally yours; they must and will be regulated, methodically secured in their just share of conquest under you; – joined with you in veritable brotherhood, sonhood, by quite other and deeper ties than those of temporary day's wages! How would mere red-coated regiments, to say nothing of chivalries, fight for you, if you could discharge them on the evening of the battle, on payment of the stipulated shillings, – and they discharge you on the morning of it! Chelsea Hospitals,[a] pensions, promotions, rigorous lasting covenant on the one side and on the other, are indispensable even for a hired fighter. The Feudal Baron, much more, – how could he subsist with mere temporary mercenaries round him, at sixpence a day; ready to go over to the other side, if sevenpence were offered? He could not have subsisted; – and his noble instinct saved him from the necessity of even trying! The Feudal Baron had a Man's Soul in him; to which anarchy, mutiny, and the other fruits of temporary mercenaries, were intolerable: he had never been a Baron otherwise, but had continued a Chactaw and Bucanier. He felt it precious, and at last it became habitual, and his fruitful enlarged existence included it as a necessity, to have men round him who in heart loved him; whose life he watched over with rigour yet with love; who were prepared to give their life for him, if need came. It was beautiful; it was human! Man lives not otherwise, nor can live contented, anywhere or anywhen. Isolation is the sum-total of wretchedness to man. To be cut off, to be left solitary: to have a world alien, not your world; all a hostile camp for you; not a home at all, of hearts and faces who are yours, whose you are! It is the frightfulest enchantment; too

---

[a] Established by Charles II for wounded or retired soldiers.

truly a work of the Evil One. To have neither superior, nor inferior, nor equal, united manlike to you. Without father, without child, without brother. Man knows no sadder destiny. 'How is each of us,' exclaims Jean Paul, 'so lonely in the wide bosom of the All!'[22] Encased each as in his transparent 'ice-palace'; our brother visible in his, making signals and gesticulations to us; – visible, but forever unattainable: on his bosom we shall never rest, nor he on ours. It was not a God that did this; no![23]

Awake, ye noble Workers, warriors in the one true war: all this must be remedied. It is you who are already half-alive, whom I will welcome into life; whom I will conjure, in God's name, to shake off your enchanted sleep, and live wholly! Cease to count scalps, gold-purses; not in these lies your or our salvation. Even these, if you count only these, will not long be left. Let bucaniering be put far from you; alter, speedily abrogate all laws of the bucaniers, if you would gain any victory that shall endure. Let God's justice, let pity, nobleness and manly valour, with more gold-purses or with fewer, testify themselves in this your brief Life-transit to all the Eternities, the Gods and Silences. It is to you I call; for ye are not dead, ye are already half-alive: there is in you a sleepless dauntless energy, the prime-matter of all nobleness in man. Honour to you in your kind. It is to you I call; ye know at least this, That the mandate of God to His creature man is: Work! The future Epic of the World rests not with those that are near dead, but with those that are alive, and those that are coming into life.

Look around you. Your world-hosts are all in mutiny, in confusion, destitution; on the eve of fiery wreck and madness! They will not march farther for you, on the sixpence a day and supply-and-demand principle: they will not; nor ought they, nor can they. Ye shall reduce them to order, begin reducing them. To order, to just subordination; noble loyalty in return for noble guidance. Their souls are driven nigh mad; let yours be sane and ever saner. Not as a bewildered bewildering mob; but as a firm regimented mass, with real captains over them, will these men march any more. All human interests, combined human endeavours, and social growths in this world, have, at a certain stage of their development, required organising: and Work, the grandest of human interests, does now require it.

God knows, the task will be hard: but no noble task was ever easy. This task will wear away your lives, and the lives of your sons and grandsons: but for what purpose, if not for tasks like this, were lives given to men? Ye shall cease to count your thousand-pound scalps, the noble of you shall cease! Nay the very scalps, as I say, will not long be left if you count only these. Ye shall cease wholly to be barbarous vulturous Chactaws, and become noble European Nineteenth-Century Men. Ye shall know that Mammon, in never such gigs and flunky 'respectabilities,'[24] is not the alone God; that of himself he is but a Devil, and even a Brute-god.

Difficult? Yes, it will be difficult. The short-fibre cotton; that too was difficult. The waste cotton-shrub, long useless, disobedient, as the thistle by the wayside, – have ye not conquered it: made it into beautiful bandana webs; white woven shirts for men; bright-tinted air-garments wherein flit goddesses? Ye have shivered mountains asunder, made the hard iron pliant to you as soft putty: the Forest-giants, Marsh-jötuns bear sheaves of golden-grain; Ægir the Sea-demon himself stretches his back for a sleek highway to you, and on Firehorses and Windhorses ye career.[a] Ye are most strong. Thor red-bearded, with his blue sun-eyes, with his cheery heart and strong thunder-hammer, he and you have prevailed. Ye are most strong, ye Sons of the icy North, of the far East, – far marching from your rugged Eastern Wildernesses, hitherward from the gray Dawn of Time! Ye are Sons of the *Jötun*-land; the land of Difficulties Conquered. Difficult? You must try this thing. Once try it with the understanding that it will and shall have to be done. Try it as ye try the paltrier thing, making of money! I will bet on you once more, against all Jötuns, Tailor-gods, Double-barrelled Law-wards, and Denizens of Chaos whatsoever!

The Gifted (book IV ch. 7)

... Dost thou know, O sumptuous Corn-Lord, Cotton-Lord, O mutinous Trades-Unionist, gin-vanquished, undeliverable; O much-enslaved World, – this man is not a slave with thee! None of thy promotions is necessary for him. His place is with the stars of Heaven: to thee it may be momentous, to thee it may be life or death, to him it is indifferent, whether thou place him in the lowest hut, or forty feet higher at the top of thy stupendous high tower, while here on Earth. The joys of Earth that are precious, they depend not on thee and thy promotions. Food and raiment, and, round a social hearth, souls who love him, whom he loves: these are already his. He

---

[a] II Kings 2:11.

wants none of thy rewards; behold also, he fears none of thy penalties. Thou canst not answer even by killing him: the case of Anaxarchus thou canst kill;[a] but the self of Anaxarchus, the word or act of Anaxarchus, in no wise whatever. To this man death is not a bugbear; to this man life is already as earnest and awful, and beautiful and terrible, as death.

Not a May-game is this man's life; but a battle and a march, a warfare with principalities and powers. No idle promenade through fragrant orange-groves and green flowery spaces, waited on by the choral Muses and the rosy Hours: it is a stern pilgrimage through burning sandy solitudes, through regions of thick-ribbed ice. He walks among men; loves men, with inexpressible soft pity, – as they *cannot* love him: but his soul dwells in solitude, in the uttermost parts of Creation. In green oases by the palm-tree wells, he rests a space; but anon he has to journey forward, escorted by the Terrors and the Splendours, the Archdemons and Archangels. All Heaven, all Pande-monium[b] are his escort. The stars keen-glancing, from the Immensi-ties, send tidings to him; the graves, silent with their dead, from the Eternities. Deep calls for him unto Deep.[c]

Thou, O World, how wilt thou secure thyself against this man? Thou canst not hire him by thy guineas; nor by thy gibbets and law-penalties restrain him. He eludes thee like a Spirit. Thou canst not forward him, thou canst not hinder him. Thy penalties, thy poverties, neglects, contumelies: behold, all these are good for him. Come to him as an enemy; turn from him as an unfriend; only do not this one thing, – infect him not with thy own delusion: the benign Genius, were it by very death, shall guard him against this! – What wilt thou do with him? He is above thee, like a god. Thou, in thy stupendous three-inch pattens, art under him. He is thy born king, thy conqueror and supreme law-giver: not all the guineas and cannons, and leather and prunella, under the sky can save thee from him. Hardest thick-skinned Mammon-world, ruggedest Caliban shall obey him, or become not Caliban but a cramp.[d] Oh, if in this man, whose eyes can flash Heaven's lightning, and make all Calibans into a cramp, there dwelt not, as the essence of his very being, a God's justice, human Nobleness, Veracity and Mercy, – I should tremble for the world. But his strength, let us rejoice to understand, is even this: The quantity of Justice, of Valour and Pity that is in him. To

[a] Greek philosopher, pounded to death in a mortar.
[b] 'the high capital/Of Satan and his peers', *Paradise Lost*, I.ll.756–7.
[c] Psalms 42:7. [d] *Tempest* 1.ii.325; 5.i.286.

hypocrites and tailored quacks in high places his eyes are lightning; but they melt in dewy pity softer than a mother's to the down-pressed, maltreated; in his heart, in his great thought, is a sanctuary for all the wretched. This world's improvement is forever sure.

Friedrich Engels and Karl Marx

(1820–1895) (1818–1883)

In 1883, delivering the funeral oration upon his friend and collaborator of almost forty years standing, Engels claimed that 'Just as Darwin discovered the law of development of organic nature, so Marx discovered the law of development of human society'. Such an appeal to scientific analogies as the foundation for a critique of capitalism was not novel. But insofar as the Political Economists had identified their discipline with the Newtonian model of a materialist science, most of our Victorian critics challenged it from an alternative standpoint – history, religion, morality, or art and culture. Engels's proposition was an attempt to relate the challenge posed to Christian views of man's origins by the biological science of evolution, and that posed by an historical science of socio-economic development to the 'ideological' character, as he saw it, of Political Economy.

A more apposite comparison than the scientific one, however, might have been that Darwin and Marx replaced the old sacred drama of struggle, death and redemption with a new secular drama. Darwin's story was the creation of man through the accidental biological mutation of animal species and their competitive battle to survive and adapt in a hostile environment. Marx's was the drama of *homo faber* (man the creator) deploying ingenuity, technology and organised social power in the struggle to dominate Nature, yet in the process forging the means of his own enslavement. History becomes a history of class struggle, between rich and poor, oppressors and oppressed, to control the means of production. Capitalism is the ultimate state of this. Uniquely dedicated to continuous economic innovation, it universalises struggle in its competitive market system, subordinates men to uncontrollable economic forces, raises class warfare to new heights. Yet the inherent instability of this dehumanised society contains within it the seeds of salvation. Communism, a society of freedom, equality and self-government, where men are no longer the victims, but the masters of their destiny, is not merely a moral alternative to capitalism, but the logical outcome of present contradictions. Not the least of these is that labour, the true source of wealth yet deprived of all access to it, is compelled to react against its subordination, to grow in organisational strength and self-consciousness, and shatter its bonds to usher in the first stage of genuinely 'human' history.

This drama, it has been observed, was a product of intellectual synthesis, of German philosophy, French socialism and English economics. Hegel's dialectical historical philosophy, in which Spirit and Reason march across the slaughterbench of history in an irresistible search for freedom and self-determination, was transmuted from the quasi-religious language of idealism into a history of dynamic economic forces. From Fourier and Saint-Simon came a sense of the waste and irrationality of uncontrolled competition, and the idea of collective economic control. From classical political economy, and particularly Ricardo, came a language and methodology to examine the 'anatomy', as Marx called it, of modern society. Drawing together these contending ideas, Marx and Engels in 1845 proclaimed their liberation from all previous schools of thought, and their commitment to a revolutionary challenge from the working class against a decaying system.

The first extract was written just before this point, and even before the beginnings of their collaboration. A review by Engels of Carlyle's *Past and Present*, it appeared in *Deutsche-Französische Jahrbücher* (1844), a short-lived radical publication edited by Marx and Arnold Ruge (1802–80) from Paris. At the same time, Marx and Engels were between two worlds. Each had toyed with the role of youthful romantic poet, had launched into radical journalism, and suffered under the Prussian censor. Marx was a refugee in Paris, Engels at work in the family firm in Manchester, both driven by new experiences and ideas to direct the abstract radical humanism they had encountered in the 'Young Hegelian' school at Berlin University into current debates about 'the social question'. Engels's piece marks a first attempt to do this. It asserts the importance of the 'critical philosophy', developed by writers such as David Strauss, Bruno Bauer and Ludwig Feuerbach against the 'alienation' inherent in attributing to God (or 'Spirit') qualities which are essentially human ones, in producing valid insights into social relations. Reviewing Carlyle's work for a radical Continental audience provided Engels with a number of opportunities. By extensive quotation from a native critic of British society, he was establishing the credibility of his own investigations, later published as *The Condition of the Working Class in England* (1845). Equally, it provided a message for Germans about their own society which might slip beneath the net of the Prussian censor. Implicit in the article is the thesis that Germany, though economically backward compared with Britain, is intellectually far in advance. Carlyle's fulminations allow him to challenge, therefore, those German radicals who, frustrated by their own society, looked upon Britain as the model for progress, and to expose Britain's much-vaunted freedoms as a cover for partisan élitist politics, stultifying social conformity, and economic oppression of the poor. Carlyle's acquaintance with German ideas, claims Engels, has provided a unique insight into this, but even he is constrained by parochialism and British 'empiricism', and more so by his outdated romantic pantheism. Unacquainted with 'critical' philosophy, Carlyle persists in seeing history as revelatory of God, lacking the capacity to construct an alternative political economy based upon human emancipation, vainly searching for a religion-inspired aristocracy of talent to guide an inchoate mass out of the machine age rather than recognising the stirrings of self-liberation in the nascent socialism of the industrial working class. Moreover, Engels subtly distorts the overall structure of *Past and Present* by making the social critique of 'The Gospel of

Mammonism' (book III, ch. 20) central, and omitting a translation of Carlyle's medieval sections.

The second extract is a chapter from Marx's *Capital* vol. I, 'The Fetishism of Commodities . . .'. Like Mill's *Principles, Capital* was cast in the Smithian mould, part of a huge project (whose scope was forecast in the MSS known as the *Grundrisse* (1857–8)) dedicated to analysing the genesis and evolution of modern capitalism as a total system of economic, social, political and intellectual relations. Marx's difficulty in amassing and organising his research material, casting it into a coherent form, and simultaneously coping with journalistic commitments, political activity and irate creditors, meant that even the three subsequent volumes, published posthumously from his notes, were but a part of the grand design. The enterprise, too, was complicated by Marx's intellectual approach. *Capital*'s subtitle, *A Critical Analysis of Capitalist Production*, reflected the heritage of neo-Hegelian philosophy, which itself was ultimately rooted in the Socratic method of discovering, through critical reflection upon everyday beliefs and opinions, the real 'Truths' which lie obscured within them. For Marx, a genuinely 'human' science of economic life must not only deploy empirical material and supply an alternative version of the 'laws' of capitalist evolution, but also reveal how, in a dehumanised society, the 'appearances' of economic activity, codified by the classical economists, obscure the underlying 'reality'. 'Fetishism' is a prime example of this method. Even the classical writers, he observes, had recognised that commodities only have an exchange value because of the relative quantity of labour (or, in Marx's revised terminology, 'labour power') embodied in them. This relationship, Marx observes (pp. 101–3), is transparent under certain forms of economic production. But, under capitalism, the impersonal nature of the market, the specialisation of tasks, and the system of monetary payments, all combine to obscure this direct connection, even from the labourer himself. Commodities become endowed with qualities which, as objects, they cannot possess; they acquire an 'inherent' value which determines the value and conditions of labour itself. Things thereby become 'fetished' as the agents, not the products, of human activity.

The third piece is an extract from a short article 'Karl Marx' by Engels in *Volkskalender*, an almanac published in Brunswick in 1878. It offers no original analysis, but rather stands as an example of the proselytising work undertaken by Engels in the later years of Marx's life and after his death. The tone of the concluding paragraph suggests a curious role as Marx's copy-writer and publicist, enacted with the piety of a John the Baptist. Playing T. H. Huxley to Marx's Darwin, Engels achieved the canonisation of Marx's complex ideas in the 'science' of 'Marxism', 'historical materialism', or 'dialectical materialism'. Indeed, the key points, and even certain phrases, in this piece recur both in Engels's more extended *Socialism: Utopian and Scientific* (1880; English publication, 1892) (which, with the *Communist Manifesto* (1848; English publication, 1850), soon became the most popular exposition of 'Marxism'), and in the 1883 funeral oration. Engels credits Marx with two central 'scientific discoveries'. First, the materialist interpretation of history, and the theme of class conflict, which he expounds here by example from the development of feudalism into capitalism, rather than paradigmatically. This 'discovery', however obvious, was impossible, he claims, before the advent of a form of society which made the continuous increase in productive goods its main goal. We see here, also, the reason for the assurance Marx and Engels had of socialism's triumph. Marx had once claimed that 'new, higher relations of production never appear before the material conditions of their existence have matured in the womb of the old society' (Preface to *A Contribution to the Critique of Political Economy* (1859)). Engels here points to the 'contradiction' of modern society, with an economy so integrated by the market that every individual act affects, however indirectly, everyone else, yet operating on the presumption of individual autonomy and private rights. 'Socialism' is the 'resolution' of this absurdity, the social form most appropriate to the economic order.

Marx's second 'discovery' is the theory of 'surplus value' which establishes the exploitation of labour as the central fact of capitalism underpinning its whole operation. Having achieved intellectual awareness during the turbulent 1840s, and during the early stages of Germany's precarious rush to industrialisation, Marx and Engels had seized upon the dark side of the forces of capitalism identified by the earlier generation of economists, and transformed them into its central feature. The displacement of labour by machinery, crises of overproduction, the tendency of wages towards subsistence level, and of the profit rate towards zero, the shift of wealth from 'productive' to 'unproductive' classes – these phenomena were not mere contingencies mutable through social policy and 'education', but endemic to a system driven by the competitive struggle for profit to find new ways of harnessing labour-power to capital. The labour theory of value, and Ricardo's account of how rent is appropriated by landlords in an expanding economy, were reworked into an account of how 'surplus value' was forcibly extracted from labour by owners of the means of production to constitute profit. It had been, Engels observes, the main purpose of *Capital* to explain all the phenomena of capitalism through this theory of exploitation.

The contrasting styles of these three pieces clearly reflect the fact that Engels is producing journalism, Marx a treatise on economic theory. Though Marx showed in his more popular pamphlets and political journalism a capacity to write vigorous prose with eye-catching phrases, he found expounding technical economics, particularly within the structure of his philosophical perspective, extremely difficult, and was always being led into refinement and sidelong references to other parts of his system. Thus, the footnotes to 'Fetishism' (mainly omitted here because of their specialised character), take up cudgels against opponents, and it often requires an insight into his thought processes to work out their precise relevance to the text. The chapter, beginning as a comment on economic value, shifts gear towards the end as the quasi-religious concept of 'fetishism', initially described as an 'analogy' (p.97), inspires ill-supported remarks on the general relations between religious belief and economic forms (p.103), and the classical economists hypostasisation of 'Nature' as a determining force. To Marx, all were related parts of his theory of the social determination of ideas; yet they operate at different level of consciousness, and are in need of more substantial discussion. Engels, by contrast, would readily scythe through complications and pin down the exposition and criticism of ideas in terms of basic principles; which explains, perhaps, why later generations tended to read Marx's convoluted philosophical economics through Engels's simplification of 'Marxism' as a new 'hard science'. Common to both writers, however, is the *ex cathedra* mode of pronouncement. Even in 'Fetishism' there is little that can be called argument, rather than mere assertion; and nothing in earlier chapters, where Marx has outlined the labour theory of value, prepares us for the sudden proposition that commodities partake of a 'mystical character' (p.96). When Engels, too, picks Carlyle up on his limitations, we are given no intellectual justification for this position, but are simply informed that, *because* Carlyle does not know German philosophy, he cannot *therefore* see the real 'truth'. This dogmatic mode of reasoning – dogmatic not simply in the pejorative sense, but in the more technical usage of 'dogmatic theology' – was a distinctive quality of German philosophical writing which often grates on English readers. It frequently manifested itself in a combative style of writing, at once contemptuous and laced with heavy irony (e.g. extract 4, p.101 on 'Robinson Crusoe' and p.105). Dogmatism was underwritten for Marx and Engels by the conviction that they had tapped a source of truth which rendered all previous explanations woefully limited or wholly void (e.g. extract 5, p.107). For, as Engels observed in the funeral oration, Marx was both a 'scientist' and a 'revolutionist'. The enthusiasm with which both propounded their new 'discoveries' joined hands with a commitment to put them at the service of the cause of labour, which imbued even the driest pages of *Capital* with an inspirational quality absent from the writings of other political economists.

3. F. Engels, 'The Condition of England: Review of *Past and Present* by Thomas Carlyle' (1844)

Marx and Engels: Collected Works (1975–), vol. III, pp. 444–7, 460–7

Of all the fat books and thin pamphlets which have appeared in England in the past year for the entertainment or edification of 'educated society', the above work is the only one which is worth reading. All the multi-volume novels with their sad and amusing intricacies, all the edifying and meditative, scholarly and unscholarly Bible commentaries – and novels and books of edification are the two staples of English literature – all these you may with an easy conscience leave unread. Perhaps you will find some books on geology, economics, history or mathematics which contain a small grain of novelty – however these are matters which one studies, but does not *read*, they represent dry, specialised branches of science, arid botanising, plants whose roots were long ago torn out of the general soil of humanity from which they derived their nourishment. Search as you will, Carlyle's book is the only one which strikes a human chord, presents human relations and shows traces of a human point of view.

It is remarkable how greatly the upper classes of society, such as the Englishman calls '*respectable people*', or '*the better sort of people*',*a* etc., have intellectually declined and lost their vigour in England. All energy, all activity, all substance are gone; the landed aristocracy goes hunting, the moneyed aristocracy makes entries in the ledger and at best dabbles in literature which is equally empty and insipid. Political and religious prejudices are inherited from one generation to another; everything is now made easy and there is no longer any need to worry about principles as one had to formerly; they are now picked up already in the cradle, ready-made, one has no notion where they come from. What more does one need? One has enjoyed a good education, that is, one has been tormented to no avail with the Romans and Greeks at school, for the rest one is 'respectable', that is, one has so many thousand pounds to one's name and thus does not have to bother about anything except marrying, if one does not already have a wife.

And now, to cap it all, this bugbear which people call 'intellect'! Where should intellect come from, in such a life, and if it did come, where might it find a home with them? Everything there is as fixed and formalised as in China – woe be to the man who oversteps the narrow bounds, woe, thrice woe to the man who offends against a time-honoured prejudice, nine times woe to him if it is a religious prejudice. For all questions they have just two answers, a Whig answer and a Tory answer; and these answers were long ago prescribed by the sage supreme masters of ceremony of both parties, you have no need of deliberation and circumstantiality, everything is cut and dried, Dicky Cobden or Lord John Russell has said this, and Bobby Peel or *the* Duke, that is, the Duke of Wellington, has said that, and that is an end of the matter.[1]

You good Germans are told year in, year out by the liberal journalists and parliamentarians what wonderful people, what independent men the English are, and all on account of their free institutions, and from a distance it all looks quite impressive. The

---

a The words in inverted commas are given by Engels in English.

debates in the Houses of Parliament, the free press, the tumultuous popular meetings, the elections, the jury system – these cannot fail to impress the timid spirit of the average German, and in his astonishment he takes all these splendid appearances for true coin. But ultimately the position of the liberal journalist and parliamentarian is really far from being elevated enough to provide a comprehensive view, whether it be of the development of mankind or just that of a single nation. The English Constitution was quite good in its day and has achieved a fair number of good things, indeed since 1828 it has set to work on its greatest achievement – that is to say, on its own destruction[2] – but it has not achieved what the liberal attributes to it. It has not made independent men of the English. The English, that is, the educated English, according to whom the national character is judged on the Continent, these English are the most despicable slaves under the sun. Only that part of the English nation which is unknown on the Continent, only the workers, the pariahs of England, the poor, are really respectable, for all their roughness and for all their moral degradation. It is from them that England's salvation will come, they still comprise flexible material; they have no education, but no prejudices either, they still have the strength for a great national deed – they still have a future. The aristocracy – and nowadays that also includes the middle classes – has exhausted itself; such ideas as it had, have been worked out and utilised to their ultimate logical limit, and its rule is approaching its end with giant strides. The Constitution is its work, and the immediate consequence of this work was that it entangled its creators in a mesh of institutions in which any free intellectual movement has been made impossible. The rule of public prejudice is everywhere the first consequence of so-called free political institutions, and in England, the politically freest country in Europe, this rule is stronger than anywhere else – except for North America, where public prejudice is legally acknowledged as a power in the state by lynch law. The Englishman crawls before public prejudice, he immolates himself to it daily – and the more liberal he is, the more humbly does he grovel in the dust before his idol. Public prejudice in 'educated society' is however either of Tory or of Whig persuasion, or at best radical – and even that no longer has quite the odour of propriety. If you should go amongst educated Englishmen and say that you are Chartists or democrats – the balance of your mind will be doubted and your company fled. Or declare you do not believe in the divinity of Christ, and you are done for; if moreover you confess that you are atheists, the next day people will pretend not to know you. And when the independent Englishman for once – and this happens rarely enough – really begins to think and shakes off the fetters of prejudice he has absorbed with his mother's milk, even then he has not the courage to speak out his convictions openly, even then he feigns an opinion before society that is at least tolerated, and is quite content if occasionally he can discuss his views with some like-minded person in private.

Thus the minds of the educated classes in England are closed to all progress and only kept to some degree of movement by the pressure of the working class. It cannot be expected that the literary diet of their decrepit culture should be different from these classes themselves. The whole of fashionable literature moves in a never-ending circle and is just as boring and sterile as this blasé and effete fashionable society.

When Strauss' *Das Leben Jesu* and its fame crossed the Channel, no respectable man dared to translate the book, nor any bookseller of repute to print it. Finally it was translated by a socialist 'lecturer' (there is no German word for this propagandist term) – a man, therefore, in one of the world's least fashionable situations – a small socialist printer printed it in instalments at a penny each,[3] and the workers of Manchester, Birmingham and London were the only readers Strauss had in England.

If, by the way, either of the two parties into which the educated section of the English people is split deserves any preference, it is the Tories. In the social circumstances of England the Whig is himself too much of an interested party to be able to judge; industry, that focal point of English society, is in his hands and makes him rich; he can find no fault in it and considers its expansion the only purpose of all legislation, for it has given him his wealth and his power. The Tory on the other hand, whose power and unchallenged dominance have been broken by industry and whose principles have been shaken by it, hates it and sees in it at best a necessary evil. This is the reason for the formation of that group of philanthropic Tories whose chief leaders are Lord Ashley, Ferrand, Walter, Oastler, etc.[4] and who have made it their duty to take the part of the factory workers against the manufacturers. Thomas Carlyle too was originally a Tory and still stands closer to that party than to the Whigs. This much is certain: a Whig would never have been able to write a book that was half so humane as *Past and Present*. ... [Engels proceeds to review *Past and Present* with extensive quotations in his own translation into German.]

From these excerpts Carlyle's position emerges fairly clearly. His whole outlook is essentially pantheistic, and, more specifically, pantheistic with German overtones. The English have no pantheism but merely scepticism; the conclusion of all English philosophising is the despair of reason, the confessed inability to solve the contradictions with which one is ultimately faced, and consequently on the one hand a relapse into faith and on the other devotion to pure practice, without a further thought for metaphysics, etc. Carlyle with his pantheism[5] derived from German literature is therefore a 'phenomenon' in England, and for the practical and sceptical English a pretty incomprehensible one. People gape at him, speak of 'German mysticism' and distorted English; others claim there is at bottom something in it, his English, though unusual, is very fine, he is a prophet, etc. – but nobody really knows what to make of it all.

For us Germans, who know the antecedents of Carlyle's position, the matter is clear enough. On the one hand vestiges of Tory romanticism and humane attitudes originating with Goethe, and on the other sceptical–empirical England, these factors are sufficient for one to deduce the whole of Carlyle's view of the world from them. Like all pantheists, Carlyle has not yet resolved the contradiction, and Carlyle's dualism is aggravated by the fact that though he is acquainted with German literature, he is not acquainted with its necessary corollary, German philosophy and all his views are in consequence ingenuous, intuitive, more like Schelling than Hegel. With Schelling – that is to say, with the old Schelling, not the Schelling of the philosophy of revelation[6] – Carlyle really has a great deal in common; with Strauss, whose outlook is similarly pantheistic, he is on common ground in his 'hero-worship' or 'cult of genius'.

The critique of pantheism has recently been so exhaustively set forth in Germany that little more remains to be said. Feuerbach's 'Theses' in the *Anekdota*[7] and Bruno Bauer's works contain all the relevant material. We will therefore be able to confine ourselves simply to following up the implications of Carlyle's position and showing that it is basically only a first step towards the position adopted by this journal.

Carlyle complains about the emptiness and hollowness of the age, about the inner rottenness of all social institutions. The complaint is fair; but by simply complaining one does not dispose of the matter; in order to redress the evil, its cause must be discovered; and if Carlyle had done this, he would have found that this desultoriness and hollowness, this 'soullessness', this irreligion and this 'atheism' have their roots in religion itself. Religion by its very essence drains man and nature of substance, and transfers this substance to the phantom of an other-worldly God, who in turn then graciously permits man and nature to receive some of his superfluity. Now as long as faith in this other-worldly phantom is vigorous and alive, thus long man will acquire in this roundabout way at least some substance. The strong faith of the Middle Ages did indeed give the whole epoch considerable energy in this way, but it was energy that did not come from without but was already present within human nature, though as yet unperceived and undeveloped. Faith gradually weakened, religion crumbled in the face of the rising level of civilisation, but still man did not perceive that he had worshipped and deified his own being in the guise of a being outside himself. Lacking awareness and at the same time faith, man can have no substance, he is *bound* to despair of truth, reason and nature, and this hollowness and lack of substance, the despair of the eternal facts of the universe will last until mankind perceives that the being it has worshipped as God was its own, as yet unknown being, until – but why should I copy Feuerbach?

The hollowness has long been there, for religion represents man's action of making himself hollow; and you are surprised that now, when the purple that concealed it has faded, when the fog that enveloped it has passed away, that now, to your consternation, it emerges in the full light of day?

Carlyle accuses the age furthermore – this is the immediate consequence of the foregoing – of hypocrisy and lying. Naturally the hollowness and enervation must be decently concealed and kept upright by accessories, padded clothes and whalebone stays! We too attack the hypocrisy of the present Christian state of the world; the struggle against it, our liberation from it and the liberation of the world from it are ultimately our sole occupation; but because through the development of philosophy we are able to discern this hypocrisy, and because we are waging the struggle scientifically, the nature of this hypocrisy is no longer so strange and incomprehensible to us as it admittedly still is to Carlyle. This hypocrisy is traced back by us to religion, the first word of which is a lie – or does religion not begin by showing us something human and claiming it is something superhuman – something divine? But because we know that all this lying and immorality follows from religion, that religious hypocrisy, theology, is the archetype of all other lies and hypocrisy, we are justified in extending the term 'theology' to the whole untruth and hypocrisy of the present, as was originally done by Feuerbach and Bruno Bauer. Carlyle should read their works if he wishes to know the origin of the immorality that plagues our whole society.

A new religion, a pantheistic hero-worship, a cult of work, ought to be set up or is to be expected; but this is impossible; all the possibilities of religion are exhausted; after Christianity, after absolute, i.e., abstract, religion, after 'religion as such', no other form of religion can arise. Carlyle himself realises that Catholic, Protestant or any other kind of Christianity is irresistibly moving towards its downfall; if he knew the nature of Christianity, he would realise that after it no other religion is possible. Not even pantheism! Pantheism itself is another consequence of Christianity and cannot be divorced from its antecedent, at least that is true of modern pantheism, of Spinoza's,[8] Schelling's, Hegel's and also Carlyle's pantheism. Once more, Feuerbach relieves me of the trouble of providing proof of this.

As I have said, we too are concerned with combating the lack of principle, the inner emptiness, the spiritual deadness, the untruthfulness of the age; we are waging a war to the death against all these things, just as Carlyle is, and there is a much greater probability that we shall succeed than that he will, because we know what we want. We want to put an end to atheism, as Carlyle portrays it, by giving back to the man the substance he has lost through religion; not as divine but as human substance, and this whole process of giving back is no more than simply the awakening of self-consciousness. We want to sweep away everything that claims to be supernatural and superhuman, and thereby get rid of untruthfulness, for the root of all untruth and lying is the pretension of the human and the natural to be superhuman and supernatural. For that reason we have once and for all declared war on religion and religious ideas and care little whether we are called atheists or anything else. If however Carlyle's pantheistic definition of atheism were correct, it is not we but our Christian opponents who would be the true atheists. We have no intention of attacking the 'eternal inner Facts of the universe', on the contrary, we have for the first time truly substantiated them by proving their perpetuity and rescuing them from the omnipotent arbitrariness of an inherently self-contradictory God. We have no intention of pronouncing 'the world, man and his life a lie'; on the contrary, our Christian opponents are guilty of this act of immorality when they make the world and man dependent on the grace of a God who in reality was only created from the reflected image of man in the crude *hyle*[a] of his own undeveloped consciousness. We have no intention whatever of doubting or despising the 'revelation of history', for history is all and everything to us and we hold it more highly than any other previous philosophical trend, more highly than Hegel even, who after all used it only as a case against which to test his logical problem.[9]

---

[a] The Greek for 'wood', used by Aristotle to mean 'matter' or 'substance'.

It is the other side that scorns history and disregards the development of mankind; it is the Christians again who, by putting forward a separate 'History of the Kingdom of God' deny that real history has any inner substantiality and claim that this substantiality belongs exclusively to their other-worldly, abstract and, what is more, fictitious history; who, by asserting that the culmination of the human species is their Christ, make history attain an imaginary goal, interrupt it in mid-course and are now obliged, if only for the sake of consistency, to declare the following eighteen hundred years to be totally nonsensical and utterly meaningless. *We* lay claim to the meaning of history; but we see in history not the revelation of 'God' but of man and only of man. We have no need, in order to see the splendour of the human character, in order to recognise the development of the human species through history, its irresistible progress, its ever-certain victory over the unreason of the individual, its overcoming of all that is apparently supernatural, its hard but successful struggle against nature until the final achievement of free, human self-consciousness, the discernment of the unity of man and nature, and the independent creation – voluntarily and by its own effort – of a new world based on purely human and moral social relationships – in order to recognise all that in its greatness, we have no need first to summon up the abstraction of a 'God' and to attribute to it everything beautiful, great, sublime and truly human; we do not need to follow this roundabout path, we do not need first to imprint the stamp of the 'divine' on what is truly human, in order to be sure of its greatness and splendour. On the contrary, the 'more divine', in other words, the more inhuman, something is, the less we shall be able to admire it. Only the *human* origin of the content of all religions still preserves for them here and there some claim to respect; only the consciousness that even the wildest superstition nevertheless has within it at bottom the eternal determinants of human nature, in however dislocated and distorted a form, only this awareness saves the history of religion, and particularly of the Middle Ages, from total rejection and *eternal* oblivion, which would otherwise certainly be the fate of these 'godly' histories. The more 'godly' they are, the more inhuman, the more bestial, and the 'godly' Middle Ages did indeed produce the culmination of human bestiality, serfdom, *jus primae noctis,*[a] etc. The god*lessness* of our age, of which Carlyle so much complains, is precisely its *saturation* with God. From this it also becomes clear why, above. I gave man as the solution to the riddle of the Sphinx. The question has previously always been: what is God?

---

[a] The feudal lord's right of first access to new brides of his dependants.

and German philosophy has answered the question in this sense: God is man. Man has only to understand himself, to take himself as the measure of all aspects of life, to judge according to his being, to organise the world in a truly human manner according to the demands of his own nature, and he will have solved the riddle of our time. Not in other-worldly, non-existent regions, not beyond time and space, not with a 'God' immanent in or opposed to the world, is the truth to be found, but much nearer, in man's own breast. Man's own substance is far more splendid and sublime than the imaginary substance of any conceivable 'God', who is after all only the more or less indistinct and distorted image of man himself. So when Carlyle follows Ben Jonson in saying, man has lost his soul and is only now beginning to notice the want of it, the right formulation would be: in religion man has lost his own substance, has alienated his humanity and now that religion, through the progress of history, has begun to totter, he notices his emptiness and instability. But there is no other salvation for him, he cannot regain his humanity, his substance, other than by thoroughly overcoming all religious ideas and returning firmly and honestly, not to 'God', but to himself.

All of this may also be found in Goethe, the 'prophet', and anyone who has his eyes open can read this between the lines. Goethe did not like to be concerned with 'God'; the word made him uncomfortable, he felt at home only in human matters, and this humanity, this emancipation of art from the fetters of religion is precisely what constitutes Goethe's greatness. Neither the ancients nor Shakespeare can measure up to him in this respect. But this consummate humanity, this overcoming of the religious dualism can only be apprehended in its full historical significance by those who are not strangers to that other aspect of German national development, philosophy. What Goethe could only express spontaneously, and therefore, it is true, in a certain sense 'prophetically', has been developed and substantiated in contemporary German philosophy. Carlyle too embodies assumptions which, logically, must lead to the position set forth above. Pantheism itself is but the last, preliminary step towards a free and human point of view. History, which Carlyle presents as the real 'revelation', contains only what is human, and only by an arbitrary act can its content be taken away from humanity and credited to the account of a 'God'. Work, free activity, in which Carlyle similarly sees a 'cult', is again a purely human matter and can only be linked with 'God' in an arbitrary manner. What is the point of continually pushing to the fore a word which *at best* only expresses the boundlessness of indetermination and, what is more, maintains the illusion of dualism, a word which in itself is the denial of nature and humanity?

So much for the inward, religious aspect of Carlyle's standpoint. It serves as a point of departure for the assessment of the outward, politico-social aspect; Carlyle has still enough religion to remain in a state of unfreedom; pantheism still recognises something higher than man himself. Hence his longing for a 'true aristocracy', for 'heroes'; as if these heroes could at best be more than *men*. If he had understood man as man in all his infinite complexity, he would not have conceived the idea of once more dividing mankind into two lots, sheep and goats, rulers and ruled, aristocrats and the rabble, lords and dolts, he would have seen the proper social function of talent not in ruling by force but in acting as a stimulant and taking the lead. The role of talent is to convince the masses of the truth of its ideas, and it will then have no need further to worry about their application, which will follow entirely of its own accord. Mankind is surely not passing through democracy to arrive back eventually at the point of departure – What Carlyle says about democracy, incidentally, leaves little to be desired, if we discount what we have just been referring to, his lack of clarity about the goal, the purpose of modern democracy. Democracy, true enough, is only a transitional stage, though not towards a new, improved aristocracy, but towards real human freedom; just as the irreligiousness of the age will eventually lead to complete emancipation from everything that is religious, superhuman and supernatural, and not to its restoration.

Carlyle recognises the inadequacy of 'competition, demand' and 'supply, Mammonism', etc., and is far removed from asserting the absolute justification of landownership. So why has he not drawn the straightforward conclusion from all these assumptions and rejected the whole concept of property? How does he think he will destroy 'competition', 'supply and demand', Mammonism, etc., as long as the root of all these things, private property, exists? 'Organisation of labour' cannot help in this respect, it cannot even be applied without a certain identity of interests. Why then does he not act consistently and decisively, proclaiming the identity of interests the only true human state of affairs, and thereby putting an end to all difficulties, all imprecision and lack of clarity?

In all Carlyle's rhapsodies, there is not a syllable mentioning the English Socialists. As long as he adheres to his present point of view, which is admittedly infinitely far in advance of that of the mass of educated people in England but still abstract and theoretical, he will indeed not be able to view their efforts with particular sympathy. The

English Socialists are purely practical and therefore also propose remedies, home-colonies,[a] etc., rather in the manner of Morison's pills; their philosophy is truly English, sceptical, in other words they despair of theory, and for all practical purposes they cling to the materialism upon which their whole social system is based; all this will have little appeal for Carlyle, but he is as one-sided as they. Both have only overcome the contradiction *within* the contradiction; the Socialists within the sphere of practice, Carlyle within the sphere of theory, and even there only spontaneously, whereas the Socialists, by means of reasoning, have definitely overcome the practical aspect of the contradiction. The Socialists are still Englishmen, when they ought to be simply men, of philosophical developments on the Continent they are only acquainted with materialism but not with German philosophy, that is their only shortcoming, and they are directly engaged on the rectification of this deficiency by working for the removal of national differences. We have no need to be very hasty in forcing German philosophy on them, they will come to it of their own accord and it could be of little use to them now. But in any case they are the only party in England which has a future, relatively weak though they may be. Democracy, Chartism must soon be victorious, and then the mass of the English workers will have the choice only between starvation and socialism.

For Carlyle and his standpoint, ignorance of German philosophy is not a matter of such indifference. He is himself a theoretician of the German type, and yet at the same time his nationality leads him to empiricism; he is beset by a flagrant contradiction which can only be resolved if he continues to develop his German-theoretical viewpoint to its final conclusion, until it is totally reconciled with empiricism. To surmount the contradiction in which he is working, Carlyle has only *one* more step to take, but as all experience in Germany has shown, it is a difficult one. Let us hope that he will take it, and although he is no longer young, he will still probably be capable of it, for the progress shown in his last book proves that his views are still developing.

All this shows that Carlyle's book is ten thousand times more worth translating into German than all the legions of English novels which every day and every hour are imported into Germany, and I can only advocate such a translation. But let our hack translators just keep their hands off it! Carlyle writes a very particular English, and a translator who does not thoroughly understand English and

[a] The name Owen gave to his communes.

references to English conditions would make the most absurd howlers. . . .

4. K. Marx, 'The Fetishism of Commodities and the Secret Thereof' (1867)

Capital: A Critical Analysis of Capitalist Production, vol. 1, ed.
F. Engels, trans. S. Moore and E. Aveling (1887), pp. 41–55

A commodity appears, at first sight, a very trivial thing, and easily understood. Its analysis shows that it is, in reality, a very queer thing, abounding in metaphysical subtleties and theological niceties. So far as it is a value in use, there is nothing mysterious about it, whether we consider it from the point of view that by its properties it is capable of satisfying human wants, or from the point that those properties are the product of human labour. It is as clear as noon-day, that man, by his industry, changes the forms of the materials furnished by Nature, in such a way as to make them useful to him. The form of wood, for instance, is altered, by making a table out of it. Yet, for all that, the table continues to be that common, every-day thing, wood. But, so soon as it steps forth as a commodity, it is changed into something transcendent. It not only stands with its feet on the ground, but, in relation to all other commodities, it stands on its head, and evolves out of its wooden brain grotesque ideas, far more wonderful than 'table-turning' ever was.

The mystical character of commodities does not originate, therefore, in their use-value. Just as little does it proceed from the nature of the determining factors of value. For, in the first place, however varied the useful kinds of labour, or productive activities, may be, it is a physiological fact, that they are functions of the human organism, and that each such function, whatever may be its nature or form, is essentially the expenditure of human brain, nerves, muscles, &c. Secondly, with regard to that which forms the ground-work for the quantitative determination of value, namely, the duration of that expenditure, or the quantity of labour, it is quite clear that there is a palpable difference between its quantity and quality. In all states of society, the labour-time that it costs to produce the means of subsistence, must necessarily be an object of interest to mankind, though not of equal interest in different stages of development. And lastly, from the moment that men in any way work for one another, their labour assumes a social form.[10]

4. 'The Fetishism of Commodities'

Whence, then, arises the enigmatical character of the product of labour, so soon as it assumes the form of commodities? Clearly from this form itself. The equality of all sorts of human labour is expressed objectively by their products all being equally values; the measure of the expenditure of labour-power by the duration of that expenditure, takes the form of the quantity of value of the products of labour; and finally, the mutual relations of the producers, within which the social character of their labour affirms itself, take the form of a social relation between the products.

A commodity is therefore a mysterious thing, simply because in it the social character of men's labour appears to them as an objective character stamped upon the product of that labour; because the relation of the producers to the sum total of their own labour is presented to them as a social relation, existing not between themselves, but between the products of their labour. This is the reason why the products of labour become commodities, social things whose qualities are at the same time perceptible and imperceptible by the senses. In the same way the light from an object is perceived by us not as the subjective excitation of our optic nerve, but as the objective form of something outside the eye itself. But, in the act of seeing, there is at all events, an actual passage of light from one thing to another, from the external object to the eye. There is a physical relation between physical things. But it is different with commodities. There, the existence of the things *quâ* commodities, and the value-relation between the products of labour which stamps them as commodities, have absolutely no connexion with their physical properties and with the material relations arising therefrom. There it is a definite social relation between men, that assumes, in their eyes, the fantastic form of a relation between things. In order, therefore, to find an analogy, we must have recourse to the mist-enveloped regions of the religious world. In that world the productions of the human brain appear as independent beings endowed with life, and entering into relation both with one another and the human race. So it is in the world of commodities with the products of men's hands. This I call the Fetishism which attaches itself to the products of labour, so soon as they are produced as commodities, and which is therefore inseparable from the production of commodities.

This Fetishism of commodities has its origin, as the foregoing analysis has already shown, in the peculiar social character of the labour that produces them.

As a general rule, articles of utility become commodities, only because they are products of the labour of private individuals or groups of individuals who carry on their work independently of each other.[11] The sum total of the labour of all these private individuals form the aggregate labour of society. Since the producers do not come into social contact with each other until they exchange their products, the specific social character of each producer's labour does not show itself except in the act of exchange. In other words, the labour of the individual asserts itself as a part of the labour of society only by means of the relations which the act of exchange establishes directly between the producers. To the latter, therefore, the relations connecting the labour of one individual with that of the rest appear, not as direct social relations between individuals at work, but as what they really are, material relations between persons and social relations between things. It is only by being exchanged that the products of labour acquire, as values, one uniform social status, distinct from their varied forms of existence as objects of utility. This division of a product into a useful thing and a value becomes practically important, only when exchange has acquired such an extension that useful articles are produced for the purpose of being exchanged, and their character as values has therefore to be taken into account, beforehand, during production. From this moment the labour of the individual producer acquires socially a two-fold character. On the one hand, it must, as a definite useful kind of labour, satisfy a definite social want, and thus hold its place as part and parcel of the collective labour of all, as a branch of a social division of labour that has sprung up spontaneously. On the other hand, it can satisfy the manifold wants of the individual producer himself, only in so far as the mutual exchangeability of all kinds of useful private labour is an established social fact, and therefore the private useful labour of each producer ranks on an equality with that of all others. The equalisation of the most different kinds of labour can be the result only of an abstraction from their inequalities, or of reducing them to their common denominator, viz., expenditure of human labour-power or human labour in the abstract. The two-fold social character of the labour of the individual appears to him, when reflected in his brain, only under those forms which are impressed upon that labour in every-day practice by the exchange of products. In this way, the character that his own labour possesses of being socially useful takes the form of the condition, that the product must be not only useful, but useful for others, and the social character that his particular labour has of being the equal of all other particular kinds of labour, takes the form that all the physically different articles that are the products of labour, have one common quality, viz., that of having value.

4. 'The Fetishism of Commodities'

Hence, when we bring the products of our labour into relations with each other as values, it is not because we see in these articles the material receptacles of homogeneous human labour. Quite the contrary: whenever, by an exchange, we equate as values our different products, by that very act, we also equate, as human labour, the different kinds of labour expended upon them. We are not aware of this, nevertheless we do it. Value, therefore, does not stalk about with a label describing what it is. It is value, rather, that converts every product into a social hieroglyphic. Later on, we try to decipher the hieroglyphic, to get behind the secret of our own social products; for to stamp an object of utility as a value, is just as much a social product as language. The recent scientific discovery, that the products of labour, so far as they are values, are but material expressions of the human labour spent in their production, marks, indeed, an epoch in the history of the development of the human race, but, by no means, dissipates the mist through which the social character of labour appears to us to be an objective character of the products themselves. The fact, that in the particular form of production with which we are dealing, viz., the production of commodities, the specific social character of private labour carried on independently, consists in the equality of every kind of that labour, by virtue of its being human labour, which character, therefore, assumes in the product the form of value – this fact appears to the producers, notwithstanding the discovery above referred to, to be just as real and final, as the fact, that, after the discovery by science of the component gases of air, the atmosphere itself remained unaltered.

What, first of all, practically concerns producers when they make an exchange, is the question, how much of some other product they get for their own? in what proportions the products are exchangeable? When these proportions have, by custom, attained a certain stability, they appear to result from the nature of the products, so that, for instance, one ton of iron and two ounces of gold appear as naturally to be of equal value as a pound of gold and a pound of iron in spite of their different physical and chemical qualities appear to be of equal weight. The character of having value, when once impressed upon products, obtains fixity only by reason of their acting and re-acting upon each other as quantities of value. These quantities vary continually, independently of the will, foresight and action of the producers. To them, their own social action takes the form of the action of objects, which rule the producers instead of being ruled by them. It requires a fully developed production of commodities before, from accumulated experience alone, the scientific conviction springs up, that all the different kinds of private labour, which are carried on independently of each other, and yet as spontaneously developed branches of the social division of labour, are continually being reduced to the quantitative proportions in which society requires them. And why? Because, in the midst of all the accidental and ever fluctuating exchange-relations between the products, the labour-time socially necessary for their production forcibly asserts itself like an over-riding law of Nature. The law of gravity thus asserts itself when a house falls about our ears. The determination of the magnitude of value by labour-time is therefore a secret, hidden under the apparent fluctuations in the relative values of commodities. Its discovery, while removing all appearance of mere accidentality from the determination of the magnitude of the values of products, yet in no way alters the mode in which that determination takes place.

Man's reflections on the forms of social life, and consequently, also, his scientific analysis of those forms, take a course directly opposite to that of their actual historical development. He begins, post festum,[a] with the results of the process of development ready to hand before him. The characters that stamp products as commodities, and whose establishment is a necessary preliminary to the circulation of commodities, have already acquired the stability of natural, self-understood forms of social life, before man seeks to decipher, not their historical character, for in his eyes they are immutable, but their meaning. Consequently it was the analysis of the prices of commodities that alone led to the determination of the magnitude of value, and it was the common expression of all commodities in money that alone led to the establishment of their characters as values. It is, however, just this ultimate money-form of the world of commodities that actually conceals, instead of disclosing, the social character of private labour, and the social relations between the individual producers. When I state that coats or boots stand in a relation to linen, because it is the universal incarnation of abstract human labour, the absurdity of the statement is self-evident. Nevertheless, when the producers of coats and boots compare those articles with linen, or, what is the same thing, with gold or silver, as the universal equivalent, they express the relation between their own private labour and the collective labour of society in the same absurd form.

The categories of bourgeois economy consist of such like forms. They are forms of thought expressing with social validity the conditions and relations of a definite, historically determined mode of production, viz., the production of commodities. The whole mystery

[a] After the festival, event.

of commodities, all the magic and necromancy that surrounds the products of labour as long as they take the form of commodities, vanishes therefore, so soon as we come to other forms of production.

Since Robinson Crusoe's experiences are a favourite theme with political economists, let us take a look at him on his island. Moderate though he be, yet some few wants he has to satisfy, and must therefore do a little useful work of various sorts, such as making tools and furniture, taming goats, fishing and hunting. Of his prayers and the like we take no account, since they are a source of pleasure to him, and he looks upon them as so much recreation. In spite of the variety of his work, he knows that his labour, whatever its form, is but the activity of one and the same Robinson, and consequently, that it consists of nothing but different modes of human labour. Necessity itself compels him to apportion his time accurately between his different kinds of work. Whether one kind occupies a greater space in his general activity than another, depends on the difficulties, greater or less as the case may be, to be overcome in attaining the useful effect aimed at. This our friend Robinson soon learns by experience, and having rescued a watch, ledger, and pen and ink from the wreck, commences, like a true-born Briton, to keep a set of books. His stock-book contains a list of the objects of utility that belong to him, of the operations necessary for their production; and lastly, of the labour-time that definite quantities of those objects have, on an average, cost him. All the relations between Robinson and the objects that form this wealth of his own creation, are here so simple and clear as to be intelligible without exertion, even to Mr Sedley Taylor.[12] And yet those relations contain all that is essential to the determination of value.

Let us now transport ourselves from Robinson's island bathed in light to the European middle ages shrouded in darkness. Here, instead of the independent man, we find everyone dependent, serfs and lords, vassals and suzerains, laymen and clergy. Personal dependence here characterises the social relations of production just as much as it does for other spheres of life organised on the basis of that production. But for the very reason that personal dependence forms the ground-work of society, there is no necessity for labour and its products to assume a fantastic form different from their reality. They take the shape, in the transactions of society, of services in kind and payments in kind. Here the particular and natural form of labour, and not, as in a society based on production of commodities, its general abstract form is the immediate social form of labour. Compulsory labour is just as properly measured by time, as commodity-producing labour; but every serf knows that what he expends in the service of his lord, is a definite quantity of his own personal labour-power. The tithe to be rendered to the priest is more matter of fact than his blessing. No matter, then, what we may think of the parts played by the different classes of people themselves in this society, the social relations between individuals in the performance of their labour, appear at all events as their own mutual personal relations, and are not disguised under the shape of social relations between the products of labour.

For an example of labour in common or directly associated labour, we have no occasion to go back to that spontaneously developed form which we find on the threshold of the history of all civilised races. We have one close at hand in the patriarchal industries of a peasant family, that produces corn, cattle, yarn, linen, and clothing for home use. These different articles are, as regards the family, so many products of its labour, but as between themselves, they are not commodities. The different kinds of labour, such as tillage, cattle tending, spinning, weaving and making clothes, which result in the various products, are in themselves, and such as they are, direct social functions, because functions of the family, which, just as much as a society based on the production of commodities, possesses a spontaneously developed system of division of labour. The distribution of the work within the family, and the regulation of the labour-time of the several members, depend as well upon differences of age and sex as upon natural conditions varying with the seasons. The labour-power of each individual, by its very nature, operates in this case merely as a definite portion of the whole labour-power of the family, and therefore, the measure of the expenditure of individual labour-power by its duration, appears here by its very nature as a social character of their labour.

Let us now picture to ourselves, by way of change, a community of free individuals, carrying on their work with the means of production in common, in which the labour-power of all the different individuals is consciously applied as the combined labour-power of the community. All the characteristics of Robinson's labour are here repeated, but with this difference, that they are social, instead of individual. Everything produced by him was exclusively the result of his own personal labour, and therefore simply an object of use for himself. The total product of our community is a social product. One portion serves as fresh means of production and remains social. But another portion is consumed by the members as a means of subsistence. A distribution of this portion amongst them is consequently necessary.

4. 'The Fetishism of Commodities'

The mode of this distribution will vary with the productive organisation of the community, and the degree of historical development attained by the producers. We will assume, but merely for the sake of a parallel with the production of commodities, that the share of each individual producer in the means of subsistence is determined by his labour-time. Labour-time would, in that case, play a double part. Its apportionment in accordance with a definite social plan maintains the proper proportion between the different kinds of work to be done and the various wants of the community. On the other hand, it also serves as a measure of the portion of the common labour borne by each individual, and of his share in the part of the total product destined for individual consumption. The social relations of the individual producers, with regard both to their labour and to its products, are in this case perfectly simple and intelligible, and that with regard not only to production but also to distribution.[13]

The religious world is but the reflex of the real world. And for a society based upon the production of commodities, in which the producers in general enter into social relations with one another by treating their products as commodities and values, whereby they reduce their individual private labour to the standard of homogeneous human labour – for such a society, Christianity with its *cultus* of abstract man, more especially in its bourgeois developments, Protestantism, Deism, &c., is the most fitting form of religion. In the ancient Asiatic and other ancient modes of production, we find that the conversion of products into commodities, and therefore the conversion of men into producers of commodities, holds a subordinate place, which, however, increases in importance as the primitive communities approach nearer and nearer to their dissolution. Trading nations, properly so called, exist in the ancient world only in its interstices, like the gods of Epicurus in the Intermundia,[14] or like Jews in the pores of Polish society. Those ancient social organisms of production are, as compared with bourgeois society, extremely simple and transparent. But they are founded either on the immature development of man individually, who has not yet severed the umbilical cord that unites him with his fellowmen in a primitive tribal community, or upon direct relations of subjection. They can arise and exist only when the development of the productive power of labour has not risen beyond a low stage, and when, therefore, the social relations within the sphere of material life, between man and man, and between man and Nature, are correspondingly narrow. This narrowness is reflected in the ancient worship of Nature, and in the other elements of the popular religions. The religious reflex of the real world can, in any case, only then finally vanish, when the practical relations of every-day life offer to man none but perfectly intelligible and reasonable relations with regard to his fellowmen and to Nature.

The life-process of society, which is based on the process of material production, does not strip off its mystical veil until it is treated as production by freely associated men, and is consciously regulated by them in accordance with a settled plan. This, however, demands for society a certain material ground-work or set of conditions of existence which in their turn are the spontaneous product of a long and painful process of development.

Political Economy has indeed analysed, however incompletely,[15] value and its magnitude, and has discovered what lies beneath these forms. But it has never once asked the question why labour is represented by the value of its product and labour-time by the magnitude of that value. These formulae, which bear it stamped upon them in unmistakable letters that they belong to a state of society, in which the process of production has the mastery over man, instead of being controlled by him, such formulae appear to the bourgeois intellect to be as much a self-evident necessity imposed by Nature as productive labour itself. Hence forms of social production that preceded the bourgeois form, are treated by the bourgeoisie in much the same way as the Fathers of the Church treated pre-Christian religions.[16]

To what extent some economists are misled by the Fetishism inherent in commodities, or by the objective appearance of the social characteristics of labour, is shown, amongst other ways, by the dull and tedious quarrel over the part played by Nature in the formation of exchange-value. Since exchange-value is a definite social manner of expressing the amount of labour bestowed upon an object, Nature has no more to do with it, than it has in fixing the course of exchange.

The mode of production in which the product takes the form of a commodity, or is produced directly for exchange, is the most general and most embryonic form of bourgeois production. It therefore makes its appearance at an early date in history, though not in the same predominating and characteristic manner as now-a-days. Hence its Fetish character is comparatively easy to be seen through. But when we come to more concrete forms, even this appearance of simplicity vanishes. Whence arose the illusions of the monetary system? To it gold and silver, when serving as money, did not represent a social relation between producers, but were natural objects with strange social properties. And modern economy, which looks down with such disdain on the monetary system, does not its superstition come out as clear as noon-day, whenever it treats of capital? How long is it since economy discarded the physiocratic illusion, that rents grow out of the soil and not out of society?[17]

But not to anticipate, we will content ourselves with yet another example relating to the commodity-form. Could commodities themselves speak, they would say: Our use-value may be a thing that interests men. It is no part of us as objects. What, however, does belong to us as objects, is our value. Our natural intercourse as commodities proves it. In the eyes of each other we are nothing but exchange-values. Now listen how those commodities speak through the mouth of the economist. 'Value' – (*i.e.*, exchange-value) 'is a property of things, riches' – (*i.e.*, use-value) 'of man. Value, in this sense, necessarily implies exchanges, riches do not.'[18] 'Riches' (use-value) 'are the attribute of men, value is the attribute of commodities. A man or a community is rich, a pearl or a diamond is valuable ... A pearl or a diamond is valuable' as a pearl or a diamond.[19] So far no chemist has ever discovered exchange-value either in a pearl or a diamond. The economic discoverers of this chemical element, who by-the-by lay special claim to critical acumen, find however that the use-value of objects belongs to them independently of their material properties, while their value, on the other hand, forms a part of them as objects. What confirms them in this view, is the peculiar circumstance that the use-value of objects is realised without exchange, by means of a direct relation between the objects and man, while, on the other hand, their value is realised only by exchange, that is, by means of a social process. Who fails here to call to mind our good friend, Dogberry, who informs neighbour Seacoal, that, 'To be a well-favoured man is the gift of fortune; but reading and writing comes by Nature.'[a]

5. F. Engels, 'Karl Marx' (1877)

Marx and Engels: Selected Works (1968), pp. 370–4

... Of the many important discoveries through which Marx has inscribed his name in the annals of science, we can here dwell on only two.

The first is the revolution brought about by him in the whole conception of world history. The whole previous view of history was based on the conception that the ultimate causes of all historical changes are to be looked for in the changing ideas of human beings,

[a] Misquotation of *Much Ado About Nothing*, III, iii, 14.

and that of all historical changes political changes are the most important and dominate the whole of history. But the question was not asked as to whence the ideas come into men's minds and what the driving causes of the political changes are. Only upon the newer school of French, and partly also of English, historians had the conviction forced itself that, since the Middle Ages at least, the driving force in European history was the struggle of the developing bourgeoisie with the feudal aristocracy for social and political domination. Now Marx has proved that the whole of previous history is a history of class struggles, that in all the manifold and complicated political struggles the only thing at issue has been the social and political rule of social classes, the maintenance of domination by older classes and the conquest of domination by newly arising classes. To what, however, do these classes owe their origin and their continued existence? They owe it to the particular material, physically sensible conditions in which society at a given period produces and exchanges its means of subsistence. The feudal rule of the Middle Ages rested on the self-sufficient economy of small peasant communities, which themselves produced almost all their requirements, in which there was almost no exchange and which received from the arms-bearing nobility protection from without and national or at least political cohesion. When the towns arose and with them separate handicraft industry and trade intercourse, at first internal and later international, the urban bourgeoisie developed, and already during the Middle Ages achieved, in struggle with the nobility, its inclusion in the feudal order as likewise a privileged estate. But with the discovery of the extra-European world, from the middle of the fifteenth century onwards, this bourgeoisie acquired a far more extensive sphere of trade and therewith a new spur for its industry; in the most important branches handicrafts were supplanted by manufacture, now on a factory scale, and this again was supplanted by large-scale industry, become possible owing to the discoveries of the previous century, especially that of the steam engine. Large-scale industry, in its turn, reacted on trade by driving out the old manual labour in backward countries, and creating the present-day new means of communication: steam engines, railways, electric telegraphy, in the more developed ones. Thus the bourgeoisie came more and more to combine social wealth and social power in its hands, while it still for a long period remained excluded from political power, which was in the hands of the nobility and the monarchy supported by the nobility. But at a certain stage – in France since the Great Revolution – it also conquered political power, and now in turn became the ruling class over the proletariat and small peasants. From this point of view all the historical phenomena are explicable in the simplest possible way – with sufficient knowledge of the particular economic condition of society, which it is true is totally lacking in our professional historians, and in the same way the conceptions and ideas of each historical period are most simply to be explained from the economic conditions of life and from the social and political relations of the period, which are in turn determined by these economic conditions. History was for the first time placed on its real basis; the palpable but previously totally overlooked fact that men must first of all eat, drink, have shelter and clothing, therefore must *work*, before they can fight for domination, pursue politics, religion, philosophy, etc. – this palpable fact at last came into its historical rights.

This new conception of history, however, was of supreme significance for the socialist outlook. It showed that all previous history moved in class antagonisms and class struggles, that there have always existed ruling and ruled, exploiting and exploited classes, and that the great majority of mankind has always been condemned to arduous labour and little enjoyment. Why is this? Simply because in all earlier stages of development of mankind production was so little developed that the historical development could proceed only in this antagonistic form, that historical progress as a whole was assigned to the activity of a small privileged minority, while the great mass remained condemned to producing by their labour their own meagre means of subsistence and also the increasingly rich means of the privileged. But the same investigation of history, which in this way provides a natural and reasonable explanation of the previous class rule, otherwise only explicable from the wickedness of man, also leads to the realisation that, in consequence of the so tremendously increased productive forces of the present time, even the last pretext has vanished for a division of mankind into rulers and ruled, exploiters and exploited, at least in the most advanced countries; that the ruling big bourgeoisie has fulfilled its historic mission, that it is no longer capable of the leadership of society and has even become a hindrance to the development of production, as the trade crises, and especially the last great collapse,[a] and the depressed condition of industry in all countries have proved; that historical leadership has passed to the proletariat, a class which, owing to its whole position in society, can only free itself by abolishing altogether all class rule, all servitude and all exploitation: and that the social productive forces, which have outgrown the control of the bourgeoisie, are only waiting for the

[a] Of 1873, ushering in the economic depression of the mid-1870s.

associated proleteriat to take possession of them in order to bring about a state of things in which every member of society will be enabled to participate not only in production but also in the distribution and administration of social wealth, and which so increases the social productive forces and their yield by planned operation of the whole of production that the satisfaction of all reasonable needs will be assured to everyone in an ever-increasing measure.

The second important discovery of Marx is the final elucidation of the relation between capital and labour, in other words, the demonstration how, within present society and under the existing capitalist mode of production, the exploitation of the worker by the capitalist takes place. Ever since political economy had put forward the proposition that labour is the source of all wealth and of all value, the question became inevitable: How is this then to be reconciled with the fact that the wage-worker does not receive the whole sum of value created by his labour but has to surrender a part of it to the capitalist? Both the bourgeois economists and the Socialists exerted themselves to give a scientifically valid answer to this question, but in vain, until at last Marx came forward with the solution. This solution is as follows: The present-day capitalist mode of production presupposes the existence of two social classes – on the one hand, that of the capitalists, who are in possession of the means of production and subsistence, and, on the other hand, that of the proletarians, who, being excluded from this possession, have only a single commodity for sale, their labour power, and who therefore have to sell this labour power of theirs in order to obtain possession of means of subsistence. The value of a commodity is, however, determined by the socially necessary quantity of labour embodied in its production, and, therefore, also in its reproduction; the value of the labour power of an average human being during a day, month or year is determined, therefore, by the quantity of labour embodied in the quantity of means of subsistence necessary for the maintenance of his labour power during a day, month or year. Let us assume that the means of subsistence of a worker for one day require six hours of labour for their production, or, what is the same thing, that the labour contained in them represents a quantity of labour of six hours; then the value of labour power for one day will be expressed in a sum of money which also embodies six hours of labour. Let us assume further that the capitalist who employs our worker pays him this sum in return, pays him, therefore, the full value of his labour power. If now the worker works six hours of the day for the capitalist, he has completely replaced the latter's outlay – six hours' labour for six hours' labour. But then there would be nothing in it for the capitalist, and the latter therefore looks at the matter quite differently. He says: I have bought the labour power of this worker not for six hours but for a whole day, and accordingly he makes the worker work 8, 10, 12, 14 or more hours, according to circumstances, so that the product of the seventh, eighth and following hours is a product of unpaid labour and wanders, to begin with, into the pocket of the capitalist. Thus the worker in the service of the capitalist not only reproduces the value of his labour power, for which he receives pay, but over and above that he also produces a *surplus value* which, appropriated in the first place by the capitalist, is in its further course divided according to definite economic laws among the whole capitalist class and forms the basic stock from which arise ground rent, profit, accumulation of capital, in short, all the wealth consumed or accumulated by the non-labouring classes. But this proved that the acquisition of riches by the present-day capitalists consists just as much in the appropriation of the unpaid labour of others as that of the slave-owner or the feudal lord exploiting serf labour, and that all these forms of exploitation are only to be distinguished by the difference in manner and method by which the unpaid labour is appropriated. This, however, also removed the last justification for all the hypocritical phrases of the possessing classes to the effect that in the present social order right and justice, equality of rights and duties and a general harmony of interests prevail and present-day bourgeois society, no less than its predecessors, was exposed as a grandiose institution for the exploitation of the huge majority of the people by a small, ever-diminishing minority.

Modern, scientific socialism is based on these two important facts. In the second volume of *Capital* these and other hardly less important scientific discoveries concerning the capitalist system, of society will be further developed, and thereby those aspects also of political economy not touched upon in the first volume will undergo revolutionisation. May it be vouchsafed to Marx to be able soon to have it ready for the press.

John Stuart Mill

(1806–1873)

Mill was forty-two when he published his first major work of social thought, the *Principles of Political Economy*. Although it underwent much revision during the course of the numerous editions its success warranted (see p. 3) it was already the product of mature thought. In his early teens he had been initiated by his father into the ideas of Ricardo's *Principles*, the work James Mill had done so much to encourage. Subsequently, Mill had often written about economic questions among the plethora of essays and reviews on politics, philosophy, literature and sociology he had published since his late teens. Unlike some of these pieces, and his later extended essays (*On Liberty* (1859), *On Representative Government* (1861), *Utilitarianism* (1863)), the *Principles* has since fallen into obscurity. Partly this is because it is not wholly original, partly because its economic theorising is regarded today as out-moded and does not fit easily into modern debates. In the contemporary context, however, its influence was enormous. For, as Mill announced in his Preface, he was producing not a mere text-book on economic theory, but a successor to Smith's *Wealth of Nations*, synthesising the development of technical economic theorising since Smith's time, and also, like its model, embedding this in a mass of information and discussion about social institutions, principles and policy. Our extracts, derived from these less technical and more speculative sections, show how Mill was able to present his unconventional views on contemporary society within the confines of an exposition of conventional economic theorising.

The impersonal story told in his *Autobiography* (published posthumously in 1873) reveals the main lines of Mill's intellectual development: the education received at his father's hand – and often seen as a model for that of Gradgrind's children in Dickens's *Hard Times* – producing a child prodigy trained to carry the message of Benthamite utilitarianism and to lead the party of philosophic radicalism; Mill's breakdown in 1826–7, from which, he believed, he recovered by experiencing for the first time genuine emotion on reading Wordsworth's poetry; his subsequent re-education through con-fronting the ideas of Coleridge, Saint-Simon, de Tocqueville and Carlyle, a close friend and mentor in the early 1830s; and his adulation of Mrs Harriet Taylor, author, libertarian feminist and socialist, to whom the *Principles* was privately dedicated, and whom he married in 1851. The *Autobiography* reveals a man enormously certain of his intellectual powers, but deeply insecure about his personal identity, his private feelings, and his capacity for wholly original thought. Having thrown off the oppressive burden of his father's narrow and rigid utilitarianism and opened his mind to the various intellectual currents of the day, he turned eclecticism into a central virtue. As the essays on Bentham (1838) and Coleridge (1840) reveal, Mill saw the moral and mental improvement of mankind, to which he was dedicated, emerging, not from the ultimate triumph of one world-view over another, but from toleration of diversity, and the laborious work of extracting and combining the elements of truth from competing intellectual systems. Our extracts highlight his dissatisfaction with the commonplace assumptions of Victorian life, and demonstrate the process of attempting to harmonise divergent ideas in the search for a richer, fuller social consensus.

In the *Principles*, Mill made two significant modifications to the socio-economic thought of his mentors. First, they, living during the early development of industrialism, had produced an economics based on the presumption of scarcity, aimed at maximising growth to cater for what were seen as man's insatiable material desires. Under the influence of romanticism's critique of capitalism, Mill, like his younger contemporary Marx, postulated an economics of abundance. In our first extract, 'Of the Stationary State', we see his preference for moral over material improvement. Once the Malthusian problem of overpopulation is conquered, which the approaching stationary state will itself assist in doing, zero economic growth offers a benison to be welcomed in terms of a better quality of life, not a danger to be feared. For readers today who passed through the 1960s, the association of ideas in this brief chapter will appear wholly familiar and modern – its attack on the economic rat-race, determination of different priorities for advanced and underdeveloped economies, contempt for consumerism and concern with conservation, personal space, and the quality of the environment.

A second innovation was the distinction, developed at the beginning of book II 'On property', which challenged the classical view that the laws of Political Economy governed both the production and the distribution of material things. Mill had absorbed the historical critique of Enlightenment rationalism, taking over Auguste Comte's word 'sociology' to describe the master science of human behaviour, and insisting that economic distribution was the product of specific property relations which were on the one hand, historically and culturally contingent, and on the other, potentially mutable. The second, much revised, extract shows Mill to have been deeply sympathetic to the moral objectives of alternative systems of property. Indeed, the third edition actually states that communism was, perhaps, the ultimate end of human progress. Yet this piece also makes clear his reservations: a communitarian society may not offer sufficient incentives for innovation and equally distributed labour; it may impose a stifling conformity and be incompatible with the need for independence; and, as our final extract suggests, it may misconceive the nature of the apparent threat posed by the idea of competition.

In this last section 'The Probable Futurity of the Labouring Classes', some of these issues are given greater immediacy. Though he flirted briefly with Saint-Simonian and Carlylean rejections of democracy, Mill generally held the enfranchisement of labour to be both desirable and inevitable. Our extract follows a discussion of contrasts between the 'theory of dependence and protection' and the 'theory of self-dependence'. The former Carlylean paternalism is dismissed as unworkable, because 'the poor have come out of leading-strings, and cannot any longer be governed or treated like children', and as morally demeaning to both the guardians and their charges. Yet, he observes, whether democracy will contribute or stifle moral progress 'depends upon the degree to which [the labouring classes] can be made rational.' Fear of the ignorant multitude, of class warfare and civil strife, stalks Mill's mind as much as that of any respectable Victorian; and 'Futurity' looks to the evolution of existing experiments in industrial partnership, profit-sharing schemes, and workers' co-operatives, to mitigate economic conflict and draw the working class from sullen resentment at 'the system' towards responsible participation and reform.

In all his works, Mill treated the end of moral improvement (happiness or 'utility in the largest sense', as he elsewhere calls it) as requiring a pragmatic approach to all intermediate principles and institutions. Just as he supports the general principle of competition, yet seeks to investigate socialism as a practical system, so elsewhere in the *Principles* he asserts a strong preference for *laissez-faire* in government policy, yet develops a whole series of qualifications. It is perhaps, therefore, no surprise that, despite his aloof intellectual status, and deep suspicion of trade unionism and the masses, he acquired a considerable reputation as a friend of the labouring poor.

The first impression Mill's writing gives is of an orderly mind at work. Compared with the extracts from Carlyle and Ruskin, Mill's spartan exposition of contending arguments may seem devoid of passion or commitment, for he had cut his stylistic teeth not upon the drama and lyricism of the Bible but upon his father's educative methods of continual précis and resumé. Work in his spare time as editor of Bentham's papers, and salaried employment as a clerk in the India Office, developed the capacity for producing lucid appraisals, which smack at times of well-written Civil Service reports. Such habits as subdividing the material by book, chapter and subsection, each of the last prefixed by a brief indication of the argument, confirm this impression. The virtues of this mode of writing emerge more clearly when it is compared not just with the average economics text-book, but particularly with that other mid-Victorian classic of political economy, Marx's *Capital*, with its often turgid prose, meandering and obscure arguments, and blustering attacks upon intellectual opponents. In the *Autobiography*, Mill claimed that, in regular debates with his friends during the 1820s, 'I greatly increased my power of effective writing; acquiring not only an ear for smoothness and rhythm, but a practical sense for *telling* sentences'. Despite the largely abstract language and complex arguments Mill uses, the thread of his thought is always easy to follow and this may help to account for the popularity this work enjoyed with a wide and varied audience. His deployment of subordinate clauses is masterly, enabling him to avoid both the monotony of continuous short statements and the stumbling lengthy sentences which are often the result of ill-digested material. The opening sentence of the fifth paragraph of our excerpt from 'On Property' gives some idea of Mill's control of long sentences: despite the accumulation of clauses and ideas, the essential movement of the sentence is never in doubt, and the resolution of the argument is given greater resonance by one of Mill's comparatively rare ventures into metaphor. A further stylistic mannerism of Mill's lends an air of balance to his writings and meliorates any impression of curt didacticism: the frequency with which he employs couplets of near synonyms (the third paragraph of the extract reveals 'unpleasing and discouraging', 'tone and tendency', 'pinched and stinted', 'natural and normal') helps, almost imperceptibly, to temper the pace of his argument so that we may the more easily absorb its drift.

Balanced appraisal is, of course, at once the virtue and the vice of the liberal temperament, yet Mill's writing is not impassive. Just as his arguments attempt to reach some conclusion rather than relying upon fence-sitting evasion, so in expressing himself he is not afraid to declare his personal views with some force (e.g. 'I cannot therefore' (p. 116), 'I know not why' (p. 117)). It is worth reminding ourselves, whilst admiring Mill's orderly control of matter and manner, of the high estimate in which he seemed to hold 'spontaneity' (pp. 125, 134). His own capacity to coin the spontaneously apt phrase may, we suspect, have been limited (reports of his parliamentary speeches speak of carefully prepared rhetoric rather than the witty riposte or quickly-turned thrust), but he could expose contrasts in a telling manner or achieve epigrammatic effect: sadly omitted after the second edition due to adverse public reaction was the splendid jibe from 'Of the Stationary State' about American life, reprinted in endnote 3 to the text. The restraint of style seen in his *Principles* was not necessarily the reflection of a cramped personality. In early essays like 'The Spirit of the Age' (1830), which first brought him to Carlyle's attention, he had proved able to assume the fashionable language of rhetorical prophecy with some skill. It was rather that, whilst asserting the importance of feeling, art and poetry, he came to recognise that it was his distinctive talent to recast the important message they might contain into the educative language of rational discourse.

Mill published editions of the *Principles* in 1848, 1849, 1852, 1857, 1862, 1867 and 1871. The text reprinted here is from the 1871 edition as representing his final thoughts. It shows only minor alterations from the 1867 version and the cheap People's Edition of 1868. In the endnotes, however, we have commented on some of the substantive, as opposed to merely stylistic, changes made by Mill over the years.

6. *Principles of Political Economy with some of their Applications to Social Philosophy*

(2 vols., 1848; 7th edn, 1871), vol. I, pp. 254–63, 266–9; vol. II, pp. 326–32, 341–5, 374–8

Of the Stationary State (bk IV, ch. 6)

1. [*Stationary state of wealth and population is dreaded and deprecated by writers*]

The preceding chapters comprise the general theory of the economical progress of society, in the sense in which those terms are commonly understood; the progress of capital, of population, and of the productive arts. But in contemplating any progressive movement, not in its nature unlimited, the mind is not satisfied with merely tracing the laws of the movement; it cannot but ask the further question, to what goal? Towards what ultimate point is society tending by its industrial progress? When the progress ceases, in what condition are we to expect that it will leave mankind?

It must always have been seen, more or less distinctly, by political economists, that the increase of wealth is not boundless: that at the end of what they term the progressive state lies the stationary state, that all progress in wealth is but a postponement of this, and that each step in advance is an approach to it. We have now been led to recognise that this ultimate goal is at all times near enough to be fully in view; that we are always on the verge of it, and that if we have not reached it long ago, it is because the goal itself flies before us. The richest and most prosperous countries would very soon attain the stationary state, if no further improvement were made in the productive arts, and if there were a suspension of the overflow of capital from those countries into the uncultivated or ill-cultivated regions of the earth.

This impossibility of ultimately avoiding the stationary state – this irresistible necessity that the stream of human industry should finally spread itself out into an apparently stagnant sea – must have been, to the political economists of the last two generations, an unpleasing and discouraging prospect; for the tone and tendency of their speculations goes completely to identify all that is economically desirable with the progressive state, and with that alone. With Mr M'Culloch,[1] for example, prosperity does not mean a large production and a good distribution of wealth, but a rapid increase of it; his test of prosperity is high profits; and as the tendency of that very increase of wealth, which he calls prosperity, is towards low profits, economical progress, according to him, must tend to the extinction of prosperity. Adam Smith always assumes that the condition of the mass of the people, though it may not be positively distressed, must be pinched and stinted in a stationary condition of wealth, and can only be satisfactory in a progressive state. The doctrine that, to however distant a time incessant struggling may put off our doom, the progress of society must 'end in shallows and in miseries,' far from being, as many people still believe, a wicked invention of Mr Malthus, was either expressly or tacitly affirmed by his most distinguished predecessors, and can only be successfully combated on his principles. Before attention had been directed to the principle of population as the active force in determining the remuneration of labour, the increase of mankind was virtually treated as a constant quantity; it was, at all events, assumed that in the natural and normal state of human affairs population must constantly increase, from which it followed that a constant increase of the means of support was essential to the physical comfort of the mass of mankind. The publication of Mr Malthus' Essay is the era from which better views of this subject must be dated; and notwithstanding the acknowledged errors of his first edition, few writers have done more than himself, in the subsequent editions, to promote these juster and more hopeful anticipations.[2]

Even in a progressive state of capital, in old countries, a conscientious or prudential restraint on population is indispensable, to prevent the increase of numbers from outstripping the increase of capital, and the condition of the classes who are at the bottom of society from being deteriorated. Where there is not, in the people, or in some very large proportion of them, a resolute resistance to this deterioration – a determination to preserve an established standard of comfort – the condition of the poorest class sinks, even in a progressive state, to the lowest point which they will consent to endure. The same determination would be equally effectual to keep up their condition in the stationary state, and would be quite as likely to exist. Indeed, even now, the countries in which the greatest prudence is manifested in the regulating of population, are often those in which capital increases least rapidly. Where there is an indefinite prospect of employment for increased numbers, there is apt to appear less necessity for prudential restraint. If it were evident that a new hand could not obtain employment but by displacing, or succeeding to, one already employed, the combined influences of prudence and public opinion might in some measure be relied on for restricting the coming generation within the numbers necessary for replacing the present.

2. [*But the stationary state is not in itself undesirable*]

I cannot, therefore, regard the stationary state of capital and wealth with the unaffected aversion so generally manifested towards it by political economists of the old school. I am inclined to believe that it would be, on the whole, a very considerable improvement on our present condition. I confess I am not charmed with the ideal of life held out by those who think that the normal state of human beings is that of struggling to get on; that the trampling, crushing, elbowing, and treading on each other's heels, which form the existing type of social life, are the most desirable lot of human kind, or anything but the disagreeable symptoms of one of the phases of industrial progress. It may be a necessary stage in the progress of civilization, and those European nations which have hitherto been so fortunate as to be preserved from it, may have it yet to undergo. It is an incident of growth, not a mark of decline, for it is not necessarily destructive of the higher aspirations and the heroic virtues; as America, in her great civil war, has proved to the world, both by her conduct as a people and by numerous splendid individual examples, and as England, it is to be hoped, would also prove, on an equally trying and exciting occasion.[3] But it is not a kind of social perfection which philanthropists to come will feel any very eager desire to assist in realizing. Most fitting, indeed, is it, that while riches are power, and to grow as rich as possible the universal object of ambition, the path to its attainment should be open to all, without favour or partiality. But the best state for human nature is that in which, while no one is poor, no one desires to be richer, nor has any reason to fear being thrust back, by the efforts of others to push themselves forward.

That the energies of mankind should be kept in employment by the struggle for riches, as they were formerly by the struggle of war, until the better minds succeed in educating the others into better things, is undoubtedly more desirable than that they should rust and stagnate. While minds are coarse they require coarse stimuli, and let them have them. In the meantime, those who do not accept the present very early stage of human improvement as its ultimate type, may be excused for being comparatively indifferent to the kind of economical progress which excites the congratulations of ordinary politicians; the mere increase of production and accumulation. For the safety of national independence it is essential that a country should not fall much behind its neighbours in these things. But in themselves they are of little importance, so long as either the increase of population or anything else prevents the mass of the people from reaping any part of the benefit of them. I know not why it should be matter of congratulation that persons who are already richer than any one needs to be, should have doubled their means of consuming things which give little or no pleasure except as representative of wealth; or that numbers of individuals should pass over, every year, from the middle classes into a richer class, or from the class of the occupied rich to that of the unoccupied. It is only in the backward countries of the world that increased production is still an important object: in those most advanced, what is economically needed is a better distribution, of which one indispensable means is a stricter restraint on population. Levelling institutions, either of a just or of an unjust kind, cannot alone accomplish it; they may lower the heights of society, but they cannot, of themselves, permanently raise the depths.

On the other hand, we may suppose this better distribution of property attained, by the joint effect of the prudence and frugality of individuals, and of a system of legislation favouring equality of fortunes, so far as is consistent with the just claim of the individual to the fruits, whether great or small, of his or her own industry. We may suppose, for instance (according to the suggestion thrown out in a former chapter[a]), a limitation of the sum which any one person may acquire by gift or inheritance, to the amount sufficient to constitute a moderate independence. Under this two-fold influence, society would exhibit these leading features: a well-paid and affluent body of labourers; no enormous fortunes, except what were earned and accumulated during a single lifetime; but a much larger body of persons than at present, not only exempt from the coarser toils, but with sufficient leisure, both physical and mental, from mechanical details, to cultivate freely the graces of life, and afford examples of them to the classes less favourably circumstanced for their growth. This condition of society, so greatly preferable to the present, is not only perfectly compatible with the stationary state, but, it would seem, more naturally allied with that state than with any other.

There is room in the world, no doubt, and even in old countries, for a great increase of population, supposing the arts of life to go on improving, and capital to increase. But even if innocuous, I confess I see very little reason for desiring it. The density of population necessary to enable mankind to obtain, in the greatest degree, all the advantages both of co-operation and of social intercourse, has, in all the most populous countries, been attained. A population may be

[a] Bk II, ch. 2, section 4.

too crowded, though all be amply supplied with food and raiment. It is not good for man to be kept perforce at all times in the presence of his species. A world from which solitude is extirpated, is a very poor ideal. Solitude, in the sense of being often alone, is essential to any depth of meditation or of character; and solitude in the presence of natural beauty and grandeur, is the cradle of thoughts and aspirations which are not only good for the individual, but which society could ill do without. Nor is there much satisfaction in contemplating the world with nothing left to the spontaneous activity of nature; with every rood of land brought into cultivation, which is capable of growing food for human beings; every flowery waste or natural pasture ploughed up, all quadrupeds or birds which are not domesticated for man's use exterminated as his rivals for food, every hedgerow or superfluous tree rooted out, and scarcely a place left where a wild shrub or flower could grow without being eradicated as a weed in the name of improved agriculture. If the earth must lose that great portion of its pleasantness which it owes to things that the unlimited increase of wealth and population would extirpate from it, for the mere purpose of enabling it to support a larger, but not a better or a happier population, I sincerely hope, for the sake of posterity, that they will be content to be stationary, long before necessity compels them to it.

It is scarcely necessary to remark that a stationary condition of capital and population implies no stationary state of human improvement. There would be as much scope as ever for all kinds of mental culture, and moral and social progress; as much room for improving the Art of Living, and much more likelihood of its being improved, when minds ceased to be engrossed by the art of getting on. Even the industrial arts might be as earnestly and as successfully cultivated, with this sole difference, that instead of serving no purpose but the increase of wealth, industrial improvements would produce their legitimate effect, that of abridging labour. Hitherto it is questionable if all the mechanical inventions yet made have lightened the day's toil of any human being. They have enabled a greater population to live the same life of drudgery and imprisonment, and an increased number of manufacturers and others to make fortunes. They have increased the comforts of the middle classes. But they have not yet begun to effect those great changes in human destiny, which it is in their nature and in their futurity to accomplish. Only when, in addition to just institutions, the increase of mankind shall be under the deliberate guidance of judicious foresight, can the conquests made from the powers of nature by the intellect and energy of scientific discoverers, become the common property of the species, and the means of improving and elevating the universal lot.

Of Property (bk. ii, ch. i)⁴

2. [*Statement of the question concerning property*]

... The assailants of the principle of individual property may be divided into two classes: those whose scheme implies absolute equality in the distribution of the physical means of life and enjoyment, and those who admit inequality, but grounded on some principle, or supposed principle, of justice or general expediency, and not, like so many of the existing social inequalities, dependent on accident alone. At the head of the first class, as the earliest of those belonging to the present generation, must be placed Mr Owen and his followers.⁵ M. Louis Blanc and M. Cabet⁶ have more recently become conspicuous as apostles of similar doctrines (though the former advocates equality of distribution only as a transition to a still higher standard of justice, that all should work according to their capacity, and receive according to their wants). The characteristic name for this economical system is Communism, a word of continental origin, only of late introduced into this country. The word Socialism, which originated among the English Communists, and was assumed by them as a name to designate their own doctrine, is now, on the Continent, employed in a larger sense; not necessarily implying Communism, or the entire abolition of private property, but applied to any system which requires that the land and the instruments of production should be the property, not of individuals, but of communities or associations, or of the government. Among such systems, the two of highest intellectual pretension are those which, from the names of their real or reputed authors, have been called St Simonism and Fourierism; the former defunct as a system, but which during the few years of its public promulgation, sowed the seeds of nearly all the Socialist tendencies which have since spread so widely in France: the second, still flourishing in the number, talent, and zeal of its adherents.⁷

3. [*Examination of Communism*]⁸

Whatever may be the merits or defects of these various schemes, they cannot be truly said to be impracticable. No reasonable person can doubt that a village community, composed of a few thousand inhabitants cultivating in joint ownership the same extent of land which at present feeds that number of people, and producing by combined labour and the most improved processes the manufactured articles which they required, could raise an amount of productions sufficient to maintain them in comfort; and would find the means of obtaining, and if need be, exacting, the quantity of labour necessary for this purpose, from every member of the association who was capable of work.

The objection ordinarily made to a system of community of property and equal distribution of the produce, that each person would be incessantly occupied in evading his fair share of the work, points, undoubtedly, to a real difficulty. But those who urge this objection, forget to how great an extent the same difficulty exists under the system on which nine-tenths of the business of society is now conducted. The objection supposes, that honest and efficient labour is only to be had from those who are themselves individually to reap the benefit of their own exertions. But how small a part of all the labour performed in England, from the lowest-paid to the highest, is done by persons working for their own benefit. From the Irish reaper or hodman to the chief justice or the minister of state, nearly all the work of society is remunerated by day wages or fixed salaries. A factory operative has less personal interest in his work than a member of a Communist association, since he is not, like him, working for a partnership of which he is himself a member. It will no doubt be said, that though the labourers themselves have not, in most cases, a personal interest in their work, they are watched and superintended, and their labour directed, and the mental part of the labour per-formed, by persons who have. Even this however, is far from being universally the fact. In all public, and many of the largest and most successful private undertakings, not only the labours of detail but the control and superintendence are entrusted to salaried officers. And though the 'master's eye,' when the master is vigilant and intelligent, is of proverbial value, it must be remembered that in a Socialist farm or manufactory, each labourer would be under the eye not of one master, but of the whole community. In the extreme case of obstinate perseverance in not performing the due share of work, the commu-nity would have the same resources which society now has for compelling conformity to the necessary conditions of the association. Dismissal, the only remedy at present, is no remedy when any other labourer who may be engaged does no better than his predecessor: the power of dismissal only enables an employer to obtain from his workmen the customary amount of labour, but that customary labour may be of any degree of inefficiency. Even the labourer who loses his employment by idleness or negligence, has nothing worse to suffer, in the most unfavourable case, than the discipline of a workhouse, and if the desire to avoid this be a sufficient motive in the one system, it would be sufficient in the other. I am not undervaluing the strength of the incitement given to labour when the whole or a large share of the benefit of extra exertion belongs to the labourer. But under the present system of industry this incitement, in the great majority of cases, does not exist. If Communistic labour might be less vigorous than that of a peasant proprietor, or a workman labouring on his own account, it would probably be more energetic than that of a labourer for hire, who has no personal interest in the matter at all. The neglect by the uneducated classes of labourers for hire, of the duties which they engage to perform, is in the present state of society most flagrant. Now it is an admitted condition of the Communist scheme that all shall be educated: and this being supposed, the duties of the members of the association would doubtless be as diligently performed as those of the generality of salaried officers in the middle or higher classes; who are not supposed to be necessarily unfaithful to their trust, because so long as they are not dismissed, their pay is the same in however lax a manner their duty is fulfilled. Undoubtedly, as a general rule, remuneration by fixed salaries does not in any class of functionaries produce the maximum of zeal: and this is as much as can be reasonably alleged against Communistic labour.

That even this inferiority would necessarily exist, is by no means so certain as is assumed by those who are little used to carry their minds beyond the state of things with which they are familiar. Mankind are capable of a far greater amount of public spirit than the present age is accustomed to suppose possible. History bears witness to the success with which large bodies of human beings may be trained to feel the public interest their own. And no soil could be more favourable to the growth of such a feeling, than a Communist association, since all the ambition, and the bodily and mental activity, which are now exerted in the pursuit of separate and self-regarding interests, would require another sphere of employment, and would naturally find it in the pursuit of the general benefit of the community. The same cause, so often assigned in explanation of the devotion of the Catholic priest or monk to the interest of his order – that he has no interest apart from it – would, under Communism, attach the citizen to the community. And independently of the public motive, every member of the association would be amenable to the most universal, and one of the strongest, of personal motives, that of public opinion. The force of this motive in deterring from any act or omission positively reproved by the community, no one is likely to deny; but the power also of emulation, in exciting to the most strenuous exertions for the sake of the approbation and admiration of others, is borne witness to by experience in every situation in which human beings publicly compete with one another, even if it be in things frivolous, or from which the public derive no benefit. A contest, who can do most for the common good, is not the kind of competition which Socialists repudiate. To what extent, therefore, the energy of labour would be diminished by Communism, or whether in the long run it would be diminished at all, must be considered for the present an undecided question.

Another of the objections to Communism is similar to that, so often urged against poor-laws: that if every member of the community were assured of subsistence for himself and any number of children, on the sole condition of willingness to work, prudential restraint on the multiplication of mankind would be at an end, and population would start forward at a rate which would reduce the community, through successive stages of increasing discomfort, to actual starvation. There would certainly be much ground for this apprehension if Communism provided no motives to restraint, equivalent to those which it would take away. But Communism is precisely the state of things in which opinion might be expected to declare itself with greatest intensity against this kind of selfish intemperance. Any augmentation of numbers which diminished the comfort or increased the toil of the mass, would then cause (which now it does not) immediate and unmistakeable inconvenience to every individual in the association; inconvenience which could not then be imputed to the avarice of employers, or the unjust privileges of the rich. In such altered circumstances opinion could not fail to reprobate, and if reprobation did not suffice, to repress by penalties of some description, this or any other culpable self-indulgence at the expense of the community. The Communistic scheme, instead of being peculiarly open to the objection drawn from danger of over-population, has the recommendation of tending in an especial degree to the prevention of that evil.

A more real difficulty is that of fairly apportioning the labour of the community among its members. There are many kinds of work, and by what standard are they to be measured one against another? Who is to judge how much cotton spinning, or distributing goods from the stores, or brick-laying, or chimney sweeping, is equivalent to so much ploughing? The difficulty of making the adjustment between different qualities of labour is so strongly felt by Communist writers, that they have usually thought it necessary to provide that all should work by turns at every description of useful labour: an arrangement which, by putting an end to the division of employments, would sacrifice so much of the advantage of co-operative production as greatly to diminish the productiveness of labour. Besides, even in the same kind of work, nominal equality of labour would be so great a real inequality, that the feeling of justice would revolt against its being enforced. All persons are not equally fit for all labour; and the same quantity of labour is an unequal burthen on the weak and the strong, the hardy and the delicate, the quick and the slow, the dull and the intelligent.

But these difficulties, though real, are not necessarily insuperable. The apportionment of work to the strength and capacities of individuals, the mitigation of a general rule to provide for cases in which it would operate harshly, are not problems to which human intelligence, guided by a sense of justice, would be inadequate. And the worst and most unjust arrangement which could be made of these points, under a system aiming at equality, would be so far short of the inequality and injustice with which labour (not to speak of remuneration) is now apportioned, as to be scarcely worth counting in the comparison. We must remember too, that Communism, as a system of society, exists only in idea; that its difficulties, at present, are much better understood than its resources; and that the intellect of mankind is only beginning to contrive the means of organizing it in detail, so as to overcome the one and derive the greatest advantage from the other.

If, therefore, the choice were to be made between Communism with all its chances, and the present state of society with all its sufferings and injustices; if the institution of private property necessarily carried with it as a consequence, that the produce of labour should be apportioned as we now see it, almost in an inverse ratio to the labour – the largest portions to those who have never worked at all, the next largest to those whose work is almost nominal, and so in a descending scale, the remuneration dwindling as the work grows harder and more disagreeable, until the most fatiguing and exhausting bodily labour cannot count with certainty on being able to earn even the necessaries of life; if this or Communism were the alternative, all the difficulties, great or small, of Communism would be but as dust in the balance. But to make the comparison applicable, we must compare Communism at its best, with the régime of individual property, not as it is, but as it might be made. The principle of private property has never yet had a fair trial in any country; and less so, perhaps, in this country than in some others. The social arrangements of modern Europe commenced from a distribution of property which was the result, not of just partition, or acquisition by industry, but of conquest and violence: and notwithstanding what industry has been doing for many centuries to modify the work of force, the system still retains many and large traces of its origin. The laws of property have never yet conformed to the principles on which the justification of private property rests. They have made property of things which never ought to be property, and absolute property where only a qualified property ought to exist. They have not held the balance fairly between human beings, but have heaped impediments upon some, to give advantage to others; they have purposely fostered inequalities, and prevented all from starting fair in the race. That all should indeed start on perfectly equal terms, is inconsistent with any law of private property: but if as much pains as has been taken to aggravate the inequality of chances arising from the natural working of the principle, had been taken to temper that inequality by every means not subversive of the principle itself; if the tendency of legislation had been to favour the diffusion, instead of the concentration of wealth – to encourage the subdivision of the large masses, instead of striving to keep them together; the principle of individual property would have been found to have no necessary connexion with the physical and social evils which almost all Socialist writers assume to be inseparable from it.

Private property, in every defence made of it, is supposed to mean, the guarantee to individuals of the fruits of their own labour and abstinence. The guarantee to them of the fruits of the labour and abstinence of others, transmitted to them without any merit or exertion of their own, is not of the essence of the institution, but a mere incidental consequence, which, when it reaches a certain height, does not promote, but conflicts with, the ends which render private property legitimate. To judge of the final destination of the institution of property, we must suppose everything rectified, which causes the institution to work in a manner opposed to that equitable principle, of proportion between remuneration and exertion, on which in every vindication of it that will bear the light, it is assumed to be grounded. We must also suppose two conditions realized, without which neither Communism nor any other laws or institutions could make the condition of the mass of mankind other than degraded and miserable. One of these conditions is, universal education; the other, a due limitation of the numbers of the community. With these, there could be no poverty, even under the present social institutions: and these being supposed, the question of Socialism is not, as generally stated by Socialists, a question of flying to the sole refuge against the evils which now bear down humanity; but a mere question of comparative advantages, which futurity must determine. We are too ignorant either of what individual agency in its best form, or Socialism in its best form, can accomplish, to be qualified to decide which of the two will be the ultimate form of human society.

If a conjecture may be hazarded, the decision will probably depend mainly on one consideration, viz. which of the two systems is consistent with the greatest amount of human liberty and spontaneity. After the means of subsistence are assured, the next in strength of the personal wants of human beings is liberty; and (unlike the physical wants, which as civilization advances become more moderate and more amenable to control) it increases instead of diminishing in intensity, as the intelligence and the moral faculties are more developed. The perfection both of social arrangements and of practical morality would be, to secure to all persons complete independence and freedom of action, subject to no restriction but that of not doing injury to others: and the education which taught or the social institutions which required them to exchange the control of their own actions for any amount of comfort or affluence, or to renounce liberty for the sake of equality, would deprive them of one of the most elevated characteristics of human nature. It remains to be discovered how far the preservation of this characteristic would be found compatible with the Communistic organization of society. No doubt, this, like all the other objections to the Socialist schemes is vastly exaggerated. The members of the association need not be required to live together more than they do now, nor need they be controlled in the disposal of their individual share of the produce, and of the probably large amount of leisure which, if they limited their production to things really worth producing, they would possess. Individuals need not be chained to an occupation, or to a particular locality. The restraints of Communism would be freedom in comparison with the present condition of the majority of the human race. The generality of labourers in this and most other countries, have as little choice of occupation or freedom of loco-motion, are practically as dependent on fixed rules and on the will of others, as they could be on any system short of actual slavery; to say nothing of the entire domestic subjection of one half the species, to which it is the signal honour of Owenism and most other forms of

Socialism that they assign equal rights, in all respects, with those of the hitherto dominant sex.[9] But it is not by comparison with the present bad state of society that the claims of Communism can be estimated; nor is it sufficient that it should promise greater personal and mental freedom than is now enjoyed by those who have not enough of either to deserve the name. The question is, whether there would be any asylum left for individuality of character; whether public opinion would not be a tyrannical yoke; whether the absolute dependence of each on all, and surveillance of each by all, would not grind all down into a tame uniformity of thoughts, feelings, and actions. This is already one of the glaring evils of the existing state of society, notwithstanding a much greater diversity of education and pursuits, and a much less absolute dependence of the individual on the mass, than would exist in the Communistic régime. No society in which eccentricity is a matter of reproach, can be in a wholesome state. It is yet to be ascertained whether the Communistic scheme would be consistent with that multiform development of human nature, those manifold unlikenesses, that diversity of tastes and talents, and variety of intellectual points of view, which not only form a great part of the interest of human life, but by bringing intellects into stimulating collision, and by presenting to each innumerable notions that he would not have conceived of himself, are the mainspring of mental and moral progression.

4. [*Examination of St Simonism and Fourierism*]

I have thus far confined my observations to the Communistic doctrine, which forms the extreme limit of Socialism; according to which not only the instruments of production, the land and capital, are the joint property of the community, but the produce is divided and the labour apportioned, as far as possible, equally. The objections, whether well or ill grounded, to which Socialism is liable, apply to this form of it in their greatest force. The other varieties of Socialism mainly differ from Communism, in not relying solely on what M. Louis Blanc calls the point of honour of industry, but retaining more or less of the incentives to labour derived from private pecuniary interest. Thus it is already a modification of the strict theory of Communism, when the principle is professed of proportioning remuneration to labour. The attempts which have been made in France to carry Socialism into practical effect, by associations of workmen manufacturing on their own account, mostly began by sharing the remuneration equally, without regard to the quantity of work done by the individual: but in almost every case this plan was after a short time abandoned, and recourse was had to working by the piece. The original principle appeals to a higher standard of justice, and is adapted to a much higher moral condition of human nature. The proportioning of remuneration to work done, is really just, only in so far as the more or less of the work is a matter of choice: when it depends on natural difference of strength or capacity, this principle of remuneration is in itself an injustice: it is giving to those who have; assigning most to those who are already most favoured by nature. Considered, however, as a compromise with the selfish type of character formed by the present standard of morality, and fostered by the existing social institutions, it is highly expedient; and until education shall have been entirely regenerated, is far more likely to prove immediately successful, than an attempt at a higher ideal.

The two elaborate forms of non-communistic Socialism known as St Simonism and Fourierism, are totally free from the objections usually urged against Communism; and though they are open to others of their own, yet by the great intellectual power which in many respects distinguishes them, and by their large and philosophic treatment of some of the fundamental problems of society and morality, they may justly be counted among the more remarkable productions of the past and present age. . . .

The most skilfully combined, and with the greatest foresight of objections, of all the forms of Socialism, is that commonly known as Fourierism.[10] This system does not contemplate the abolition of private property, nor even of inheritance; on the contrary, it avowedly takes into consideration, as an element in the distribution of the produce, capital as well as labour. It proposes that the operations of industry should be carried on by associations of about two thousand members, combining their labour on a district of about a square league in extent, under the guidance of chiefs selected by themselves.[a] In the distribution, a certain minimum is first assigned for the subsistence of every member of the community, whether capable or not of labour. The remainder of the produce is shared in certain proportions, to be determined beforehand, among the three elements, Labour, Capital, and Talent. The capital of the community may be owned in unequal shares by different members, who would in that case receive, as in any other joint-stock company, proportional dividends. The claim of each person on the share of the produce apportioned to talent, is estimated by the grade or rank

[a] Fourier called these organisations 'phalanxes'.

which the individual occupies in the several groups of labourers to which he or she belongs; these grades being in all cases conferred by the choice of his or her companions. The remuneration, when received, would not of necessity be expended or enjoyed in common; there would be separate *ménages* for all who preferred them, and no other community of living is contemplated, than that all the members of the association should reside in the same pile of buildings; for saving of labour and expense, not only in building, but in every branch of domestic economy; and in order that, the whole of the buying and selling operations of the community being performed by a single agent, the enormous portion of the produce of industry now carried off by the profits of mere distributors might be reduced to the smallest amount possible.

This system, unlike Communism, does not, in theory at least, withdraw any of the motives to exertion which exist in the present state of society. On the contrary, if the arrangement worked according to the intentions of its contrivers, it would even strengthen those motives; since each person would have much more certainty of reaping individually the fruits of increased skill or energy, bodily or mental, than under the present social arrangements can be felt by any but those who are in the most advantageous positions, or to whom the chapter of accidents is more than ordinarily favourable. The Fourierists, however, have still another resource. They believe that they have solved the great and fundamental problem of rendering labour attractive. That this is not impracticable, they contend by very strong arguments; in particular by one which they have in common with the Owenites, viz., that scarcely any labour, however severe, undergone by human beings for the sake of subsistence, exceeds in intensity that which other human beings, whose subsistence is already provided for, are found ready and even eager to undergo for pleasure. This certainly is a most significant fact, and one from which the student in social philosophy may draw important instruction. But the argument founded on it may easily be stretched too far. If occupations full of discomfort and fatigue are freely pursued by many persons as amusements, who does not see that they are amusements exactly because they are pursued freely, and may be discontinued at pleasure? The liberty of quitting a position often makes the whole difference between its being painful and pleasurable. Many a person remains in the same town, street, or house from January to December, without a wish or a thought tending towards removal, who, if confined to that same place by the mandate of authority, would find the imprisonment absolutely intolerable.

6. Principles of Political Economy

According to the Fourierists, scarcely any kind of useful labour is naturally and necessarily disagreeable, unless it is either regarded as dishonourable, or is immoderate in degree, or destitute of the stimulus of sympathy and emulation. Excessive toil need not, they contend, be undergone by any one, in a society in which there would be no idle class, and no labour wasted, as so enormous an amount of labour is now wasted, in useless things; and where full advantage would be taken of the power of association, both in increasing the efficiency of production, and in economizing consumption. The other requisites for rendering labour attractive would, they think, be found in the execution of all labour by social groups, to any number of which the same individual might simultaneously belong, at his or her own choice: their grade in each being determined by the degree of service which they were found capable of rendering, as appreciated by the suffrages of their comrades. It is inferred from the diversity of tastes and talents, that every member of the community would be attached to several groups, employing themselves in various kinds of occupation, some bodily, others mental, and would be capable of occupying a high place in some one or more; so that a real equality, or something more nearly approaching to it than might at first be supposed, would practically result: not, from the compression, but, on the contrary, from the largest possible development, of the various natural superiorities residing in each individual.

Even from so brief an outline, it must be evident that this system does no violence to any of the general laws by which human action, even in the present imperfect state of moral and intellectual culti-vation, is influenced; and that it would be extremely rash to pro-nounce it incapable of success, or unfitted to realize a great part of the hopes founded on it by its partisans. With regard to this, as to all other varieties of Socialism, the thing to be desired, and to which they have a just claim, is opportunity of trial. They are all capable of being tried on a moderate scale, and at no risk, either personal or pecuniary, to any except those who try them. It is for experience to determine how far or how soon any one or more of the possible systems of community of property will be fitted to substitute itself for the 'organization of industry' based on private ownership of land and capital. In the meantime we may, without attempting to limit the ultimate capabilities of human nature, affirm, that the political economist, for a considerable time to come, will be chiefly concerned with the conditions of existence and progress belonging to a society founded on private property and individual competition; and that the object to be principally aimed at in the present stage of human improvement, is not the subversion of the system of individual property, but the improvement of it, and the full participation of every member of the community in its benefits.

Of the Probable Futurity of the Labouring Classes (bk IV, ch. 7)[11]

4. [*Tendency of society towards the disuse of the relation of hiring and service*]

The political consequences of the increasing power and importance of the operative classes, and of the growing ascendancy of numbers, which, even in England and under the present institutions, is rapidly giving to the will of the majority at least a negative voice in the acts of government, are too wide a subject to be discussed in this place. But, confining ourselves to economical considerations, and notwithstanding the effect which improved intelligence in the working classes, together with just laws, may have in altering the distribution of the produce to their advantage, I cannot think that they will be permanently contented with the condition of labouring for wages as their ultimate state. They may be willing to pass through the class of servants in their way to that of employers; but not to remain in it all their lives. To begin as hired labourers, then after a few years to work on their own account, and finally employ others, is the normal condition of labourers in a new country, rapidly increasing in wealth and population, like America or Australia. But in an old and fully peopled country, those who begin life as labourers for hire, as a general rule, continue such to the end, unless they sink into the still lower grade of recipients of public charity. In the present stage of human progress, when ideas of equality are daily spreading more widely among the poorer classes, and can no longer be checked by anything short of the entire suppression of printed discussion and even of freedom of speech, it is not to be expected that the division of the human race into two hereditary classes, employers and employed, can be permanently maintained. The relation is nearly as unsatisfactory to the payer of wages as to the receiver. If the rich regard the poor as, by a kind of natural law, their servants and dependents, the rich in their turn are regarded as a mere prey and pasture for the poor; the subject of demands and expectations wholly indefinite, increasing in extent with every concession made to them. The total absence of regard for justice or fairness in the relations between the two, is as marked on the side of the employed as on that of the employers. We look in vain among the working classes in general for the just pride which will choose to give good work for good wages; for the most part, their sole endeavour is to receive as much, and return as little in the shape of service, as possible. It will sooner or later become insupportable to the employing classes, to live in close and hourly contact with persons whose interests and feelings are in hostility to them. Capitalists are almost as much interested as labourers in placing the operations of industry on such a footing, that those who labour for them may feel the same interest in the work, which is felt by those who labour on their own account.

The opinion expressed in a former part of this treatise respecting small landed properties and peasant proprietors,[a] may have made the reader anticipate that a wide diffusion of property in land is the resource on which I rely for exempting at least the agricultural labourers from exclusive dependence on labour for hire. Such, however, is not my opinion. I indeed deem that form of agricultural economy to be most groundlessly cried down, and to be greatly preferable, in its aggregate effects on human happiness, to hired labour in any form in which it exists at present; because the prudential check to population acts more directly, and is shown by experience to be more efficacious; and because, in point of security, of independence, of exercise of any other than the animal faculties, the state of a peasant proprietor is far superior to that of an agricultural labourer in this or any other old country. Where the former system already exists, and works on the whole satisfactorily, I should regret, in the present state of human intelligence, to see it abolished in order to make way for the other, under a pedantic notion of agricultural improvement as a thing necessarily the same in every diversity of circumstances. In a backward state of industrial improvement, as in Ireland, I should urge its introduction, in preference to an exclusive system of hired labour; as a more powerful instrument for raising a population from semi-savage listlessness and recklessness, to persevering industry and prudent calculation.

But a people who have once adopted the large system of production, either in manufactures or in agriculture, are not likely to recede from it; and when population is kept in due proportion to the means of support, it is not desirable that they should. Labour is unquestionably more productive on the system of large industrial enterprises; the produce, if not greater absolutely, is greater in proportion to the labour employed: the same number of persons can

[a] Discussed in bk II, chs. 6–10.

be supported equally well with less toil and greater leisure; which will be wholly an advantage, as soon as civilization and improvement have so far advanced, that what is a benefit to the whole shall be a benefit to each individual composing it. And in the moral aspect of the question, which is still more important than the economical, something better should be aimed at as the goal of industrial improvement, than to disperse mankind over the earth in single families, each ruled internally, as families now are, by a patriarchal despot, and having scarcely any community of interest, or necessary mental communion, with other human beings. The domination of the head of the family over the other members, in this state of things, is absolute; while the effect on his own mind tends towards concentration of all interests in the family, considered as an expansion of self, and absorption of all passions in that of exclusive possession, of all cares in those of preservation and acquisition. As a step out of the merely animal state into the human, out of reckless abandonment to brute instincts into prudential foresight and self-government, this moral condition may be seen without displeasure. But if public spirit, generous sentiments, or true justice and equality are desired, association, not isolation, of interests, is the school in which these excellences are nurtured. The aim of improvement should be not solely to place human beings in a condition in which they will be able to do without one another, but to enable them to work with or for one another in relations not involving dependence. Hitherto there has been no alternative for those who lived by their labour, but that of labouring either each for himself alone, or for a master. But the civilizing and improving influences of association, and the efficiency and economy of production on a large scale, may be obtained without dividing the producers into two parties with hostile interests and feelings, the many who do the work being mere servants under the command of the one who supplies the funds, and having no interest of their own in the enterprise except to earn their wages with as little labour as possible. The speculations and discussions of the last fifty years, and the events of the last thirty, are abundantly conclusive on this point. If the improvement which even triumphant military despotism[a] has only retarded, not stopped, shall continue its course, there can be little doubt that the *status* of hired labourers will gradually tend to confine itself to the description of workpeople whose low moral qualities render them unfit for anything more independent: and that the relation of masters and workpeople will be

---

[a] A reference to Emperor Louis Napoleon III in France after 1851. Napoleon was deposed during the Franco-Prussian War of 1870–1.

gradually superseded by partnership, in one of two forms: in some cases, association of the labourers with the capitalist; in others, and perhaps finally in all, association of labourers among themselves.

5. [*Examples of the association of labourers with capitalists*]

This first of these forms of association has long been practised, not indeed as a rule, but as an exception. In several departments of industry there are already cases in which every one who contributes to the work, either by labour or by pecuniary resources, has a partner's interest in it, proportional to the value of his contribution. It is already a common practice to remunerate those in whom peculiar trust is reposed, by means of a percentage on the profits: and cases exist in which the principle is, with excellent success, carried down to the class of mere manual labourers. . . .

6. [*Examples of the association of labourers among themselves*]

. . . Under the most favourable supposition, it will be desirable, and perhaps for a considerable length of time, that individual capitalists, associating their work people in the profits, should coexist with even those co-operative societies which are faithful to the co-operative principle. Unity of authority makes many things possible, which could not or would not be undertaken subject to the chance of divided councils or changes in the management. A private capitalist, exempt from the control of a body, if he is a person of capacity, is considerably more likely than almost any association to run judicious risks, and originate costly improvements. Co-operative societies may be depended on for adopting improvements after they have been tested by success, but individuals are more likely to commence things previously untried. Even in ordinary business, the competition of capable persons who in the event of failure are to have all the loss, and in case of success the greater part of the gain, will be very useful in keeping the managers of co-operative societies up to the due pitch of activity and vigilance.

When, however, co-operative societies shall have sufficiently multiplied, it is not probable that any but the least valuable workpeople will any longer consent to work all their lives for wages merely; both private capitalists and associations will gradually find it necessary to make the entire body of labourers participants in profits. Eventually, and in perhaps a less remote future than may be supposed, we may, through the co-operative principle, see our way to a change in society, which would combine the freedom and independence of the individual, with the moral, intellectual, and economical advantages of aggregate production; and which, without violence or spoliation, or even any sudden disturbance of existing habits and expectations, would realize, at least in the industrial department, the best aspirations of the democratic spirit, by putting an end to the division of society into the industrious and the idle, and effacing all social distinctions but those fairly earned by personal services and exertions. Associations like those which we have described, by the very process of their success, are a course of education in those moral and active qualities by which alone success can be either deserved or attained. As associations multiplied, they would tend more and more to absorb all work-people, except those who have too little understanding, or too little virtue, to be capable of learning to act on any other system than that of narrow selfishness. As this change proceeded, owners of capital would gradually find it to their advantage, instead of maintaining the struggle of the old system with work-people of only the worst description, to lend their capital to the associations; to do this at a diminishing rate of interest, and at last, perhaps, even to exchange their capital for terminable annuities. In this or some such mode, the existing accumulations of capital might honestly, and by a kind of spontaneous process, become in the end the joint property of all who participate in their productive employment: a transformation which, thus effected, (and assuming of course that both sexes participate equally in the rights and in the government of the association) would be the nearest approach to social justice, and the most beneficial ordering of industrial affairs for the universal good, which it is possible at present to foresee.

7. [*Competition is not pernicious, but useful and indispensable*]

I agree, then, with the Socialist writers in their conception of the form which industrial operations tend to assume in the advance of improvement; and I entirely share their opinion that the time is ripe for commencing this transformation, and that it should by all just and effectual means be aided and encouraged. But while I agree and sympathize with Socialists in this practical portion of their aims, I utterly dissent from the most conspicuous and vehement part of their teaching, their declamations against competition. With moral conceptions in many respects far ahead of the existing arrangements of society, they have in general very confused and erroneous notions of its actual working; and one of their greatest errors, as I conceive, is to charge upon competition all the economical evils which at present exist. They forget that wherever competition is not, monopoly is; and that monopoly, in all its forms, is the taxation of the industrious for the support of indolence, if not of plunder. They forget, too, that with the exception of competition among labourers, all other competition is for the benefit of the labourers, by cheapening the articles they consume; that competition even in the labour market is a source not of low but of high wages, wherever the competition *for* labour exceeds the competition *of* labour, as in America, in the colonies, and in the skilled trades; and never could be a cause of low wages, save by the oversticking of the labour market through the too great numbers of the labourers' families; while, if the supply of labourers is excessive, not even Socialism can prevent their remuneration from being low. Besides, if association were universal, there would be no competition between labourer and labourer; and that between association and association would be for the benefit of the consumers, that is, of the associations; of the industrious classes generally.

I do not pretend that there are no inconveniences in competition, or that the moral objections urged against it by Socialist writers, as a source of jealousy and hostility among those engaged in the same occupation, are altogether groundless. But if competition has its evils, it prevents greater evils. . . . It is the common error of Socialists to overlook the natural indolence of mankind; their tendency to be passive, to be the slaves of habit, to persist indefinitely in a course once chosen. Let them once attain any state of existence which they consider tolerable, and the danger to be apprehended is that they will thenceforth stagnate; will not exert themselves to improve, and by letting their faculties rust, will lose even the energy required to preserve them from deterioration. Competition may not be the best conceivable stimulus, but it is at present a necessary one, and no one can foresee the time when it will not be indispensable to progress. Even confining ourselves to the industrial department, in which, more than in any other, the majority may be supposed to be competent judges of improvements; it would be difficult to induce the general assembly of an association to submit to the trouble and inconvenience of altering their habits by adopting some new and promising invention, unless their knowledge of the existence of rival associations made them apprehend that what they would not consent to do, others would, and that they would be left behind in the race.

Instead of looking upon competition as the baneful and anti-social principle which it is held to be by the generality of Socialists, I conceive that, even in the present state of society and industry, every restriction of it is an evil, and every extension of it, even if for the time injuriously affecting some class of labourers, is always an ultimate good. To be protected against competition is to be protected in idleness, in mental dulness; to be saved the necessity of being as active and as intelligent as other people; and if it is also to be protected against being underbid for employment by a less highly paid class of labourers, this is only where old custom, or local and partial monopoly, has placed some particular class of artizans in a privileged position as compared with the rest; and the time has come when the interest of universal improvement is no longer promoted by prolonging the privileges of a few. If the slopsellers and others of their class have lowered the wages of tailors, and some other artizans, by making them an affair of competititon instead of custom, so much the better in the end. What is now required is not to bolster up old customs, whereby limited classes of labouring people obtain partial gains which interest them in keeping up the present organization of society, but to introduce new general practices beneficial to all; and there is reason to rejoice at whatever makes the privileged classes of skilled artizans feel that they have the same interests, and depend for their remuneration on the same general causes, and must resort for the improvement of their condition to the same remedies, as the less fortunately circumstanced and comparatively helpless multitude.

John Ruskin

(1819–1900)

Perhaps because it cost him the most effort, Ruskin once expressed the wish that, of all his writings, this essay should be preserved. Unreliable judges as authors often are of their own work, in this case Ruskin's wish was eventually to be fulfilled. The circumstances surrounding its initial publication were, however, inauspicious. 'Ad Valorem' is the fourth and last of a series of pieces written for the *Cornhill Magazine* in 1860; they produced so adverse a reaction from the readership that the editor, Thackeray, declined any successor. It was seventeen years before a second edition of the pieces, collected under the title *Unto This Last* (1862), appeared. Thereafter, its reputation soared. A survey of London libraries in 1894 revealed it to be the best-read work of 'the most popular author who deals with political economy and sociology' ('What London Reads', *London* (19 April 1894) p. 243), while a questionnaire circulated to Labour Members of Parliament in 1906 showed that Ruskin was the most frequently cited influence on their thinking.

It seems likely that if he provided these MPs with the foundations of an economic strategy (and it was by the older, not the younger ones he was most mentioned), it was as a moralist, not as a social scientist. Ruskin had little interest in the workings of the nineteenth-century economy compared with the vision he offered of a world in which production and consumption were but components of an absolute moral economy. As the footnotes indicate, biblical allusion is endemic to Ruskin's style; and, long after his loss of faith in 1858, he continued to advocate as an educational practice the systematic learning of biblical passages which had formed so important a part of his own upbringing. The prose of the Authorised Version supplied him with a tool and model sufficiently flexible to incorporate writing ranging from the expository to the prophetic in mode, the denunciatory to the visionary in tone. Yet this is no mere stylistic mannerism. The moral imperatives of the Bible, or occasionally of Greece and Rome, are Ruskin's touchstone. Political Economy is treated, not merely as intellectually inadequate, nor as a mere misreading of contemporary evidence, but as an instance of man's tendency to align himself with the satanic powers of self-destruction (see paragraphs 67, 77).

This absolutist moral position determines Ruskin's political stance. Despite his subsequent elevation into the ranks of socialist saints, Ruskin himself once identified the paradox of his position – 'I am a Socialist – of the most stern sort – but I am also a Tory of the sternest sort'. Shaw later characterised him as a Bolshevik by leaning rather than a democrat (G. B. Shaw, *Ruskin's Politics* (1921)), but this anachronistic comparison merely shows how misleading it is retrospectively to apply partisan labels to thinkers whose work predated the emergence of modern labour and socialist movements. Ruskin's guide to the regeneration of society was not the egalitarian individualism of that other proto-socialist, Mill, but Carlyle's conception of a paternalistic ruling élite, guiding justly and effectively a hierarchically structured organism. And in other works where Ruskin contemplates the moral and practical role of the state, he reveals few of Mill's qualms about its potential dangers to personal freedom. The true Carlylean bent of *Unto This Last* is revealed in the Preface, where Ruskin explains the purpose of the work as that of restoring 'honesty' to the captains of industry, which would ensure that 'the organization of labour is easy, and will develop itself without quarrel or difficulty'.

Like Carlyle, Ruskin had in earlier writings conveyed his vision through an imaginative reconstruction of medieval Europe, Carlyle through the records of the Camden Society, Ruskin from direct aesthetic judgements in such works as 'The Nature of Gothic' (*The Stones of Venice*, 3 vols., 1853). Here Ruskin had revealed a vision at once more substantial and less political. The moral absolute of work in Carlyle was fleshed out into a picture of the meaning which everyday toil must have had before machine production destroyed both its inherent satisfaction and the faith that labour was dedicated to higher spiritual purposes. Ruskin expanded Carlyle's preoccupation with 'leaders' and 'led' into a richer idea of the way in which the division of labour could be integrated into a social system of mutual interdependence and hierarchy. Each, too, transmuted the romance and chivalry of medievalism in a different direction – Carlyle into charismatic political 'heroes', Ruskin into the ill-starred League of St George, a guild of craftsmen redolent of the Owenite communities.

Though idealisation of the medieval world may underlie *Unto This Last*, it is notably absent from the text. For Ruskin here takes up the gauntlet declined by Carlyle, that of tackling Political Economy on its own ground, adopting like his contemporary, Marx, the view that it was far more effective during its period of ascendancy to undermine Political Economy from within than to snipe at it from 'outside'. The result is a work of demolition deploying barbed irony, logic-chopping, and even, where necessary, convenient distortion of his opponents' views, delivered in a tone which led one outraged reviewer (*Saturday Review*) to maintain that Smith, Ricardo and Mill deserved better treatment than 'to be preached to death by a mad governess'. The desire to produce such an accumulation of arguments means, however, that many misfire. In attacking the labour theory of value (para. 60), he hints at a *reductio ad absurdum* in the question of whether the fisherman catches whales or whitebait, but the alliterative jibe is in danger of distracting the reader's attention from the main thrust of his argument. Elsewhere, Adam Smith's hymn to the productive advantages of the division of labour is savaged as inhumane, ignoring the fact that Smith himself acknowledged its morally debilitating effects. Nor does Ruskin acknowledge that his attack upon the potential unfairness implicit in exchange relation between people unequal in power or education (para. 67) would have been endorsed by, among others, J. S. Mill, the stalking-horse of this piece. Indeed, Mill was altogether an unfortunate choice to take for his prime object of attack. For he, like Ruskin, had once sat at Carlyle's feet, differentiated clearly between the quantity of goods and quality of life, advocated co-operative modes of work, and looked on education as a means of improving the status and responsibility of labour. Ruskin, however, rejects Mill's distinction between revising, on the one hand, the technical apparatus, and, on the other, the moral implications of earlier economic writings. Thus, his assertion that utility, rather than labour, is the true determination of commodity values (para. 62ff) foreshadowed the revisionist attack by Jevons and the neo-classical economists of the 1870s on their predecessors; but the theoretical consequences of this are ignored in favour of defining 'utility' in moral terms to which Mill might well have assented.

Characteristic also of Ruskin's technique is that, whereas Marx and Engels adopted the terminology of Political Economy in order to subvert its central message, Ruskin attempts a subversion of its very language. Virtually the whole of the essay rests upon challenging common definitions and meanings, disintegrating the theoretical precision of key concepts by a succession of examples which purport to destroy their validity, and offering a more 'logical' account of the central terminology. Taking Mill's definition of 'wealth', for instance, (para. 62), he breaks it down into component parts, and slips in the word 'possession', which is then defined, not by analysis, but by example. The dramatic form of the given illustration not only grasps the reader's attention, but predetermines the nature and extent of the following discussion; for Ruskin is anxious to point to the contrary implications of the noun 'possession' depending upon whether it is derived from the active or passive voice of the verb. He takes his cue here from the language of the Authorised Version which refers to a man 'possessed of the palsy'; but throughout, there is a fondness for word-coinage (e.g. 'illth' and 'pluses') and for producing etymologies which are ingenious to the point of whimsy, so idiosyncratic we are reminded of Lewis Carroll's Humpty Dumpty – 'When *I* use a word . . . it means just what I choose it to mean, neither more nor less'. Though such techniques reflect both a Carlylean proclivity for word-play, and a cast of mind which operated more by lateral association than by logical sequence, their impact is sometimes to restore to the pun that seriousness of intent possible in its Jacobean usage, reminiscent of the carefully manipulated confusion of values when Ben Jonson came to play with the word 'possess' in *Volpone*.

But further, the nature of the examples chosen in para. 62 is related to a train of imagery which gathers symbolic moral value. Just as the metaphor of the fog in *Bleak House*, or the dust heaps in *Our Mutual Friend*, bear slowly growing accretions of moral significance, so do jewellery and gold for Ruskin. The economists' use of gold as a standard measure of currency, and the role played by this inert metal as a stock of value, become symbolic of the degradation of society – suborning changing human tastes and values to a uniform material base, distorting the fact that England's inhabitants, not her possessions, constitute her real wealth (see end of essay II, 'The Veins of Wealth').

The contraries of life and death Ruskin uses here, and in his further mention of gladiatorial ritual, are not merely dramatic exaggerations, but a parable of the romantic conception of society as an organic whole, a living thing defying the dissection of economists who treat it as a static mechanism resoluble into individual components. The truest understanding of Ruskin's paradoxical political position is to be found, finally, in attention to his style. The socialist message of wealth distributed 'Unto this last even as unto thee' is enunciated with the authoritative assurance of a Tory patriarch. Olympian prescience alone can determine the wisdom of curbing individual self-interest for the ultimate benefit of a society always greater than the sum of its parts.

7. Ad Valorem,[a] *Unto This Last*,[1] essay IV (1862)

The Works of John Ruskin, eds. E. T. Cook and A. Wedderburn (36 vols., 1903–12), vol. XVII, pp. 77–114

56. IN THE LAST paper we saw that just payment of labour consisted in a sum of money which would approximately obtain equivalent labour at a future time: we have now to examine the means of obtaining such equivalence. Which question involves the definition of Value, Wealth, Price, and Produce.

None of these terms are yet defined so as to be understood by the public. But the last, Produce, which one might have thought the clearest of all, is, in use, the most ambiguous; and the examination of the kind of ambiguity attendant on its present employment will best open the way to our work.

In his chapter on Capital,[2] Mr J. S. Mill instances, as a capitalist, a hardware manufacturer, who, having intended to spend a certain portion of the proceeds of his business in buying plate and jewels, changes his mind, and 'pays it as wages to additional workpeople.' The effect is stated by Mr Mill to be, that 'more food is appropriated to the consumption of productive labourers.'

57. Now I do not ask, though, had I written this paragraph, it would surely have been asked of me, What is to become of the silversmiths? If they are truly unproductive persons, we will acqui-

---

[a] 'Concerning value'; but see para. 61 below.

esce in their extinction. And though in another part of the same passage, the hardware merchant is supposed also to dispense with a number of servants, whose 'food is thus set free for productive purposes,' I do not inquire what will be the effect, painful or otherwise, upon the servants, of this emancipation of their food. But I very seriously inquire why ironware is produce, and silverware is not? That the merchant consumes the one, and sells the other, certainly does not constitute the difference, unless it can be shown (which, indeed, I perceive it to be becoming daily more and more the aim of tradesmen to show) that commodities are made to be sold, and not to be consumed. The merchant is an agent of conveyance to the consumer in one case, and is himself the consumer in the other. But the labourers are in either case equally productive, since they have produced goods to the same value, if the hardware and the plate are both goods.

And what distinction separates them? It is indeed possible that in the 'comparative estimate of the moralist,' with which Mr Mill says political economy has nothing to do (III.i.2), a steel fork might appear a more substantial production than a silver one: we may grant also that knives, no less than forks, are good produce; and scythes and ploughshares serviceable articles. But, how of bayonets? Supposing the hardware merchant to effect large sales of *these*, by help of the 'setting free' of the food of his servants and his silversmith, – is he still employing productive labourers or, in Mr Mill's words, labourers who increase 'the stock of permanent means of enjoyment' (I.iii.4)? Or if, instead of bayonets, he supply bombs, will not the absolute and final 'enjoyment' of even these energetically productive articles (each of which costs ten pounds) be dependent on a proper choice of time and place for their *enfantement*,[a] choice, that is to say, depending on those philosophical considerations with which political economy has nothing to do?[3]

58. I should have regretted the need of pointing out inconsistency in any portion of Mr Mill's work, had not the value of his work proceeded from its inconsistencies. He deserves honour among economists by inadvertently disclaiming the principles which he states, and tacitly introducing the moral considerations with which he declares his science has no connection. Many of his chapters are, therefore, true and valuable; and the only conclusions of his which I have to dispute are those which follow from his premises.

Thus, the idea which lies at the root of the passage we have just been examining, namely, that labour applied to produce luxuries will

[a] Creation.

not support so many persons as labour applied to produce useful articles, is entirely true; but the instance given fails – and in four directions of failure at once – because Mr Mill has not defined the real meaning of usefulness. The definition which he has given – 'capacity to satisfy a desire, or serve a purpose' (III.i.2) – applies equally to the iron and silver; while the true definition – which he has not given, but which nevertheless underlies the false verbal definition in his mind, and comes out once or twice by accident (as in the words 'any support to life or strength' in I.iii.5) – applies to some articles of iron, but not to others, and to some articles of silver, but not to others. It applies to ploughs, but not to bayonets and to forks but not to filigree.[4]

59. The eliciting of the true definitions will give us the reply to our first question, 'What is value?' respecting which, however, we must first hear the popular statements.

'The word "Value," when used without adjunct, always means, in political economy, value in exchange' (Mill, III.i.2). So that, if two ships cannot exchange their rudders, their rudders are, in politico-economic language, of no value to either.

But 'the subject of political economy is wealth.' – (Preliminary remarks, page 1.)

And wealth 'consists of all useful and agreeable objects which possess exchangeable value' – (Preliminary remarks, page 10.)

It appears, then, according to Mr Mill, that usefulness and agreeableness underlie the exchange value, and must be ascertained to exist in the thing, before we can esteem it an object of wealth.

Now, the economical usefulness of a thing depends not merely on its own nature, but on the number of people who can and will use it. A horse is useless, and therefore unsaleable, if no one can ride, – a sword, if no one can strike, and meat, if no one can eat. Thus every material utility depends on its relative human capacity.

Similarly: The agreeableness of a thing depends not merely on its own likeableness, but on the number of people who can be got to like it. The relative agreeableness, and therefore saleableness, of 'a pot of the smallest ale,' and of 'Adonis painted by a running brook,' depends virtually on the opinion of Demos,[a] in the shape of Christopher Sly. That is to say, the agreeableness of a thing depends on its relatively human disposition.[5] Therefore, political economy, being a science of wealth, must be a science respecting human capacities and dispositions. But moral considerations have nothing to do with political

---

[a] The common man.

economy (III.i.2). Therefore, moral considerations have nothing to do with human capacities and dispositions.

60. I do not wholly like the look of this conclusion from Mr Mill's statements: – let us try Mr Ricardo's.[6]

'Utility is not the measure of exchangeable value, though it is absolutely essential to it.' – (Chap. I.sect.i) Essential in what degree, Mr Ricardo? There may be greater and less degrees of utility. Meat, for instance, may be so good as to be fit for any one to eat, or so bad as to be fit for no one to eat. What is the exact degree of goodness which is 'essential' to its exchangeable value, but not 'the measure' of it? How good must the meat be, in order to possess any exchangeable value? and how bad must it be – (I wish this were a settled question in London markets) – in order to possess none?

There appears to be some hitch, I think, in the working even of Mr Ricardo's principles; but let him take his own example. 'Suppose that in the early stages of society the bows, and arrows of the hunter were of equal value with the implements of the fisherman. Under such circumstances the value of the deer, the produce of the hunter's day's labour, would be *exactly'* (italics mine) 'equal to the value of the fish, the product of the fisherman's day's labour. The comparative value of the fish and game would be *entirely* regulated by the quantity of labour realized in each.' (Ricardo, Chap. I,sect.iii On Value.)

Indeed! Therefore, if the fisherman catches one sprat, and the huntsman one deer, one sprat will be equal in value to one deer; but if the fisherman catches no sprat and the huntsman two deer, no sprat will be equal in value to two deer?

Nay; but – Mr Ricardo's supporters may say – he means, on an average; – if the average product of a day's work of fisher and hunter be one fish and one deer, the one fish will always be equal in value to the one deer.

Might I inquire the species of fish? Whale? or whitebait?

It would be waste of time to pursue these fallacies farther; we will seek for a true definition.

61. Much store has been set for centuries upon the use of our English classical education. It were to be wished that our well-educated merchants recalled to mind always this much of their Latin schooling, – that the nominative of *valorem* (a word already suffi-ciently familiar to them) is *valor*; a word which, therefore, ought to be familiar to them. *Valor*, from *valere*, to be well or strong (ὑγιαίνω); – strong, *in* life (if a man), or valiant; strong, *for* life (if a thing), or valuable. To be 'valuable', therefore, is to 'avail towards life.' A truly valuable or availing thing is that which leads to life with

its whole strength. In proportion as it does not lead to life, or as its strength is broken, it is less valuable; in proportion as it leads away from life, it is unvaluable or malignant.

The value of a thing, therefore, is independent of opinion, and of quantity. Think what you will of it, gain how much you may of it, the value of the thing itself is neither greater nor less. For ever it avails, or avails not; no estimate can raise, no disdain repress, the power which it holds from the Maker of things and of men.

The real science of political economy, which has yet to be distinguished from the bastard science, as medicine from witchcraft, and astronomy from astrology, is that which teaches nations to desire and labour for the things that lead to life: and which teaches them to scorn and destroy the things that lead to destruction. And if, in a state of infancy, they supposed indifferent things, such as excrescences of shell-fish, and pieces of blue and red stone, to be valuable, and spent large measures of the labour which ought to be employed for the extension and ennobling of life, in diving or digging for them, and cutting them into various shapes, – or if, in the same state of infancy, they imagine precious and beneficent things, such as air, light, and cleanliness, to be valueless, – or if, finally, they imagine the conditions of their own existence, by which alone they can truly possess, or use anything, such, for instance, as peace, trust and love, to be prudently exchangeable, when the markets offer, for gold, iron, or excrescences of shells – the great and only science of Political Economy teaches them, in all these cases, what is vanity, and what substance; and how the service of Death, the Lord of Waste, and of eternal emptiness, differs from the service of Wisdom, the Lady of Saving, and of eternal fulness; she who has said, 'I will cause those that love me to inherit SUBSTANCE; and I will FILL their treasures.'[a]

The 'Lady of Saving,' in a profounder sense than that of the savings bank, though that is a good one: Madonna della Salute,[7] – Lady of Health, – which, though commonly spoken of as if separate from wealth, is indeed a part of wealth. This word, 'wealth,' it will be remembered, is the next we have to define.

62. 'To be wealthy,' says Mr Mill, 'is to have a large stock of useful articles.'

I accept this definition. Only let us perfectly understand it. My opponents often lament my not giving them enough logic: I fear I must at present use a little more than they will like; but this business of Political Economy is no light one, and we must allow no loose terms in it.

[a] Proverbs 8:21

We have, therefore, to ascertain in the above definition, first, what is the meaning of 'having,' or the nature of Possession. Then what is the meaning of 'useful,' or the nature of Utility.

And first of possession. At the crossing of the transepts of Milan Cathedral has lain, for three hundred years, the embalmed body of St Carlo Borromeo. It holds a golden crosier, and has a cross of emeralds on its breast. Admitting the crosier and emeralds to be useful articles, is the body to be considered as 'having' them? Do they, in the politico-economical sense of property, belong to it? If not, and if we may, therefore, conclude generally that a dead body cannot possess property, what degree and period of animation in the body will render possession possible?

As thus: lately in a wreck of a Californian ship, one of the passengers fastened a belt about him with two hundred pounds of gold in it, with which he was found afterwards at the bottom. Now, as he was sinking – had he the gold? or had the gold him?[8]

And if, instead of sinking him in the sea by its weight, the gold had struck him on the forehead, and thereby caused incurable disease – suppose palsy or insanity, – would the gold in that case have been more a 'possession' than in the first? Without pressing the inquiry up through instances of gradually increasing vital power over the gold (which I will, however, give, if they are asked for), I presume the reader will see that possession, or 'having,' is not an absolute, but a gradated, power; and consists not only in the quantity or nature of the thing possessed, but also (and in a greater degree) in its suitableness to the person possessing it and in his vital power to use it.

And our definition of Wealth, expanded, becomes: 'The possession of useful articles, *which we can use.*' This is a very serious change. For wealth, instead of depending merely on a 'have,' is thus seen to depend on a 'can.' Gladiator's death, on a 'habet'; but soldier's victory, and State's salvation, on a 'quo plurimum posset.' (Liv. VII.6).[9] And what we reasoned of only as accumulation of material, is seen to demand also accumulation of capacity.

63. So much for our verb. Next for our adjective. What is the meaning of 'useful'?

The inquiry is closely connected with the last. For what is capable of use in the hands of some persons, is capable, in the hands of others, of the opposite of use, called commonly 'from-use', or 'ab-use.' And it depends on the person, much more than on the article, whether its usefulness or ab-usefulness will be the quality developed in it. Thus, wine, which the Greeks, in their Bacchus, made rightly the type of all passion, and which, when used, 'cheereth god and man'[a] that is to say, strengthens both the divine life, or reasoning power, and the earthy, or carnal power, of man); yet, when abused, becomes 'Dionusos,' hurtful especially to the divine part of man, or reason.[10] And again, the body itself, being equally liable to use and to abuse, and, when rightly disciplined, serviceable to the State, both for war and labour, – but when not disciplined, or abused, valueless to the State, and capable only of continuing the private or single existence of the individual (and that but feebly) – the Greeks called such a body an 'idiotic' or 'private' body, from their word signifying a person employed in no way directly useful to the State; whence finally, our 'idiot,' meaning a person entirely occupied with his own concerns.

Hence, it follows that if a thing is to be useful, it must be not only of an availing nature, but in availing hands. Or, in accurate terms, usefulness is value in the hands of the valiant; so that this science of wealth being, as we have just seen, when regarded as the science of Accumulation, accumulative of capacity as well as of material, – when regarded as the Science of Distribution, is distribution not absolute, but discriminate; not of every thing to every man, but of the right thing to the right man. A difficult science, dependent on more than arithmetic.

64. Wealth, therefore, is 'THE POSSESSION OF THE VALUABLE BY THE VALIANT'; and in considering it as a power existing in a nation, the two elements, the value of the thing, and the valour of its possessor, must be estimated together. Whence it appears that many of the persons commonly considered wealthy, are in reality no more wealthy than the locks of their own strong boxes are, they being inherently and eternally incapable of wealth; and operating for the nation, in an economical point of view, either as pools of dead water, and eddies in a stream (which, so long as the stream flows, are useless, or serve only to drown people, but may become of importance in a state of stagnation should the stream dry); or else, as dams in a river, of which the ultimate service depends not on the dam, but the miller; or else, as mere accidental stays and impediments, acting not as wealth, but (for we ought to have a correspondent term) as 'illth,' causing various devastation and trouble around them in all directions; or lastly, act not at all, but are merely animated conditions of delay, (no use being possible of anything they have until they are dead,) in which last condition they are nevertheless often useful *as* delays, and 'impedimenta',[b] if a nation is apt to move too fast.

65. This being so, the difficulty of the true science of Political

---

[a] Judges 9:13   [b] Obstacles.

Economy lies not merely in the need of developing manly character to deal with material value, but in the fact, that while the manly character and material value only form wealth by their conjunction, they have nevertheless a mutually destructive operation on each other. For the manly character is apt to ignore, or even cast away, the material value:– whence that of Pope:–

> Sure, of qualities demanding praise,
> More go to ruin fortunes, than to raise.[11]

And on the other hand, the material value is apt to undermine the manly character; so that it must be our work, in the issue, to examine what evidence there is of the effect of wealth on the minds of its possessors; also, what kind of person it is who usually sets himself to obtain wealth, and succeeds in doing so; and whether the world owes more gratitude to rich or to poor men, either for their moral influence upon it, or for chief goods, discoveries, and practical advancements. I may, however, anticipate future conclusions, so far as to state that in a community regulated only by laws of demand and supply, but protected from open violence, the persons who become rich are, generally speaking, industrious, resolute, proud, covetous, prompt, methodical, sensible, unimaginative, insensitive, and ignorant. The persons who remain poor are the entirely foolish, the entirely wise, the idle, the reckless, the humble, the thoughtful, the dull, the imaginative, the sensitive, the well-informed, the improvident, the irregularly and impulsively wicked, the clumsy knave, the open thief, and the entirely merciful, just, and godly person.

66. Thus far, then, of wealth. Next, we have to ascertain the nature of Price; that is to say, of exchange value, and its expression by currencies.

Note first, of exchange, there can be no *profit* in it. It is only in labour there can be profit – that is to say, a 'making in advance,' or 'making in favour of' (from proficio). In exchange, there is only advantage, *i.e.*, a bringing of vantage or power to the exchanging persons. Thus, one man, by sowing and reaping, turns one measure of corn into two measures. That is Profit. Another, by digging and forging, turns one spade into two spades. That is Profit. But the man who has two measures of corn wants sometimes to dig; and the man who has two spades wants sometimes to eat:– They exchange the gained grain for gained tool; and both are the better for the exchange; but though there is much advantage in the transaction, there is no profit. Nothing is constructed or produced. Only that which has been before constructed is given to the person by whom it can be used. If labour is necessary to effect the exchange, that labour is in reality involved in the production, and, like all other labour, bears profit. Whatever number of men are concerned in the manufacture, or in the conveyance, have share in the profit; but neither the manufacture nor the conveyance are the exchange, and in the exchange itself there is no profit.

There may, however, be acquisition, which is a very different thing. If, in the exchange, one man is able to give what cost him little labour for what has cost the other much, he 'acquires' a certain quantity of the produce of the other's labour. And precisely what he acquires, the other loses. In mercantile language, the person who thus acquires is commonly said to have 'made a profit'; and I believe that many of our merchants are seriously under the impression that it is possible for everybody, somehow, to make a profit in this manner. Whereas, by the unfortunate constitution of the world we live in, the laws both of matter and motion have quite rigorously forbidden universal acquisition of this kind. Profit, or material gain, is attainable only by construction or by discovery; not by exchange. Whenever material gain follows exchange, for every *plus* there is a precisely equal *minus*.

Unhappily for the progress of the science of Political Economy, the plus quantities, or – if I may be allowed to coin an awkward plural – the pluses, make a very positive and venerable appearance in the world, so that every one is eager to learn the science which produces results so magnificent; whereas the minuses have, on the other hand, a tendency to retire into back streets, and other places of shade, – or even to get themselves wholly and finally put out of sight in graves: which renders the algebra of this science peculiar, and difficultly legible; a large number of its negative signs being written by the account-keeper in a kind of red ink, which starvation thins, and makes strangely pale, or even quite invisible ink, for the present.

67. The Science of Exchange, or, as I hear it has been proposed to call it, of 'Catallactics,'[12] considered as one of gain, is therefore, simply nugatory; but considered as one of acquisition, it is a very curious science, differing in its data and basis from every other science known. Thus:– If I can exchange a needle with a savage for a diamond, my power of doing so depends either on the savage's ignorance of social arrangements in Europe, or on his want of power to take advantage of them, by selling the diamond to any one else for more needles. If, farther, I make the bargain as completely advantageous to myself as possible, by giving to the savage a needle with no

eye in it (reaching, thus a sufficiently satisfactory type of the perfect operation of catallactic science), the advantage to me in the entire transaction depends wholly upon the ignorance, powerlessness, or heedlessness of the person dealt with. Do away with these, and catalactic advantage becomes impossible. So far, therefore, as the science of exchanging relates to the advantage of one of the exchanging persons only, it is founded on the ignorance or incapacity of the opposite person. Where these vanish, it also vanishes. It is therefore a science founded on nescience, and an art founded on artlessness. But all other sciences and arts, except this, have for their object the doing away with their opposite nescience and artlessness. *This* science, alone of sciences, must, by all available means, promulgate and prolong its opposite nescience; otherwise the science itself is impossible. It is, therefore, peculiarly and alone the science of darkness; probably a bastard science – not by any means a *divina scientia*, but one begotten of another father, that father who, advising his children to turn stones into bread, is himself employed in turning bread into stones, and who, if you ask a fish of him (fish not being producible on his estate), can but give you a serpent.[a]

68. The general law, then, respecting just or economical exchange, is simply this:– there must be one advantage on both sides (or if only advantage on one, at least no disadvantage on the other) to the persons exchanging; and just payment for his time, intelligence, and labour, to any intermediate person effecting the transaction (commonly called a merchant); and whatever advantage there is on either side, and whatever pay is given to the intermediate person, should be thoroughly known to all concerned. All attempt at concealment implies some practice of the opposite, or undivine science, founded on nescience. Whence another saying of the Jew merchant's – 'As a nail between the stone joints, so doth sin stick fast between buying and selling.'[b] Which peculiar riveting of stone and timber, in men's dealings with each other, is again set forth in the house which was to be destroyed – timber and stones together – when Zechariah's roll (more probably 'curved sword') flew over it: 'the curse that goeth forth over all the earth upon every one that stealeth and holdeth himself guiltless,' instantly followed by the vision of the Great Measure; – the measure 'of the injustice of them in all the earth' (αὕτη ἡ ἀδικία αὐτῶν ἐν πάσῃ τῇ γῇ), with the weight of lead for its lid, and the woman, the spirit of wickedness, within it; – that is to say, Wickedness hidden by dulness, and formalized, outwardly, into

<hr />

[a] See Luke 11:11–13.   [b] Ecclesiasticus 27:2.

ponderously established cruelty, 'It shall be set upon its own base in the land of Babel.'[13]

69. I have hitherto carefully restricted myself, in speaking of exchange, to the use of the term 'advantage'; but that term includes two ideas: the advantage, namely, of getting what we *need*, and that of getting what we *wish for*. Three-fourths of the demands existing in the world are romantic; founded on visions, idealisms, hopes, and affections; and the regulation of the purse is, in its essence, regulation of the imagination and the heart. Hence, the right discussion of the nature of price is a very high metaphysical and psychical problem; sometimes to be solved only in a passionate manner, as by David in his counting the price of the water of the well by the gate of Bethlehem;[14] but its first conditions are the following:– The price of anything is the quantity of labour given by the person desiring it, in order to obtain possession of it. This price depends on four variable quantities. A. The quantity of wish the purchaser has for the thing; opposed to α, the quantity of wish the seller has to keep it. B. The quantity of labour the purchaser can afford, to obtain the thing; opposed to β, the quantity of labour the seller can afford, to keep it. These quantities are operative only in excess: *i.e.*, the quantity of wish (A) means the quantity of wish for this thing, above wish for other things; and the quantity of work (B) means the quantity which can be spared to get this thing from the quantity needed to get other things.

Phenomena of price, therefore, are intensely complex, curious and, interesting – too complex, however, to be examined yet; every one of them, when traced far enough, showing itself at last as a part of the bargain of the Poor of the Flock (or 'flock of slaughter'), 'If ye think good, give ME my price, and if not, forbear' – Zech. xi. 12;[15] but as the price of everything is to be calculated finally in labour, it is necessary to define the nature of that standard.

70. Labour is the contest of the life of man with an opposite; – the term 'life' including his intellect, soul, and physical power, contending with question, difficulty, trial, or material force.

Labour is of a higher or lower order, as it includes more or fewer of the elements of life: and labour of good quality, in any kind, includes always as much intellect and feeling as will fully and harmoniously regulate the physical force.

In speaking of the value and price of labour, it is necessary always to understand labour of a given rank and quality, as we should speak of gold or silver of a given standard. But (that is, heartless, inexperienced, or senseless) labour cannot be valued; it is like gold of uncertain alloy, or flawed iron.

The quality and kind of labour being given, its value, like that of all other valuable things, is invariable. But the quantity of it which must be given for other things is variable: and in estimating this variation, the price of other things must always be counted by the quantity of labour; not the price of labour by the quantity of other things.

71. Thus, if we want to plant an apple sapling in rocky ground, it may take two hours' work; in soft ground, perhaps only half an hour. Grant the soil equally good for the tree in each case. Then the value of the sapling planted by two hours' work is nowise greater than that of the sapling planted in half an hour. One will bear no more fruit than the other. Also, one half-hour of work is as valuable as another half-hour; nevertheless, the one sapling has cost four such pieces of work, the other only one. Now, the proper statement of this fact is, not that the labour on the hard ground is cheaper than on the soft; but that the tree is dearer. The exchange value may, or may not, afterwards depend on this fact. If other people have plenty of soft ground to plant in, they will take no cognizance of our two hours' labour in the price they will offer for the plant on the rock. And if, through want of sufficient botanical science, we have planted an upas-tree[a] instead of an apple, the exchange value will be a negative quantity; still less proportionate to the labour expended.

What is commonly called cheapness of labour, signifies, therefore, in reality, that many obstacles have to be overcome by it; so that much labour is required to produce a small result. But this should never be spoken of as cheapness of labour, but as dearness of the object wrought for. It would be just as rational to say that walking was cheap, because we had ten miles to walk home to our dinner, as that labour was cheap, because we had to work ten hours to earn it.

72. The last word which we have to define is 'Production.'

I have hitherto spoken of all labour as profitable; because it is impossible to consider under one head the quality or value of labour, and its aim. But labour of the best quality may be various in aim. It may be either constructive ('gathering,' from con and struo), as agriculture; nugatory, as jewel-cutting; or destructive ('scattering,' from de and struo), as war. It is not, however, always easy to prove labour, apparently nugatory, to be actually so; generally, the formula holds good: 'he that gathereth not, scattereth';[b] thus, the jeweller's art is probably very harmful in its ministering to a clumsy and inelegant pride. So that, finally, I believe nearly all labour may be shortly divided into positive and negative labour: positive, that which produces life; negative, that which produces death; the most

---

[a] Javanese tree supposed to poison all life in its vicinity.   [b] Matthew 12:30.

directly negative labour being murder, and the most directly positive, the bearing and rearing of children: so that in the precise degree in which murder is hateful, on the negative side of idleness, in that exact degree child-rearing is admirable, on the positive side of idleness. For which reason, and because of the honour that there is in rearing children, while the wife is said to be as the vine (for cheering), the children are as the olive branch, for praise:[a] nor for praise only but for peace (because large families can only be reared in times of peace): though since, in their spreading and voyaging in various directions, they distribute strength, they are, to the home strength, as arrows in the hand of the giant[b] – striking here and there far away.

Labour being thus various in its result, the prosperity of any nation is in exact proportion to the quantity of labour which it spends in obtaining and employing means of life. Observe, – I say, obtaining and employing; that is to say, not merely wisely producing, but wisely distributing and consuming. Economists usually speak as if there were no good in consumption absolute. So far from this being so, consumption absolute is the end, crown, and perfection of production; and wise consumption is a far more difficult art than wise production. Twenty people can gain money for one who can use it; and the vital question, for individual and for nation, is, never 'how much do they make?' but 'to what purpose do they spend?'

73. The reader may, perhaps, have been surprised at the slight reference I have hitherto made to 'capital,' and its functions. It is here the place to define them.

Capital signifies 'head, or source, or root material' – it is material by which some derivative or secondary good is produced. It is only capital proper (caput vivum, not caput mortuum)[16] when it is thus producing something different from itself. It is a root, which does not enter into vital function till it produces something else than a root: namely, fruit. That fruit will in time again produce roots; and so all living capital issues in reproduction of capital; but capital which produces nothing but capital is only root producing root; bulb issuing in bulb, never in tulip; seed issuing in seed, never in bread. The Political Economy of Europe has hitherto devoted itself wholly to the multiplication, or (less even) the aggregation, of bulbs. It never saw, nor conceived, such a thing as a tulip. Nay, boiled bulbs they might have been – glass bulbs – Prince Rupert's drops,[17] consummated in powder (well, if it were glasspowder and not gunpowder), for any end or meaning the economists had in defining the laws of aggregation. We will try and get a clearer notion of them.

---

[a] Psalm 128:3   [b] Psalm 127:3–5.

The best and simplest general type of capital is a well-made ploughshare. Now, if that ploughshare did nothing but beget other ploughshares, in a polypous manner, – however the great cluster of polypous plough, might glitter in the sun it would have lost its function of capital. It becomes true capital only by another kind of splendour, – when it is seen 'splendescere sulco,' to grow bright in the furrow,*a* rather with diminution of its substance, than addition, by the noble friction. And the true home question, to every capitalist and to every nation, is not, 'how many ploughs have you?' but, 'where are your furrows?' not – 'how quickly will this capital reproduce itself?' – but, 'what will it do during reproduction?' What substance will it furnish, good for life? what work construct, protective of life? if none, its own reproduction is useless – if worse than none, – (for capital may destoy life as well as support it), its own reproduction is worse than useless; it is merely an advance from Tisiphone,*b* on mortgage – not a profit by any means.

74. Not a profit, as the ancients truly saw, and showed in the type of Ixion;[18] – for capital is the head, or fountain head, of wealth – the 'well-head' of wealth, as the clouds are the well-heads of rain: but when clouds are without water,*c* and only beget clouds, they issue in wrath at last, instead of rain, and in lightning instead of harvest; whence Ixion is said first to have invited his guests to a banquet, and then made them fall into a pit filled with fire; which is the type of the temptation of riches issuing in imprisoned torment, – torment in a pit, (as also Demas' silver mine,) after which, to show the rage of riches passing from lust of pleasure to lust of power, yet power not truly understood, Ixion is said to have desired Juno, and instead, embracing a cloud (or phantasm), to have begotten the Centaurs; the power of mere wealth being, in itself, as the embrace of a shadow, – comfortless, (so also 'Ephraim feedeth on wind and followeth after the east wind'; or 'that which is not' – Prov. xxiii. 5; and again Dante's Geryon, the type of avaricious fraud, as he flies, gathers the *air* up with retractile claws, – 'l'aer a se raccolse,') but in its offspring, a mingling of the brutal with the human nature: human in sagacity – using both intellect and arrow; but brutal in its body and hoof, for consuming, and trampling down. For which sin Ixion is at last bound upon a wheel – fiery and toothed, and rolling perpetually in the air; – the type of human labour when selfish and fruitless (kept far into the Middle Ages in their wheel of fortune); the wheel which has in it no breath or spirit, but is whirled by chance only; whereas of all true work the Ezekiel vision is true, that the Spirit of the living creature is

---

a Virgil, *Georgics* i, 46.   *b* One of the three avenging furies.   *c* Jude 12.

in the wheels, and where the angels go, the wheels go by them; but move no otherwise.[a]

75. This being the real nature of capital, it follows that there are two kinds of true production, always going on in an active State: one of seed, and one of food; or production for the Ground, and for the Mouth; both of which are by covetous persons thought to be production only for the granary; whereas the function of the granary is but intermediate and conservative, fulfilled in distribution; else it ends in nothing but mildew, and nourishment of rats and worms. And since production for the Ground is only useful with future hope of harvest, all *essential* production is for the Mouth; and is finally measured by the mouth; hence, as I said above,[b] consumption is the crown of production; and the wealth of a nation is only to be estimated by what it consumes.

The want of any clear sight of this fact is the capital error, issuing in rich interest and revenue of error among the political economists. Their minds are continually set on money-gain, not on mouth-gain; and they fall into every sort of net and snare, dazzled by the coin-glitter as birds by the fowler's glass; or rather (for there is not much else like birds in them) they are like children trying to jump on the heads of their own shadows; the money-gain being only the shadow of the true gain, which is humanity.

78. The final object of political economy, therefore, is to get good method of consumption and great quantity of consumption: in other words, to use everything, and to use it nobly; whether it be substance, service, or service perfecting substance. The most curious error in Mr Mill's entire work, (provided for him originally by Ricardo,) is his endeavour to distinguish between direct and indirect services, and consequent assertion that a demand for commodities is not demand for labour (1.v.9, *et seq.*).[19] He distinguishes between labourers employed to lay out pleasure grounds, and to manufacture velvet; declaring that it makes material difference to the labouring classes in which of these two ways a capitalist spends his money; because the employment of the gardeners is a demand for labour, but the purchase of velvet is not. Error colossal, as well as strange. It will, indeed, make a difference to the labourer whether we bid him swing his scythe in the spring winds, or drive the loom in pestilential air; but, so far as his pocket is concerned, it makes to him absolutely no difference whether we order him to make green velvet, with seed and a scythe, or red velvet, with silk and scissors. Neither does it anywise concern him whether, when the velvet is made, we consume it by

---

[a] Ezekiel 1:15–21.   [b] Para.73.

walking on it, or wearing it, so long as our consumption of it is wholly selfish. But if our consumption is to be in anywise unselfish, not only our mode of consuming the articles we require interests him, but also the *kind* of article we require with a view to consumption. As thus (returning for a moment to Mr Mill's great hardware theory):[a] it matters, so far as the labourer's immediate profit is concerned, not an iron filing whether I employ him in growing a peach, or forging a bombshell; but my probable mode of consumption of those articles matters seriously. Admit that it is to be in both cases 'unselfish,' and the difference, to him, is final, whether when his child is ill, I walk into his cottage and give it the peach, or drop the shell down his chimney, and blow his roof off.

The worst of it, for the peasant, is that the capitalist's consumption of the peach is apt to be selfish, and of the shell, distributive; but, in all cases, this is the broad and general fact, that on due catallactic commercial principles, *somebody's* roof must go off in fulfilment of the bomb's destiny. You may grow for your neighbour, at your liking, grapes or grape-shot; he will also, catallactically, grow grapes or grape-shot for you, and you will each reap what you have sown.[b]

77. It is, therefore, the manner and issue of consumption which are the real tests of production. Production does not consist in things laboriously made, but in things serviceably consumable; and the question for the nation is not how much labour it employs, but how much life it produces. For as consumption is the end and aim of production, so life is the end and aim of consumption.

I left this question to the reader's thought two months ago,[20] choosing rather that he should work it out for himself than have it sharply stated to him. But now, the ground being sufficiently broken (and the details into which the several questions, here opened, must lead us, being too complex for discussion in the pages of a periodical, so that I must pursue them elsewhere),[21] I desire, in closing the series of introductory papers, to leave this one great fact clearly stated. THERE IS NO WEALTH BUT LIFE. Life, including all its powers of love, of joy, and of admiration. That country is the richest which nourishes the greatest number of noble and happy human beings; that man is richest who, having perfected the functions of his own life to the utmost, has also the widest helpful influence, both personal, and by means of his possessions, over the lives of others.

A strange political economy; the only one, nevertheless, that ever was or can be: all political economy founded on self-interest being

---

[a] See para. 56.   [b] Galatians 6:7.

but the fulfilment of that which once brought schism into the Policy of angels, and ruin into the Economy of Heaven.

78. 'The greatest number of human beings noble and happy.' But is the nobleness consistent with the number? Yes, not only consistent with it, but essential to it. The maximum of life can only be reached by the maximum of virtue. In this respect the law of human population differs wholly from that of animal life. The multiplication of animals is checked only by want of food, and by the hospitality of races; the population of the gnat is restrained by the hunger of the swallow, and that of the swallow by the scarcity of gnats. Man, considered as an animal, is indeed limited by the same laws: hunger, or plague, or war, are the necessary and only restraints upon his increase, – effectual restraints hitherto, – his principal study having been how most swiftly to destroy himself, or ravage his dwelling-places, and his highest skill directed to give range to the famine, seed to the plague, and sway to the sword. But, considered as other than an animal, his increase is not limited by these laws. It is limited only by the limits of his courage and his love. Both of these *have* their bounds; and ought to have; his race has its bounds also; but these have not yet been reached, nor will be reached for ages.

79. In all the ranges of human thought I know none so melancholy as the speculations of political economists on the population question. It is proposed to better the condition of the labourer by giving him higher wages, he will either people down to the same point of misery at which you found him, or drink your wages away.' He will. I know it. Who gave him this will? Suppose it were your own son of whom you spoke, declaring to me that you dared not take him into your firm, nor even give him his just labourer's wages, because if you did he would die of drunkenness, and leave half a score of children to the parish. 'Who gave your son these dispositions?' – I should enquire. Has he them by inheritance or by education? By one or other they *must* come; and as in him, so also in the poor. Either these poor are of a race essentially different from ours, and unredeemable (which, however often implied, I have heard none yet openly say), or else by such care as we have ourselves received, we may make them continent and sober as ourselves – wise and dispassionate as we are – models arduous of imitation. 'But,' it is answered, 'they cannot receive education.' Why not? That is precisely the point at issue. Charitable persons suppose the worst fault of the rich is to refuse the people meat; and the people cry for their meat, kept back by fraud, to the Lord of Multitudes.[a] Alas! it is not meat of which the refusal is

[a] James 5:4.

cruelest, or to which the claim is validest. The life is more than the meat.[a] The rich not only refuse food to the poor; they refuse wisdom; they refuse virtue; they refuse salvation. Ye sheep without shepherd,[b] it is not the pasture that has been shut from you, but the Presence. Meat! perhaps your right to that may be pleadable; but other rights have to be pleaded first. Claim your crumbs from the table if you will; but claim them as children, not as dogs,[c] claim your right to be fed, but claim more loudly your right to be holy, perfect, and pure.

Strange words to be used of working people! 'What! holy; without any long robes or anointing oils; these rough-jacketed, rough-worded persons; set to nameless, dishonoured service? Perfect! – these, with dim eyes and cramped limbs, and slowly wakening minds? Pure! – these, with sensual desire and grovelling thought; foul of body and coarse of soul?' It may be so; nevertheless, such as they are, they are the holiest, perfectest, purest persons the earth can at present show. They may be what you have said; but if so, they yet are holier than we who have left them thus.

But what can be done for them? Who can clothe – who teach – who restrain their multitudes? What end can there be for them at last, but to consume one another?

I hope for another end, though not, indeed, from any of the three remedies for over-population commonly suggested by economists.

80. These three are, in brief – Colonization; Bringing in of waste lands; or Discouragement of Marriage.

The first and second of these expedients merely evade or delay the question. It will, indeed, be long before the world has been all colonized, and its deserts all brought under cultivation. But the radical question is, not how much habitable land is in the world, but how many human beings ought to be maintained on a given space of habitable land.

Observe, I say, *ought* to be, not how many *can* be. Ricardo, with his usual inaccuracy, defines what he calls the 'natural rate of wages' as 'that which will maintain the labourer.' Maintain him! yes; but how? – the question was instantly thus asked of me by a working girl, to whom I read the passage. I will amplify her question for her. 'Maintain him, how?' As, first, to what length of life? Out of a given number of fed persons, how many are to be old – how many young? that is to say, will you arrange their maintenance so as to kill them early – say at thirty or thirty-five on the average, including deaths of weakly or ill-fed children? – or so as to enable them to live out a

[a] Matthew 6:25.   [b] Matthew 9:36.   [c] Matthew 15:26–7.

natural life? You will feed a greater number, in the first case, by rapidity of succession; probably a happier number in the second: which does Mr Ricardo mean to be their natural state, and to which state belongs the natural rate of wages?

Again: A piece of land which will only support ten idle, ignorant, and improvident persons, will support thirty or forty intelligent and industrious ones. Which of these is their natural state, and to which of them belongs the natural rate of wages?

Again: If a piece of land support forty persons in industrious ignorance; and if, tired of this ignorance, they set apart ten of their number to study the properties of cones, and the sizes of stars; the labour of these ten being withdrawn from the ground, must either tend to the increase of food in some transitional manner, or the persons set apart for sidereal and conic purposes must starve, or some one else starve instead of them. What is, therefore, the natural rate of wages of the scientific persons, and how does this rate relate to, or measure, their reverted or transitional productiveness?[22]

Again: if the ground maintains, at first, forty labourers in a peaceable and pious state of mind, but they become in a few years so quarrelsome and impious that they have to set apart five, to meditate upon and settle their disputes; – ten, armed to the teeth with costly instruments, to enforce the decisions; and five to remind everybody in an eloquent manner of the existence of a God; – what will be the result upon the general power of production, and what is the 'natural rate of wages' of the meditative, muscular, and oracular labourers?

81. Leaving these questions to be discussed, or waived, at their pleasure, by Mr Ricardo's followers, I proceed to state the main facts bearing on that probable future of the labouring classes which has been partially glanced at by Mr Mill. That chapter and the preceding one differ from the common writing of political economists in admitting some value in the aspect of nature, and expressing regret at the probability of the destruction of natural scenery.[a] But we may spare our anxieties on this head. Men can neither drink steam, nor eat stone. The maximum of population on a given space of land implies also the relative maximum of edible vegetable, whether for men or cattle; it implies a maximum of pure air, and of pure water. Therefore; a maximum of wood, to transmute the air, and of sloping ground, protected by herbage from the extreme heat of the sun, to feed the streams. All England may, if it so chooses, become one manufacturing town; and Englishmen, sacrificing themselves to the food of general humanity, may live diminished lives in the midst of

[a] See above, p. 118.

noise, of darkness, and of deadly exhalation. But the world cannot become a factory nor a mine. No amount of ingenuity will ever make iron digestible by the million, nor substitute hydrogen for wine. Neither the avarice nor the rage of men will ever feed them; and however the apple of Sodom and the grape of Gomorrah may spread their table for a time with dainties of ashes, and nectar of asps,[a] – so long as men live by bread, the far away valleys must laugh as they are covered with the gold of God, and the shouts of His happy multitudes ring round the winepress and the well.

82. Nor need our more sentimental economists fear the too wide spread of the formalities of a mechanical agriculture. The presence of a wise population implies the search for felicity as well as for food; nor can any population reach its maximum but through that wisdom which 'rejoices' in the habitable parts of the earth.[b] The desert has its appointed place and work; the eternal engine, whose beam is the earth's axle, whose beat is its year, and whose breath is its ocean, will still divide imperiously to their desert kingdoms bound with unfur-rowable rock, and swept by unarrested sand, their powers of frost and fire: but the zones and lands between, habitable, will be loveliest in habitation. The desire of the heart is also the light of the eyes.[c] No scene is continually and untiringly loved, but one rich by joyful human labour; smooth in field; fair in garden; full in orchard; trim, sweet, and frequent in homestead; ringing with voices of vivid existence. No air is sweet that is silent; it is only sweet when full of low currents of under sound – triplets of birds, and murmur and chirp of insects, and deep-toned words of men, and wayward trebles of childhood. As the art of life is learned, it will be found at last that all lovely things are also necessary; the wild flower by the wayside, as well as the tended corn; and the wild birds and creatures of the forest, as well as the tended cattle; because man doth not live by bread only, but also by the desert manna; by every wondrous word and un-knowable work of God.[d] Happy, in that he knew them not, nor did his fathers know; and that round about him reaches yet into the infinite, the amazement of his existence.

83. Note, finally, that all effectual advancement towards this true felicity of the human race must be by individual, not public effort. Certain general measures may aid, certain revised laws guide, such advancement; but the measure and law which have *first* to be determined are those of each man's home. We continually hear it recommended by sagacious people to complaining neighbours

---

[a] Genesis 18:20–33; 19:1–29.   [b] Proverbs 8:31.   [c] Cf Proverbs 15:30.
[d] Deuteronomy 8:3.

(usually less well placed in the world than themselves), that they should 'remain content in the station in which Providence has placed them'.[23] There are perhaps some circumstances of life in which Providence has no intention that people *should* be content. Nevertheless, the maxim is on the whole a good one; but it is peculiarly for home use. That your neighbour should, or should not, remain content with *his* position, is not your business; but it is very much your business to remain content with your own. What is chiefly needed in England at the present day is to show the quantity of pleasure that may be obtained by a consistent, well-administered competence, modest, confessed, and laborious. We need examples of people who, leaving Heaven to decide whether they are to rise in the world, decide for themselves that they will be happy in it, and have resolved to seek – not greater wealth, but simpler pleasure; not higher fortune, but deeper felicity; making the first of possessions, self-possession; and honouring themselves in the harmless pride and calm pursuits of peace.

Of which lowly peace it is written that 'justice and peace have kissed each other';[a] and that the fruit of justice is 'sown in peace of them and that peace',[b] not 'peace-makers' in the common understanding – reconcilers of quarrels; (though that function also follows on the greater one;) but peace-Creators; Givers of Calm. Which you cannot give, unless you first gain; nor is this gain one which will follow assuredly on any course of business, commonly so called. No form of gain is less probable, business being (as is shown in the language of all nations – (πωλεῖν from πέλω, πρᾶσις from περάω, venire, vendre, and venal, from venio, etc.) essentially restless,[24] – and probably contentious; – having a raven-like mind to the motion to and fro, as to the carrion food; whereas the olive-feeding and bearing birds look for the rest for their feet;[c] thus it is said of Wisdom that she 'hath builded her house, and hewn out her seven pillars',[d] and even when, though apt to wait long at the doorposts, she has to leave her house and go abroad, her paths are peace also.[e]

84. For us, at all events, her work must begin at the entry of the doors: all true economy is 'Law of the house.' Strive to make that law strict, simple, generous: waste nothing, and grudge nothing. Care in nowise to make more of money, but care to make much of it; remembering always the great, palpable, inevitable fact – the rule and root of all economy – that what one person has, another cannot have; and that every atom of substance, of whatever kind, used or con-

[a] Psalm 85:10.   [b] James 3:18.   [c] Genesis 8:7–8.   [d] Proverbs 9:1.
[e] Proverbs 3:17.

sumed, is so much human life spent; which, if it issue in the saving present life, or gaining more, is well spent, but if not is either so much life prevented, or so much slain. In all buying, consider, first, what condition of existence you cause in the producers of what you buy; secondly, whether the sum you have paid is just to the producer, and in due proportion, lodged in his hands; thirdly, to how much clear use, for food, knowledge, or joy, this that you have bought can be put; and fourthly, to whom and in what way it can be most speedily and serviceably distributed; in all dealings whatsoever insisting on entire openness and stern fulfilment; and in all doings, on perfection and loveliness of accomplishment; especially on fineness and purity of all marketable commodity: watching at the same time for all ways of gaining, or teaching, powers of simple pleasure; and of showing 'ὅσον ἐν ἀσφοδέλῳ μέγ' ὄνειαρ'[25] – the sum of enjoyment depending not on the quantity of things tasted, but on the vivacity and patience of taste.

85. And if, on due and honest thought over these things, it seems that the kind of existence to which men are now summoned by every plea of pity and claim of right, may, for some time at least, not be a luxurious one; – consider whether, even supposing it guiltless, luxury would be desired by any of us, if we saw clearly at our sides the suffering which accompanies it in the world. Luxury is indeed possible in the future – innocent and exquisite; luxury for all, and by the help of all; but luxury at present can only be enjoyed by the ignorant; the cruelest man living could not sit at his feast, unless he sat blindfold. Raise the veil boldly; face the light, and if, as yet, the light of the eye can only be through tears, and the light of the body through sackcloth, go thou forth weeping, bearing precious seed, until the time come, and the kingdom, when Christ's gift of bread, and bequest of peace, shall be 'Unto this last as unto thee;' and when, for earth's severed multitudes of the wicked and the weary, there shall be holier reconciliation than that of the narrow home, and calm economy, where the Wicked cease – not from trouble, but from troubling – and the Weary are at rest.[a][26]

[a] Job 3:17.

Matthew Arnold

(1822–1888)

These extracts from Arnold's writing come from the period 1866–70 during which he addressed himself to political and social criticism in a series of articles. One, published in the *Pall Mall Gazette* (1866–7 and 1869–70) as 'My Countrymen', and purporting to be a series of letters between Arnold and 'Baron Arminius', was subsequently collected in *Friendship's Garland* (1871); the second, appearing in the *Cornhill Magazine* (1867–8), became *Culture and Anarchy* (1869).

Arnold's employment, from 1861, as Inspector of Schools involved him on a daily basis with the effects of government thinking, and encouraged him to think of the long-term consequences of particular events and measures as they might affect future generations. An additional factor in the perspective Arnold adopted was the opportunities he had enjoyed for detailed comparison with other systems of government and their fruit. In 1861 he produced *Popular Education in France*, the result of close observation of the machinery employed in France to organise, legislate for, and control the educational requirements of the nation in pursuit of an ideal state.

The events leading up to the 1867 Reform Bill may have fired Arnold to write these articles for periodicals, but the range of his inquiry goes far beyond the realms of party politics.Confronted with cabinets largely composed of aristocrats, and a House of Commons in which the landed interest predominated, various nostrums were being advocated. Some favoured strengthening the hand of the present establishment to resist working-class agitation, others recommended widening the franchise or appeasing sectional interests, such as Nonconformity. To Arnold, who wished to see a more radical assessment of national debts and assets, virtues and limitations, out of which a new synthesis might be made, all these seemed measures designed to paper over cracks.

In common with Mill (*On Liberty*) and Carlyle (*Shooting Niagara*), Arnold diagnosed a central conflict between individual liberty and collective interests, between anarchy and authority (this last phrase being the first title for *Culture and Anarchy*). Carlyle's call in later life for aristocratic leadership dissatisfied Arnold, since it did no more than shore up a class who had shown themselves bankrupt of ideas and inefficient in the exercise of power. Mill's emphasis on voluntary co-operation as the safeguard of individual liberty seemed too fragile a mould into which to pour the competing interests currently visible. Instead Arnold elevated the concept of the state as the guarantor of the order needed for reform, and the embodiment of right reason. This ideal state, different in composition and effect from the actual state of Great Britain in the mid-1860s, is to combine and lend its sanction to the best interests of all classes. To achieve this, the state will require an authority and dignity beyond that implied by Mill's voluntary agreement. As guardian and instigator of culture, or the study of perfection, Arnold accords the state a sanctity, violation of which would be tantamount to sacrilege.

Just as the longest extract, from *Culture and Anarchy*, must originally have read like a political manifesto, canvassing the issues which would be raised in the General Election of November 1868, so Letter v of the Arminius correspondence may seem merely to be pleading a particular topical cause. Irish land tenure had long been a vexed question. Arnold's period of service as Private Secretary to the Marquess of Lansdowne had alerted him to the way in which the landed interests of the great Whig peers always worked against the reforming bent of the Liberal party when Ireland was under discussion. The membership of his brother-in-law, the prominent Liberal Member of Parliament W. E. Forster, of a parliamentary select committee on the subject, induced Matthew to write to him whilst visiting Prussia in July 1865 to recommend his study of land measures undertaken there, and subsequently to explain their significance to readers of the *Pall Mall Gazette* on 8 November 1865. Yet, ultimately, the land question interested Arnold because it provided in stark form a paradigmatic example of English behaviour. Opposition to the state's functioning as a government for the benefit of all its subjects could here most easily be demonstrated to be the embodiment of vested interests masquerading as the spokesman of political principle. In this case, the *laissez-faire* constituent of political economy was offered as a weapon with which to legitimise anti-reforming instincts. Later, Arnold was to be no less hard on Gladstone for using Ireland as a pawn in his political strategy, rather than treating it as an integral part of the nation, as worthy of consideration in its own right as any other.

The adoption of the *persona* Arminius was a strategic ploy on Arnold's part, designed to underline, and so bring into question, England's mistaken insular complacency. As a Prussian, Arminius unites the expertise and success of a rapidly rising European nation, together with a Teutonic bluntness which Arnold can use to voice his most trenchant criticisms. In turn, under his own name, Arnold can voice both the resentment of an Englishman who feels his country impugned, and the intellectual curiosity which will surmount such spontaneous reactions to investigate the justice of Arminius's assertions. Wittily, Arnold challenges those critics who have stigmatized his urbanity of manner as complacency by attributing the grand style or solemnity of the pulpit with its epigrammatic flourishes to the gauche, rough Arminius, whilst presenting himself as barely under control and forced to resort to outbursts of slang to convey his feelings. By establishing his criticism in dialectical form, Arnold risked his reader being distracted from the thread of his argument through his interest in the characters themselves, but the central issue is carefully kept to the fore by the device of habitual repetition of key-phrases as one voice takes over from another.

Matthew Arnold (1822–1888)

The sustained game of fictionality disappears in *Culture and Anarchy*, although frequently the examples Arnold chooses from real life attain mythic proportions as one deed or attitude is reiterated, stretched and remoulded so that the original achieves a semi-fictional status. Yet Arnold is just as certainly creating a particular 'voice' for himself in this series of essays – a voice that wishes to share with its listener or reader 'our' doubts and the worries of 'every one of us', a voice that employs phrases such as 'Well, then,' or 'Now', derived from aural explanation, to ensure that it carries its audience with it. This voice operates at ease with long sentences whose qualificatory clauses give an impression of measured judgement and a fair-minded desire to take all views into account. Won by an air of well-considered argument, readers are lulled into accepting phrases which entirely side-step the processes of logic (e.g. 'Whereas the real truth is'), or irony so blandly presented that its sting takes a moment to penetrate (e.g. the reference to the radical Bright as 'one who loves to walk in the old ways of the Constitution' or the allusion to 'the middle class with its incomparable Parliament'). Arnold's theme is further helped by a pervasive but never obtrusive metaphor which runs throughout the book as a whole, unifying and cementing his argument. Just as the state and the culture which it embodies are finally shown to be a matter of sacred, and therefore eternal, truth, so the forces which threaten them are linked with the anarchic tendencies of unreason. The state has 'stringent', 'controlling' powers and the notion of culture is 'immovably fixed', whereas 'the assertion of personal liberty' is associated with 'drifting towards anarchy'. In uncertainty and anxiety men clutch at the 'mechanical fetishes' and 'talismans' of ideological axioms. They succumb, not from inherent wickedness, but because, ignoring reason, they are 'dazzled and borne away' by the attraction of magic and hypnotic compulsion.

In one other respect, Arnold's language is vital to his argument. In opposing the divisive material interests of different social classes, Arnold redefines these classes in such a way as to suggest that his ideal solution could dissolve these barriers. For he does not simply attack the middle class and aristocracy for their barbarism and philistinism, but renames them in terms of these cultural concepts. Society, for Arnold, *is* its culture (or lack of it), and the 'objective' circumstances of classes a reflection of 'subjective' attributes. Re-attuning cultural consciousness thus becomes the means by which 'objective' distinctions will fade into insignificance.

8. Letter v

Friendship's Garland (1871), pp. 35–42

I Communicate a Valuable Exposition, by Arminius, of the System of Tenant-Right in Prussia

GRUB STREET, November 8, 1866.

SIR,—

My love for intellect has made me seek a reconciliation with Arminius, in spite of all I had to complain of in him, and any one who had looked in here to-night might have seen him puffing away at his pipe, and laying down the law just in his old style. He was so immensely tickled at the *Daily Telegraph* calling his poor friend, – artless and obscure garretteer that he knows him to be, – 'a high priest of the kid-glove persuasion,'[1] that he has been in a good humour ever since, and to-night he had been giving me some information which I do think, notwithstanding the horrid *animus* he betrays in delivering it, is highly curious and interesting, and therefore I hasten to communicate it to you.

It is about the Prussian land reforms, and this is how I got it out of him. 'You made me look rather a fool, Arminius,' I began, 'by what you primed me with in Germany last year about Stein[2] settling your land question.' 'I dare say you looked a fool,' says my Prussian boor, 'but what did I tell you?' 'Why,' says I, 'you told me Stein had settled a land question like the Irish land question, and I said so in the *Cornhill Magazine*,[3] and now the matter has come up again by Mr Bright talking at Dublin of what Stein did, and it turns out he settled nothing like the Irish land question at all, but only a sort of tithe-commutation affair.' 'Who says that?' asked Arminius. 'A very able writer in the *Times*,' I replied.[4]

I don't know that I have ever described Arminius's personal appearance. He has the true square Teutonic head, a blond and disorderly mass of tow-like hair, a podgy and sanguine countenance, shaven cheeks, and a whity-brown moustache. He wears a rough pilot-coat, and generally smokes away with his hands in the pockets of it, and his light blue eyes fixed on his interlocutor's face. When he takes his hands out of his pockets, his pipe out of his mouth, and his eyes off his friend's face, it is a sign that he is deeply moved. He did all this on the present occasion, and passing his short thick fingers two or three times through his blond hair: 'That astonishing paper!' muttered he.

Then he began as solemn as if he was in a pulpit. 'My dear friend,' says he, 'of the British species of the great genus Philistine there are three main varieties.[5] There is the religious Philistine, the well-to-do Philistine, and the rowdy Philistine. The religious Philistine is represented by—' 'Stop, Arminius,' said I, 'you will oblige me by letting religion alone!' 'As you please,' answered he; 'well, then, the rowdy Philistine is represented by the *Daily Telegraph*, and the well-to-do Philistine by the *Times*. The well-to-do Philistine looks to get his own view of the British world, – that it is the best of all possible worlds as it is, because he has prospered in it, – preached back to him *ore rotundo*[a] in the columns of the *Times*. There must be no uncertain sound in his oracle, no faltering, nothing to excite misgivings or doubts; like his own bosom, everything his oracle utters must be positive, pleasant, and comfortable. So of course about the great first article of his creed, the sacrosanctity of property, there must in the *Times* be no trifling. But what amuses me is that his oracle must not even admit, if these matters come to be talked of, that Stein trifled with it in another country. The ark is so sacred, the example so abominable, and the devotee so sensitive. And therefore Stein's reforms become in the *Times*, for the reassurance of the well-to-do British Philistine, a sort of tithe-commutation affair – nothing in the world more! nothing in the world more!'

'Don't go on in that absurd way, Arminius,' said I; 'I don't tell you it was a tithe-commutation, but a commutation like the tithe-commutation. It was simply, the *Times* says, the conversion of serf-tenures into produce-rents. I hope that gives you a perfectly clear notion of what the whole thing was, for it doesn't me. But I make out from the *Times* that the *leibeigener*—' 'Rubbish about the *leibeigener*,'[b] cries Arminius, in a rage, 'and all this jargon to keep your stupid mind in a mist; do you want to know what really happened?' 'Yes, I do,' said I, quietly, my love for knowledge making me take no notice of his impertinence. 'Yes, I do, and particularly this: In the first place, was the land, before Stein's reforms, the landlord's or the tenant's?' 'The landlord's,' says Arminius. 'You mean,' said I, 'that the landlord could and did really eject his tenant from it if he chose.' 'Yes, I do,' says Arminius. 'Well, then, what did Stein do?' asked I. 'He did this,' Arminius answered. 'In these estates, where the landlord had his property-right on the one hand, and the tenant his tenant-right on the other, he made a compromise. In the first place he assigned, say, two-fifths of the estate to the landlord in absolute property, without any further claim of tenant-right upon it thenceforth for ever. But the

---

[a] 'In well-rounded phrase' (Horace, *Ars Poetica*).   [b] Serf.

remaining three-fifths he compelled the landlord to sell to the tenant at eighteen years' purchase, so that this part should become the tenant's absolute property thenceforth for ever. You will ask, where could the tenant find money to buy? Stein opened rent-banks in all the provincial chief towns, to lend the tenant the purchase-money required, for which the State thus became his creditor, not the landlord. He had to repay this loan in a certain number of years. To free his land from this State mortgage on it and make it his own clear property, he had every inducement to work hard, and he did work hard; and this was the grand source of the frugality, industry, and thrivingness of the Prussian peasant. It was the grand source, too, of his attachment to the State.' 'It was rotten bad political economy, though,' exclaimed I. 'Now I see what the *Times* meant by saying in its leading article yesterday[6] that Ireland is comparably better governed than the United States, France, Germany, or Italy, because the excellence of government consists in keeping obstacles out of the way of individual energy, and you throw obstacles in the way of your great proprietors' energy, and we throw none in the way of ours. Talk of a commutation like the tithe-commutation, indeed! Why it was downright spoliation; it was just what Lord Clanricarde says some people are driving at in Ireland, a system of confiscation.'[7] 'Well,' says Arminius, calmly, 'that is exactly what the Prussian junkers[a] called it. They did not call it commutation, they called it confiscation. They will tell you to this day that Stein confiscated their estates. But you will be shocked to hear that the Prussian Government had, even before Stein's time, this sad habit of playing tricks with political economy. To prevent the absorption of small proprietors by a great landed aristocracy, the Prussian Government made a rule that a *bauer-gut*, – a peasant property, – could not, even if the owner sold it, be bought up by the Lord Clanricarde of the neighbourhood; it must remain a *bauer-gut* still.[8] I believe you in England are for improving small proprietors off the face of the earth, but I assure you in Prussia we are very proud of ours, and think them the strength of the nation. Of late years the Hohenzollerns have taken up with the junkers, but for a long time their policy was to uphold the *bauer* class against the *junker* class; and, if you want to know the secret of the hold which the house of Hohenzollern has upon the heart of the Prussian people, it is not in Frederick the Great's victories that you will find it, it is in this policy of their domestic government.' 'My dear Arminius,' said I, 'you make me perfectly sick. Government here, government there! We English are

---

[a] Reactionary Prussian aristocracy.

for self-government. What business has any Mr Stein to settle that this or that estate is too large for Lord Clanricarde's virtues to expand in? Let each class settle its own affairs, and don't let us have Governments and Hohenzollerns pretending to be more enlightened than other people, and cutting and carving for what they call the general interest, and God knows what nonsense of that kind. If the landed class with us has got the magistracy and settled estates*ᵃ* and game laws, has not the middle class got the vestries, and business, and civil and religious liberty? I remember when the late Sir George Cornewall Lewis wanted to get some statistics about the religious denominations, your friend Bottles, who is now a millionaire and a Churchman, was then a Particular Baptist. 'No,' says Bottles, 'here I put down my foot. No Government on earth shall ask me whether I am a particular Baptist or a Muggletonian.' And Bottles beat the Government, because of the thorough understanding the upper and middle classes in this country have with one another that each is to go its own way, and Government is not to be thrusting its nose into the concerns of either. There is a cordial alliance between them on this basis.'⁹ 'Yes, yes, I know,' Arminius sneeringly answered; 'Herod and Pontius Pilate have shaken hands.'*ᵇ*

'But I will show you, Arminius,' I pursued, 'on plain grounds of political economy—' 'Not to-night,' interrupted Arminius, yawning; 'I am going home to bed.' And off he went, descending the garret stairs three at a time, and leaving me to burn the midnight oil in order to send you, Sir, what is really, I flatter myself, an interesting, and I may even say a valuable communication.

Your humble servant,

MATTHEW ARNOLD.

To the EDITOR *of the* PALL MALL GAZETTE.

9. *Culture and Anarchy: An Essay in Political and Social Criticism* (1869)

pp. 55–7, 68, 87–9, 229–43, 259–60

Our familiar praise of the British Constitution under which we live, is that it is a system of checks,¹⁰– a system which stops and paralyses any power in interfering with the free action of individuals. To this effect Mr Bright, who loves to walk in the old ways of the Constitution,¹¹ said forcibly in one of his great speeches, what many other

---

ᵃ Entailed estates.   *ᵇ* Luke 23:11–12.

people are every day saying less forcibly, that the central idea of English life and politics is *the assertion of personal liberty*. Evidently this is so; but evidently, also, as feudalism, which with its ideas and habits of subordination was for many centuries silently behind the British Constitution, dies out, and we are left with nothing but our system of checks, and our notion of its being the great right and happiness of an Englishman to do as far as possible what he likes, we are in danger of drifting towards anarchy. We have not the notion, so familiar on the Continent and to antiquity, of *the State* – the nation in its collective and corporate character, entrusted with stringent powers for the general advantage, and controlling individual wills in the name of an interest wider than that of individuals. We say, what is very true, that this notion is often made instrumental to tyranny; we say that a State is in reality made up of the individuals who compose it, and that every individual is the best judge of his own interests. Our leading class is an aristocracy, and no aristocracy likes the notion of a State-authority greater than itself, with a stringent administrative machinery superseding the decorative inutilities of lord-lieutenancy, deputy-lieutenancy, and the *posse comitatûs,*[a] which are all in its own hands. Our middle class, the great representative of trade and Dissent, with its maxims of every man for himself in business, every man for himself in religion, dreads a powerful administration which might somehow interfere with it; and besides, it has its own decorative inutilities of vestrymanship and guardianship, which are to this class what lord-lieutenancy and the county magistracy are to the aristocratic class, and a stringent administration might either take these functions out of its hands, or prevent its exercising them in its own comfortable, independent manner, as at present. . . .

The *State*, the power most representing the right reason of the nation, and most worthy, therefore, of ruling, – of exercising, when circumstances require it, authority over us all, – is for Mr Carlyle the aristocracy.[12] For Mr Lowe,[13] it is the middle class with its incomparable Parliament. For the Reform League,[14] it is the working class, the class with 'the brightest powers of sympathy and readiest powers of action.' Now, culture, with its disinterested pursuit of perfection, culture, simply trying to see things as they are, in order to seize on the best and to make it prevail, is surely well fitted to help us to judge rightly, by all the aids of observing, reading, and thinking, the qualifications and titles to our confidence of these three candidates for authority, and can thus render us a practical service of no mean value. . . .

[a] A body of men whose services the Sheriff may enlist to aid him in enforcing the law.

Well, then, what if we tried to rise above the idea of class to the idea of the whole community, *the State*, and to find our centre of light and authority there? Every one of us has the idea of country, as a sentiment; hardly any one of us has the idea of *the State*, as a working power. And why? Because we habitually live in our ordinary selves, which do not carry us beyond the ideas and wishes of the class to which we happen to belong. And we are all afraid of giving to the State too much power, because we only conceive of the State as something equivalent to the class in occupation of the executive government, and are afraid of that class abusing power to its own purposes.... People of the aristocratic class want to affirm their ordinary selves, their likings and dislikings; people of the middle class the same, people of the working class the same. By our every-day selves, however, we are separate, personal, at war; we are only safe from one another's tyranny when no one has any power; and this safety, in its turn, cannot save us from anarchy. And when, therefore, anarchy presents itself as a danger to us, we know not where to turn.

But by our *best self* we are united, impersonal, at harmony. We are in no peril from giving authority to this, because it is the truest friend we all of us can have; and when anarchy is a danger to us, to this authority we may turn with sure trust. Well, and this is the very self which culture, or the study of perfection, seeks to develop in us; at the expense of our old untransformed self, taking pleasure only in doing what it likes or is used to do, and exposing us to the risk of clashing with every one else who is doing the same! So that our poor culture, which is flouted as so unpractical, leads us to the very ideas capable of meeting the great want of our very present embarrassed times! We want an authority, and we find nothing but jealous classes, checks, and a deadlock; culture suggests the idea of *the State*. We find no basis for a firm State-power in our ordinary selves; culture suggests one to us in our *best self*. ...

Now, having first saluted free-trade and its doctors with all respect, let us see whether even here, too, our Liberal friends do not pursue their operations in a mechanical way, without reference to any firm intelligible law of things, to human life as a whole, and human happiness; and whether it is not more for our good, at this particular moment at any rate, if, instead of worshipping free-trade with them Hebraistically,[15] as a kind of fetish, and helping them to pursue it as an end in and for itself, we turn the free stream of our thought upon their treatment of it, and see how this is related to the intelligible law of human life, and to national well-being and happiness. In short, suppose we Hellenise a little with free-trade, as we Hellenised with the Real Estate Intestacy Bill,[16] and with the disestablishment of the Irish Church by the power of Nonconformists' antipathy to religious establishments and endowments, and see whether what our reprovers beautifully call ministering to the diseased spirit of our time[a] is best done by the Hellenising method of proceeding, or by the other.

But first let us understand how the policy of free-trade really shapes itself for our Liberal friends, and how they practically employ it as an instrument of national happiness and salvation. For as we said that it seemed clearly right to prevent the Church-property of Ireland from being all taken for the benefit of the Church of a small minority, so it seems clearly right that the poor man should eat untaxed bread, and, generally, that restrictions and regulations which, for the supposed benefit of some particular person or class of persons, make the price of things artificially high here, or artificially low there, and interfere with the natural flow of trade and commerce, should be done away with. But in the policy of our Liberal friends free-trade means more than this, and is specially valued as a stimulant to the production of wealth, as they call it, and to the increase of the trade, business, and population of the country. We have already seen how these things, – trade, business, and population, – are mechanically pursued by us as ends precious in themselves, and are worshipped as what we call fetishes; and Mr Bright, I have already said, when he wishes to give the working class a true sense of what makes glory and greatness, tells it to look at the cities it has built, the railroads it has made, the manufactures it has produced. So to this idea of glory and greatness the free-trade which our Liberal friends extol so solemnly and devoutly has served, – to the increase of trade, business, and population; and for this it is prized. Therefore, the untaxing of the poor man's bread has, with this view of national happiness, been used not so much to make the existing poor man's bread cheaper or more abundant, but rather to create more poor men to eat it; so that we cannot precisely say that we have fewer poor men than we had before free-trade, but we can say with truth that we have many more centres of industry, as they are called, and much more business, population, and manufactures. And if we are sometimes a little troubled by our multitude of poor men, yet we know the increase of manufactures and population to be such a salutary thing in itself, and our free-trade policy begets such an admirable movement, creating fresh centres of industry and fresh poor men here, while we were thinking about our poor men there, that we are quite dazzled and borne away, and more

[a] Cf. *Macbeth* 5.iii.40.

171

and more industrial movement is called for, and our social progress seems to become one triumphant and enjoyable course of what is sometimes called, vulgarly, outrunning the constable.[a]

If, however, taking some other criterion of man's well-being than the cities he has built and the manufactures he has produced, we persist in thinking that our social progress would be happier if there were not so many of us so very poor, and in busying ourselves with notions of in some way or other adjusting the poor man and business one to the other, and not multiplying the one and the other mechanically and blindly, then our Liberal friends, the appointed doctors of free-trade, take us up very sharply. 'Art is long,' says the *Times*, 'and life is short; for the most part we settle things first and understand them afterwards. Let us have as few theories as possible; what is wanted is not the light of speculation. If nothing worked well of which the theory was not perfectly understood, we should be in sad confusion. The relations of labour and capital, we are told, are not understood, yet trade and commerce, on the whole, work satisfactorily.' I quote from the *Times* of only the other day.[17] But thoughts like these, as I have often pointed out, are thoroughly British thoughts, and we have been familiar with them for years.

Or, if we want more of a philosophy of the matter than this, our free-trade friends have two axioms for us, axioms laid down by their justly esteemed doctors, which they think ought to satisfy us entirely. One is that other things being equal, the more population increases, the more does production increase to keep pace with it; because men by their numbers and contact call forth all manner of activities and resources in one another and in nature, which, when men are few and sparse, are never developed. The other is, that, although population always tends to equal the means of subsistence, yet people's notions of what subsistence is enlarge as civilisation advances, and take in a number of things beyond the bare necessaries of life; and thus, therefore, is supplied whatever check on population is needed. But the error of our friends is, just perhaps, that they apply axioms of this sort as if they were self-acting laws which will put themselves into operation without trouble or planning on our part, if we will only pursue free-trade, business, and population zealously and staunchly. Whereas the real truth is, that, however the case might be under other circumstances, yet in fact, as we now manage the matter, the enlarged conception of what is included in *subsistence* does not operate to prevent the bringing into the world of numbers of people who but just attain to the barest necessaries of life or who even fail to

[a] Overspending.

attain to them; while, again, though production may increase as population increases, yet it seems that the production may be of such a kind, and so related, or rather non-related, to population, that the population may be little the better for it. For instance, with the increase of population since Queen Elizabeth's time the production of silk-stockings has wonderfully increased, and silk-stockings have become much cheaper, and procurable in greater abundance by many more people, and tend perhaps, as population and manufactures increase, to get cheaper and cheaper, and at last to become, according to Bastiat's[18] favourite image, a common free-property of the human race, like light and air. But bread and bacon have not become much cheaper with the increase of population since Queen Elizabeth's time, nor procurable in much greater abundance by many more people; neither do they seem at all to promise to become, like light and air, a common free property of the human race. And if bread and bacon have not kept pace with our population, and we have many more people in want of them now than in Queen Elizabeth's time, it seems vain to tell us that silk-stockings have kept pace with our population, or even more than kept pace with it, and that we are to get our comfort out of that. In short, it turns out that our pursuit of free-trade, as of so many other things, has been too mechanical. We fix upon some object, which in this case is the production of wealth, and the increase of manufactures, population, and commerce through free-trade, as a kind of one thing needful[19] or end in itself; and then we pursue it staunchly and mechanically, and say that it is our duty to pursue it staunchly and mechanically, not to see how it is related to the whole intelligible law of things and to full human perfection, or to treat it as the piece of machinery, of varying value as its relations to the intelligible law of things vary, which it really is.

So it is of no use to say to the *Times*, and to our Liberal friends rejoicing in the possession of their talisman of free-trade, that about one in nineteen of our population is a pauper,[20] and that, this being so, trade and commerce can hardly be said to prove by their satisfactory working that it matters nothing whether the relations between labour and capital are understood or not; nay, that we can hardly be said not to be in sad confusion. For here our faith in the staunch mechanical pursuit of a fixed object comes in, and covers itself with that imposing and colossal necessitarianism of the *Times* which we have before noticed. And this necessitarianism, taking for granted that an increase in trade and population is a good in itself, one of the chiefest of goods, tells us that disturbances of human happiness caused by ebbs and flows in the tide of trade and business, which, on the whole, steadily mounts, are inevitable and not to be quarrelled with. This firm philosophy I seek to call to mind when I am in the East of London, whither my avocations often lead me; and, indeed, to fortify myself against the depressing sights which on these occasions assail us, I have transcribed from the *Times* one strain of this kind, full of the finest economical doctrine, and always carry it about with me. The passage is this:–

'The East End is the most commercial, the most industrial, the most fluctuating region of the metropolis. It is always the first to suffer; for it is the creature of prosperity, and falls to the ground the instant there is no wind to bear it up. The whole of that region is covered with huge docks, shipyards, manufactories, and a wilderness of small houses, all full of life and happiness in brisk times, but in dull times withered and lifeless, like the deserts we read of in the East. Now their brief spring is over. There is no one to blame for this; it is the result of Nature's simplest laws!'[21] We must all agree that it is impossible that anything can be firmer than this, or show a surer faith in the working of free-trade, as our Liberal friends understand and employ it.

But, if we still at all doubt whether the indefinite multiplication of manufactories and small houses can be such an absolute good in itself as to counterbalance the indefinite multiplication of poor people, we shall learn that this multiplication of poor people, too, is an absolute good in itself, and the result of divine and beautiful laws. This is indeed a favourite thesis with our Philistine friends, and I have already noticed the pride and gratitude with which they receive certain articles in the *Times*, dilating in thankful and solemn language on the majestic growth of our population. But I prefer to quote now, on this topic, the words of an ingenious young Scotch writer, Mr Robert Buchanan, because he invests with so much imagination and poetry this current idea of the blessed and even divine character which the multiplying of population is supposed in itself to have. 'We move to multiplicity,' says Mr Robert Buchanan. 'If there is one quality which seems God's, and his exclusively, it seems that divine philoprogenitiveness, that passionate love of distribution and expansion into living forms. Every animal added seems a new ecstasy to the Maker; every life added, a new embodiment of his love. He would *swarm* the earth with beings. There are never enough. Life, life, life, – faces gleaming, hearts beating, must fill every cranny. Not a corner is suffered to remain empty. The whole earth breeds, and God glories.'[22]

It is a little unjust, perhaps, to attribute to the Divinity exclusively this philoprogenitiveness, which the British Philistine, and the poorer class of Irish, may certainly claim to share with him; yet how inspiriting is here the whole strain of thought! and these beautiful words, too, I carry about with me in the East of London, and often read them there. They are quite in agreement with the popular language one is accustomed to hear about children and large families, which describes children as *sent*. And a line of poetry, which Mr Robert Buchanan throws in presently after the poetical prose I have quoted, –

'Tis the old story of the fig-leaf time –

this fine line, too, naturally connects itself, when one is in the East of London, with the idea of God's desire to *swarm* the earth with beings; because the swarming of the earth with beings does indeed, in the East of London, so seem to revive *the old story of the fig-leaf time*, such a number of the people one meets there having hardly a rag to cover them; and the more the swarming goes on, the more it promises to revive this old story. And when the story is perfectly revived, the swarming quite completed, and every cranny choke full, then, too, no doubt, the faces in the East of London will be gleaming faces, which Mr Robert Buchanan says it is God's desire they should be, and which every one must perceive they are not at present, but, on the contrary, very miserable.

But to prevent all this philosophy and poetry from quite running away with us, and making us think with the *Times*, and our practical Liberal free-traders, and the British Philistines generally, that the increase of houses and manufactories, or the increase of population, are absolute goods in themselves, to be mechanically pursued, and to be worshipped like fetishes, – to prevent this, we have got that notion of ours immovably fixed, of which I have long ago spoken, the notion that culture, or the study of perfection, leads us to conceive of no perfection as being real which is not a *general* perfection, embracing all our fellow-men with whom we have to do. Such is the sympathy which binds humanity together, that we are indeed, as our religion says, members of one body, and if one member suffer, all the members suffer with it.[a] Individual perfection is impossible so long as the rest of mankind are not perfected along with us. 'The *multitude of the wise* is the welfare of the world,' says the Wise Man.[b] And to this effect that excellent and often quoted guide of ours, Bishop Wilson, has some striking words: – 'It is not,' says he, 'so much our neighbour's interest as our own that we love him.' And again he says:

[a] I Corinthians 12:12–27.   [b] Wisdom 6:26.

'Our salvation does in some measure depend upon that of others.' And the author of the *Imitation*[a] puts the same thing admirably when he says: – '*Obscurior etiam via ad cœlum videbatur quando tam pauci regnum cœlorum quærere curabant*; the fewer there are who follow the way to perfection, the harder that way is to find.' So all our fellow-men, in the East of London and elsewhere, we must take along with us in the progress towards perfection, if we ourselves really, as we profess, want to be perfect; and we must not let the worship of any fetish, any machinery, such as manufactures or population, – which are not, like perfection, absolute goods in themselves, though we think them so, – create for us such a multitude of miserable, sunken, and ignorant human beings, that to carry them all along with us is impossible, and perforce they must for the most part be left by us in their degradation and wretchedness. But evidently the conception of free-trade, on which our Liberal friends vaunt themselves, and in which they think they have found the secret of national prosperity, – evidently, I say, the mere unfettered pursuit of the production of wealth, and the mere mechanical multiplying, for this end, of manufactures and population, threatens to create for us, if it has not created already, those vast, miserable, unmanageable masses of sunken people, – one pauper at the present moment, for every nineteen of us, – to the existence of which we are, as we have seen, absolutely forbidden to reconcile ourselves, in spite of all that the philosophy of the *Times* and the poetry of Mr Robert Buchanan may say to persuade us. . . .

Hebraism in general seems powerless, almost as powerless as our free-trading Liberal friends, to deal efficaciously with our ever-accumulating masses of pauperism, and to prevent their accumulating still more. Hebraism builds churches, indeed, for these masses, and sends missionaries among them; above all, it sets itself against the social necessitarianism of the *Times*, and refuses to accept their degradation as inevitable.

Thus, in our eyes, the very framework and exterior order of the State, whoever may administer the State, is sacred; and culture is the most resolute enemy of anarchy, because of the great hopes and designs for the State which culture teaches us to nourish. But as, believing in right reason, and having faith in the progress of humanity towards perfection, and ever labouring for this end, we grow to have clearer sight of the ideas of right reason, and of the elements and helps of perfection, and come gradually to fill the framework of the State with them, to fashion its internal composition

[a] Thomas à Kempis, *De Imitatione Christi.*

and all its laws and institutions conformably to them, and to make the State more and more the expression, as we say, of our best self, which is not manifold, and vulgar, and unstable, and contentious, and ever-varying, but one, and noble, and secure, and peaceful, and the same for all mankind, – with what aversion shall we not *then* regard anarchy, with what firmness shall we not check it, when there is so much that is so precious which it will endanger!

Thomas Hill Green

(1836–1882)

'Liberal Legislation' was initially delivered as a lecture to the Leicester Liberal Association in 1880, and published as a pamphlet the following year. A *piece d'occasion*, it represented the hopes held out by many reformers of the recently elected Gladstone government, having, said Green in his preface, 'nothing original about it in the way either of information or of theory'. Rather, it contained a popularisation of social doctrines that he had been inculcating into his Oxford students, and which were to receive a more formal philosophical treatment in his *Principles of Political Obligation* (1883), published posthumously. Fastening upon the common complaint that recent legislation had become increasingly illiberal and paternalistic, Green challenges the identification of a free society with one characterised by governmental non-intervention, in part by reinterpreting conventional conceptions of 'freedom' and 'progress'. Defining 'freedom' in the traditional English liberal manner as the possession of rights to do as one *wants* entailed, for Green, ignoring man's essence as a moral being and legitimating a selfish indifference to the fate of others. Instead, he proposes an alternative definition (pp. 186–7). This 'positive' conception of freedom provides the foundation for identifying progress, not with overall material improvement nor with the limitation of public intervention in private rights, but with the broadening of opportunities for the underprivileged and morally inadequate to live a life of personal worth within a community of equal citizenship.

Green was once described as 'an ultra-radical in politics, an ultra-liberal in religious opinion' (quoted in *Works* III, xlv). Though the lecture reveals few signs on the surface of theological thinking, underlying it is a deeply religious conception of the world. Born in a Yorkshire vicarage, Green was the product of a notable evangelical family background. From early reading of Wordsworth, Carlyle, Kingsley and F. D. Maurice (whose Christian Socialism he found expressed in the parochial work of his uncle, and Maurice's friend, the Rev. D. J. Vaughan in Leicester), he had developed his ideas to the extent that, on his appointment in 1861 as the first lay fellow of Balliol College, Oxford, he was closely identified with the liberal theology of *Essays and Reviews* (1860), contributed to by his tutor and friend, Benjamin Jowett. Green and Jowett were to be largely responsible for establishing Balliol's reputation as the intellectual powerhouse of late-Victorian England, and it was Jowett who directed him into studying the German idealist school of philosophy represented by Kant and Hegel which formed the basis of Green's lectures and popular lay sermons in the University. Like his mentors,

Green was inspired by the desire to isolate the gospel message of Christian duty and fellowship from ritualism and biblical literalism, and to reconcile it with the challenge of secular rationalism. In a conception of the divine as Reason, immanent in human history and evolving towards perfection in a community of individuals self-consciously acknowledging their spiritual unity and mutual obligations, he found an alternative to understanding human life as the determinant either of an extraneous providence or of mechanical scientific laws.

This theology issued forth in what contemporary parlance termed a 'social gospel', which summoned the relatively privileged in society to set about improving the well-being of those morally cramped by environmental deprivation. The impact of this message on generations of Oxford under-graduates was represented in Mrs Humphrey Ward's highly-successful novel, dedicated to Green's memory, *Robert Elsmere* (1888). In it, the eponymous hero is inspired as a student by the words of 'Professor Grey', a figure based on Green, first to take up Holy Orders, and then to shake off the doctrinal constraints of the Established Church and dedicate himself to good works in the East End slums, where he meets a tragic but worthy death. Green himself set an example of such 'improving' work, sitting on local and national committees to promote education, temperance and social welfare, and becoming the first elected university member of Oxford city council.

The reprinted lecture reveals how this social gospel was connected to Green's 'ultra-radical' politics. In attempting to display an unfolding pattern of legislative change in the nineteenth century (p. 184), he relates the theme of progress to an increasing recognition, on the part of society and its political representatives, of their duty to erode arbitrary divisions created by privilege. Liberalism is to be identified, not with fixed principles, but as the dynamic spirit of reform, pursuing 'the same old goal of social good against class interests' (p. 183), and pointing beyond freedom of contract towards legislation favouring the weak and deprived. A certain tension emerges here between Green's partisan liberalism and his neo-Hegelian view of history, which is inclined to see the spirit of freedom operating cumulatively through human actors irrespective of their precise intentions. Contrasted with his expositions of liberal measures, he is singularly uncharitable about the reform legislation of conservatives (e.g. p. 183), and their role in repealing the Corn Laws is skated over with the words 'With the ministry of Sir R. Peel began the struggle of society against monopolies ...' (p. 184).

Unlike our mid-century writers, Green does not feel impelled in this lecture to confront Political Economy directly. This is partly because he shares with most progressives after Mill a belief that the economic problem of wealth-creation has been superseded by the political problem of its distribution, partly because his historical philosophy itself denied the validity of universal economic laws, and the presumption of unchanging human motives of self-interest on which the discipline was founded; he was, for instance, sympathetic to the humanitarian instincts behind the attempts of Mill and of his own Cambridge friend and contemporary, Henry Sidgwick, to reconcile utilitarian economics with a doctrine of moral perfection, but felt them doomed to failure. Even so, Green stands full-square in the tradition of Mill's liberalism. By insisting (p. 189) that the state cannot itself promote moral goodness, but only provide an environment for individual self-improvement, he was distancing himself from the paternalism characteristic of Carlyle and Ruskin. All the reforms commended in this lecture were familiar features of mid-Victorian radical platforms, rather than pointers towards the 'collectivist' social legislation characteristic of twentieth-century governments. Green's aim was not, therefore, to change the 'Liberal Programme', but, by linking it to his own humanitarian sentiments through the medium of philosophical Idealism, to provide both with firmer intellectual foundations.

Whether he succeeded is open to question. To Jowett, for instance, German philosophy was a bedrock, not for Green's liberalised Hebraism which taught commitment to 'good works', but for reviving the spirit of ancient Hellenism, an almost pagan belief in worldly achievement and in the need to train a new Platonic élite of public servants. The terminology of this distinction calls Arnold to mind, and, despite the age difference, there were recognisable parallels between Green and Arnold. Both products of Rugby and Balliol, and sometime friends of Jowett, they shared the same neo-Idealist conception of reason and perfection as man's ends, and of 'the state' as an embodiment of the 'higher selves' of its members. Yet, while Arnold disavows commitment in favour of a superior critical stance, for Green commitment is all. In relation to the liberal belief that government has the twin function of maintaining order and advancing progress, Green's emphasis is on the second, Arnold's on the first. Arnold's arch-philistines, the middle classes, were for Green the source of progress; and John Bright, so roundly attacked in the preface to *Culture and Anarchy*, was Green's political hero.

Equally ambiguous were the lessons Green's followers drew from his writings. Some underplayed the religious source of his thought, and preached agnosticism and purely secular politics in such organisations as the London Ethical Society; others, believing he had revived the message of Christian Socialism, became engaged in the Christian Social Union and the *Lux Mundi* movement. Former pupils like Charles Loch and Bernard Bosanquet became the backbone of the Charity Organisation Society and its defence of personal responsibility against indiscriminate humanitarianism and state welfare; others, like Arnold Toynbee, J. H. Muirhead and L. T. Hobhouse, provided an inspiration for the 'New Liberalism' of the early 1900s which had close personal and intellectual links with the Fabian collectivists. Green's significance lay not, therefore, in laying down a clear path of liberal progress, but in defining a tone and ethos in the increasingly turbulent politics of late-Victorian Britain, offering sections of the middle-class intelligentsia which had lost their faith in the imperatives both of a transcendent God and of immutable economic laws, the prospect that 'good intentions' would restore harmony to society.

Despite the moral urgency which lay behind Green's writing, this lecture reveals none of the heat and passion which characterise our passages from Ruskin, Carlyle or Morris. Clearly, too, he could not have treated a popular audience to the dry, convoluted Hegelian language which permeated his technical writings, but, as befitted England's premier contemporary philosopher, the lecturer reveals his academic origins. The well-prepared organisation of arguments leaves little room for spontaneous engagement with the audience. We have a clear sense that Green knows himself to be cutting through intellectual complexities, but cannot avoid qualification and care for precise definition (e.g. p. 188). There is, at the same time, an immediacy and force about the language which explains the popularity of his Oxford lectures and lay sermons. Debating techniques, not unexpected, perhaps, in a former President of the Oxford Union, abound. The accumulation of p. 182 ('They all ... They all ... There is other ...') drives home the point that there is one central conflict raised by recent legislation. The classic techniques of antithesis and repetition draw the audience in to accept his argument ('We shall probably all agree ... But when we thus ... We do not mean ... We do not mean ... We do not mean ... When we speak on freedom ...' (p. 186). The language is terse and assertive ('Society is therefore plainly ...' (p. 189)), rhetorical questions are interpolated to revive the audience's attention, sentences are foreshortened to encompass but a single idea, with occasional signs of strain in construction ('It was just so much ...' (p. 185), 'Of compulsion by natural necessity ... Nor can he deliver ...' (p. 187)) However clear the argument, though, and however quotable many of the phrases, we are left with an uneasy sense that Green has failed to specify the meaning of his most important ideas. The concepts of 'reform' and 'reforming work' (p. 183) are left as vague as in the old Liberal motto 'Peace, Retrenchment, Reform'; and what precisely *is* 'a positive power or capacity of doing something worth doing or enjoying ...' (p. 186), a definition of freedom so central to his whole argument? This emerges particularly in the concealed change of tone identifiable in his concluding pages on the temperance question. While apparently maintaining the earlier *ex cathedra* manner of pronouncing upon issues of the day, the language shifts gear into that of the moral crusade – 'social nuisance', 'social evil', 'weakness', 'temptation', 'vice'. When we realise that Green had witnessed, and failed to avert, his brother's unhappy decline into alcoholism, and that temperance had become his chief preoccupation in the 1870s, it is easier to see how the question could accentuate an inherent tension between his academic role as a professional philosopher and his personal commitment to 'good causes'.

10. *Liberal Legislation and Freedom of Contract* (1881)

pp. 5–12, 13–22

That a discussion on this subject is opportune will hardly be disputed by any one who noticed the line of argument by which at least two of the Liberal measures of last session were opposed. To the Ground

Game Act it was objected that it interfered with freedom of contract between landlord and tenant. It withdrew the sanction of law from any agreement by which the occupier of land should transfer to the owner the exclusive right of killing hares and rabbits on the land in his occupation. The Employers' Liability Act was objected to on similar grounds.[1] It did not indeed go the length of preventing masters and workmen from contracting themselves out of its operation. But it was urged that it went on the wrong principle of encouraging the workman to look to the law for the protection which he ought to secure for himself by voluntary contract. 'The workman,' it was argued, 'should be left to take care of himself by the terms of his agreement with the employer. It is not for the State to step in and say, as by the new act it says, that when a workman is hurt in carrying out the instructions of the employer or his foreman, the employer, in the absence of a special agreement to the contrary, shall be liable for compensation. If the law thus takes to protecting men, whether tenant-farmers, or pitmen, or railway servants, who ought to be able to protect themselves, it tends to weaken their self reliance, and thus in unwisely seeking to do them good, it lowers them in the scale of moral beings.'

Such is the language which was everywhere in the air last summer, and which many of us, without being convinced by it, may have found it difficult to answer. The same line of objection is equally applicable to other legislation of recent years – to our Factory Acts, Education Acts, and laws relating to public health. They all, in one direction or another, limit a man's power of doing what he will with what he considers his own. They all involve the legal prohibition of certain agreements between man and man, and as there is nothing to force men into these agreements, it might be argued that, supposing them to be mischievous, men would, in their own interest, gradually learn to refuse them. There is other legislation which the Liberal party is likely to demand, and which is sure to be objected to on the same ground – with what justice we shall see as we proceed. If it is proposed to give the Irish tenant some security in his holding, to save him from rack-renting and from the confiscation of the results of his labour in the improvement of the soil, it will be objected that in so doing the State goes out of its way to interfere with the contracts, possibly beneficial to both sides, which landlord and tenant would otherwise make with each other. Leave the tenant, it will be said, to secure himself by contract. Meanwhile the demand for greater security of tenure is growing stronger amongst our English farmers, and should it be proposed – as it must before this Parliament expires

– to give legal effect to it, the proposal will be met by the same cry, that it is an interference with the freedom of contract – unless, indeed, like Lord Beaconsfield's Act of 1875, it undoes with one hand what it professes to do with the other.[2]

There are two other matters with which the Liberal leaders have virtually promised to deal, and upon which they are sure to be met by an appeal to the supposed inherent right of every man to do what he will with his own. One is the present system of settling land, the other the liquor traffic. The only effectual reform of the Land Laws is to put a stop to those settlements or bequests by which at present a landlord may prevent a successor from either converting any part of his land into money or from dividing it among his children.[3] But if it is proposed to take away from the landlord this power of hampering posterity, it will be said to be an interference with his free disposal of his property. As for the liquor traffic, it is obvious that even the present Licensing Laws, ineffectual as some of us think them, interfere with the free sale of an article in large consumption, and that with the concession of 'local option' the interference would, to say the least, be probably carried much further.[4] I have said enough to show that the most pressing political questions of our time are questions of which the settlement, I do not say necessarily involves an interference with freedom of contract, but is sure to be resisted in the sacred name of individual liberty, not only by all those who are interested in keeping things as they are but by others to whom freedom is dear for its own sake, and who do not sufficiently consider the conditions of its maintenance in such a society as ours. In this respect there is a noticeable difference between the present position of political reformers and that in which they stood a generation ago. Then they fought the fight of reform in the name of individual freedom against class privilege. Their opponents could not with any plausibility invoke the same name against them. Now, in appearance – though, as I shall try to show, not in reality – the case is changed. The nature of the genuine political reformer is perhaps always the same. The passion for improving mankind, in its ultimate object, does not vary. But the immediate object of reformers, and the forms of persuasion by which they seek to advance them, vary much in different generations. To a hasty observer they might even seem contradictory, and to justify the notion that nothing better than a desire for change, selfish or perverse, is at the bottom of all reforming movements. Only those who will think a little longer about it can discern the same old cause of social good against class interests, for which, under altered names, Liberals are fighting now as they were fifty years ago.

Thomas Hill Green (1836–1882)

Our political history since the first Reform Act naturally falls into three divisions. The first, beginning with the reform of Parliament, and extending to Sir R. Peel's administration, is marked by the struggle of free society against close privileged corporations. Its greatest achievement was the establishment of representative municipal governments in place of the close bodies which had previously administered the affairs of our cities and boroughs – a work which after an interval of nearly half a century we hope shortly to see extended to the rural districts. Another important work was the overhauling of the immense charities of the country, and the placing them under something like adequate public control. And the natural complement of this was the removal of the grosser abuses in the administration of the Church – the abolition of pluralities and sinecures, and the reform of cathedral chapters.[5] In all this, while there was much that contributed to the freedom of our civil life, there was nothing that could possibly be construed as an interference with the rights of the individual. No one was disturbed in doing what he would with his own. Even those who had fattened on abuses had their vested interests duly respected, for the House of Commons then as now had 'quite a passion for compensation.' With the Ministry of Sir R. Peel began the struggle of society against monopolies; in other words, the liberation of trade. Some years later Mr Gladstone, in his famous budgets, was able to complete the work which his master began, and it is now some twenty years since the last vestige of protection for any class of traders or producers disappeared. The taxes on knowledge, as they were called, followed the taxes on food, and since most of us grew up there has been no exchangeable commodity in England except land – no doubt a large exception – of which the exchange has not been perfectly free.[6]

The realisation of complete freedom of contract was the special object of this reforming work. It was to set men at liberty to dispose of what they had made their own that the free-trader worked. He only interfered to prevent interference. He would put restraint on no man in doing anything that did not directly check the free dealing of some one in something else. But of late reforming legislation has taken, as I have pointed out, a seemingly different direction. It has not at any rate been so readily identifiable with the work of liberation. In certain respects it has put restraints on the individual in doing what he will with his own. And it is noticeable that this altered tendency begins, in the main, with the more democratic Parliament of 1868. It is true that earlier Factory Acts, limiting as they do by law the conditions under which certain kinds of labour may be bought

184

and sold, had been passed some time before. The first approach to an effectual Factory Act dates as far back as the time of the first Reform Act, but it only applied to the cotton industry, and was very imperfectly put in force. It aimed at limiting the hours of labour for children and young persons. Gradually the limitation of hours came to be enforced, other industries were brought under the operation of the restraining laws, and the same protection extended to women as to young persons. But it was only alongside of the second Reform Act of 1867 that an attempt was made by Parliament to apply the same rule to every kind of factory and workshop; only later still, in the first Parliament elected partly by household suffrage, that efficient measures were taken for enforcing the restraints which previous legislation had in principle required. Improvements and extensions in detail have since been introduced – largely through the influence of Mr Mundella[7] – and now we have a system of law by which in all our chief industries except the agricultural, the employment of children except as half-timers is effectually prevented, the employment of women and young persons is effectually restricted to ten hours a day, and in all places of employment health and bodily safety have all the protection which rules can give them.

If factory regulation had been attempted, though only in a piecemeal way, some time before we had a democratic House of Commons, the same cannot be said of educational law. It was the Parliament elected by a more popular suffrage in 1868 that passed, as we know, the first great Education Act. That act introduced compulsory schooling. It left the compulsion, indeed, optional with local School Boards, but compulsion is the same in principle – is just as much compulsion by the State – whether exercised by the central Government or delegated by that Government to provincial authorities. The Education Act of 1870 was a wholly new departure in English legislation, though Mr Forster was wise enough to proceed tentatively, and leave the adoption of compulsory bye-laws to the discretion of School Boards. It was so just as much as if he had attempted at once to enforce compulsory attendance through the action of the central Government. The principle was established once for all that parents were not to be allowed to do as they willed with their children, if they willed either to set them to work or to let them run wild without elementary education. Freedom of contract in respect of all dealings with the labour of children was so far limited.[8]

I need not trouble you with recalling the steps by which the principle of the act of 1870 has since been further applied and enforced. It is evident that in the body of school and factory

legislation which I have noticed we have a great system of interference with freedom of contract. The hirer of labour is prevented
from hiring it on terms to which the person of whom he hires it could
for the most part have been readily brought to agree. If children and
young persons and women were not ready in many cases, either from
their own wish, or under the influence of parents and husbands, to
accept employment of the kind which the law prohibits, there would
have been no occasion for the prohibition. It is true that adult men
are not placed directly under the same restriction. The law does not
forbid them from working as long hours as they please. But I need
not point out here that in effect the prevention of the employment of
juvenile labour beyond certain hours, amounts, at least in the textile
industries, to the prevention of the working of machinery beyond
those hours. It thus indirectly puts a limit on the number of hours
during which the manufacturer can employ his men. And if it is only
accidentally, so to speak, that the hiring of men's labour is interfered
with by the half-time and ten hours' system, the interference on
grounds of health and safety is as direct as possible. The most mature
man is prohibited by law from contracting to labour in factories, or
pits, or workshops, unless certain rules for the protection of health
and limb are complied with. In like manner he is prohibited from
living in a house which the sanitary inspector pronounces unwholesome. The free sale or letting of a certain kind of commodity is
thereby prevented. Here, then, is a great system of restriction, which
yet hardly any impartial person wishes to see reversed; which many of
us wish to see made more complete. Perhaps, however, we have
never thoroughly considered the principles on which we approve it.
It may be well, therefore, to spend a short time in ascertaining those
principles. We shall then be on surer ground in approaching those
more difficult questions of legislation which must shortly be dealt
with, and of which the settlement is sure to be resisted in the name of
individual liberty.

We shall probably all agree that freedom, rightly understood, is the
greatest of blessings – that its attainment is the true end of all our
effort as citizens. But when we thus speak of freedom, we should
consider carefully what we mean by it. We do not mean merely
freedom from restraint or compulsion. We do not mean merely
freedom to do as we like irrespectively of what it is that we like. We
do not mean a freedom that can be enjoyed by one man or one set of
men at the cost of a loss of freedom to others. When we speak of
freedom as something to be so highly prized, we mean a positive
power or capacity of doing or enjoying something worth doing or

enjoying, and that, too, something that we do or enjoy in common with others. We mean by it a power which each man exercises through the help or security given him by his fellow-men, and which he in turn helps to secure for them. When we measure the progress of a society by its growth in freedom, we measure it by the increasing development and exercise on the whole of those powers of contributing to social good with which we believe the members of the society to be endowed – in short, by the greater power on the part of the citizens as a body to make the most and best of themselves. Thus, though of course there can be no freedom among men who act not willingly, but under compulsion, yet on the other hand the mere removal of compulsion, the mere enabling a man to do as he likes is in itself no contribution to true freedom. In one sense no man is so well able to do as he likes as the wandering savage. He has no master. There is no one to say him nay. Yet we do not count him really free, because the freedom of savagery is not strength, but weakness. The actual powers of the noblest savage do not admit of comparison with those of the humblest citizen of a law-abiding state. He is not the slave of man, but he is the slave of nature. Of compulsion by natural necessity he has plenty of experience, though of restraint by society none at all. Nor can he deliver himself from that compulsion except by submitting to this restraint. So to submit is the first step in true freedom, because the first step towards the full exercise of the faculties with which man is endowed. But we rightly refuse to recognise the highest development on the part of an exceptional individual or exceptional class, as an advance towards the true freedom of man, if it is founded on a refusal of the same opportunity to other men. The powers of the human mind have probably never attained such force and keenness – the proof of what society can do for the individual has never been so strikingly exhibited – as among the small groups of men who possessed civil privileges in the small republics of antiquity. The whole framework of our political ideas, to say nothing of our philosophy, is derived from them. But in them this extraordinary efflorescence of the privileged class was accompanied by the slavery of the multitude. That slavery was the condition on which it depended, and for that reason it was doomed to decay. There is no clearer ordinance of that supreme reason, often dark to us, which governs the course of man's affairs, than that no body of men should in the long run be able to strengthen itself at the cost of others' weakness. The civilisation and freedom of the ancient world were short-lived because they were partial and exceptional. If the ideal of true freedom is the maximum of power for all members of human society alike to make the best of themselves, we are right in refusing to ascribe the glory of freedom to a state in which the apparent elevation of the few is founded on the degradation of the many, and in ranking modern society, founded as it is on free industry, with all its confusion and ignorant license and waste of effort, above the most splendid of ancient republics.

If I have given a true account of that freedom which forms the goal of social effort, we shall see that freedom of contract – freedom in all the forms of doing what one will with one's own – is valuable only as a means to an end. That end is what I call freedom in the positive sense: in other words, the liberation of the powers of all men equally for contribution to a common good. No one has a right to do what he will with his own in such a way as to contravene this end. It is only through the guarantee which society gives him that he has property at all or, strictly speaking, any right to his possessions. This guarantee is founded on a sense of common interest. Every one has an interest in securing to every one else the free use and enjoyment and disposal of his possessions, so long as that freedom on the part of one does not interfere with a like freedom on the part of others, because such freedom contributes to that equal development of the faculties of all which is the highest good for all. This is the true and the only justification of rights of property. Rights of property, however, have been and are claimed which cannot be thus justified. We are all now agreed that men cannot rightly be the property of men. The institution of property being only justifiable as a means to the free exercise of the social capabilities of all, there can be no true right to property of a kind which debars one class of men from such free exercise altogether. We condemn slavery no less when it arises out of a voluntary agreement on the part of the enslaved person. A contract by which any one agreed for a certain consideration to become the slave of another we should reckon a void contract. Here, then, is a limitation upon freedom of contract which we all recognise as rightful. No contract is valid in which human persons, willingly or unwillingly, are dealt with as commodities, because such contracts of necessity defeat the end for which alone society enforces contracts at all.

Are there no other contracts which, less obviously perhaps but really, are open to the same objection? In the first place, let us consider contracts affecting labour. Labour, the economist tells us, is a commodity exchangeable like other commodities. This is in a certain sense true, but it is a commodity which attaches in a peculiar manner to the person of man. Hence restrictions may need to be placed on the sale of this commodity which would be unnecessary in other cases in order to prevent labour from being sold under conditions which make it impossible for the person selling it ever to become a free contributor to social good in any form. This is most plainly the case when a man bargains to work under conditions fatal to health, *e.g.*, in an unventilated factory. Every injury to the health of the individual is, so far as it goes, a public injury. It is an impediment to the general freedom; so much deduction from our power, as members of society, to make the best of ourselves. Society is, therefore, plainly within its right when it limits freedom of contract for the sale of labour, so far as is done by our laws for the sanitary regulations of factories, workshops and mines. It is equally within its right in prohibiting the labour of women and young persons beyond certain hours. If they work beyond those hours, the result is demonstrably physical deterioration; which, as demonstrably, carries with it a lowering of the moral forces of society. For the sake of that general freedom of its members to make the best of themselves, which is the object of civil society to secure, a prohibition should be put by law, which is the deliberate voice of society, on all such contracts of service as in a general way yield such a result. The purchase of hire or unwholesome dwellings is properly forbidden on the same principle. Its application to compulsory education may not be quite so obvious, but it will appear on a little reflection. Without a command of certain elementary arts and knowledge, the individual in modern society is as effectually crippled as by the loss of a limb or a broken constitution. He is not free to develope his faculties. With a view to securing such freedom among its members it is as certainly within the province of the State to prevent children from growing up in that kind of ignorance which practically excludes them from a free career in life, as it is within its province to require the sort of building and drainage necessary for public health.

Our modern legislation then with reference to labour, and education, and health – involving as it does manifold interference with freedom of contract – is justified on the ground that it is the business of the State – not indeed directly to promote moral goodness, for that, from the very nature of moral goodness, it cannot do – but to maintain the conditions without which a free exercise of the human faculties is impossible. It does not indeed follow that it is advisable for the State to do all which it is justified in doing. ...

Now, we shall probably all agree that a society in which the public health was duly protected, and necessary education duly provided for, by the spontaneous action of individuals, was in a higher condition than one in which the compulsion of law was needed to secure these ends. But we must take men as we find them. Until such a condition of society is reached it is the business of the State to take the best security it can for the young citizens growing up in such health and with so much knowledge as is necessary for their real freedom. In so doing it need not at all interfere with the independence and self-reliance of those whom it requires to do what they would otherwise do for themselves. The man who, of his own right feeling, saves his wife from overwork and sends his children to school, suffers no moral degradation from a law which, if he did not do this for himself, would seek to make him do it. Such a man does not feel the law as constraint at all. To him it is simply a powerful friend. It gives him security for that being done efficiently which, with the best wishes, he might have much trouble in getting done efficiently if left to himself. No doubt it relieves him from some of the responsibility which would otherwise fall to him as head of a family, but, if he is what we are supposing him to be, in proportion as he is relieved of responsibilities in one direction he will assume them in another. The security which the State gives him for the safe housing and sufficient schooling for his family will only make him the more careful for their well-being in other respects, which he is left to look after for himself. We need have no fear, then, of such legislation having an ill-effect on those who, without the law, would have seen to that being done, though probably less efficiently, which the law requires to be done. But it was not their case that the laws we are considering were especially meant to meet. It was the overworked women, the ill-housed and untaught families for whose benefit they were intended. And the question is whether without these laws the suffering classes could have been delivered quickly or slowly from the condition they were in. Could the enlightened self-interest or benevolence of individuals, working under a system of unlimited freedom of contract, have ever brought them into a state compatible with the free development of the human faculties? No one considering the facts can have any doubt as to the answer to this question. Left to itself, or to the operation of casual benevolence, a degraded population perpetuates and increases itself. Read any of the authorised accounts, given before Royal or Parliamentary Commissions, of the state of the labourers, especially of the women and children, as they were in our great industries before the law was first brought to bear on them, and before freedom of contract was first interfered with in them. Ask yourself what chance there was of a generation, inborn and bred under such conditions, ever contracting itself out of them.

Given a certain standard of moral and material well-being, people may be trusted not to sell their labour, or the labour of their children, on terms which would not allow that standard to be maintained. But with large masses of our population, until the laws we have been considering took effect, there was no such standard. There was nothing on their part, in the way either of self-respect or established demand for comforts, to prevent them from working and living, or from putting their children to work and live, in a way in which no one who is to be a healthy and free citizen can work and live. No doubt there were many high-minded employers who did their best for their work-people before the days of State-interference, but they could not prevent less scrupulous hirers of labour from hiring it on the cheapest terms. It is true that cheap labour is in the long run dear labour, but it is so only in the long run, and eager traders do not think of the long run. If labour is to be had under conditions incompatible with the health or decent housing or education of the labourer, there will always be plenty of people to buy it under those conditions, careless of the burden in the shape of rates and taxes which they may be laying up for posterity. Either the standard of well-being on the part of the sellers of labour must prevent them from selling their labour under these conditions, or the law must prevent it. With a population such as ours was forty years ago, and still largely is, the law must prevent it and continue the prevention for some generations, before the sellers will be in a state to prevent it for themselves. . . . [Here Green begins a long discussion about reform of landlord–tenant relations.]

. . . I have left myself little time to speak of the principles on which some of us hold that in the matter of intoxicating drinks a further limitation of freedom of contract is needed in the interest of general freedom. I say a further limitation, because there is no such thing as a free sale of these drinks at present. Men are not at liberty to buy and sell them when they will, where they will, and as they will. But our present licensing system, while it creates a class of monopolists especially interested in resisting any effectual restraint of the liquor traffic, does little to lessen the facilities for obtaining strong drink. Indeed the principle upon which licenses have been generally given has been avowedly to make it easy to get drink. The restriction of the hours of sale is no doubt a real check so far as it goes, but it remains the case that every one who has a weakness for drink has the temptation staring him in the face during all hours but those when he ought to be in bed. The effect of the present system, in short, is to prevent the drink shops from coming unpleasantly near the houses of well-to-do people, and to crowd them upon the quarters occupied by the poorer classes, who have practically no power of keeping the nuisance from them. Now it is clear that the only remedy which the law can afford for this state of things must take the form either of more stringent rules of licensing, or of a power entrusted to the householders in each district of excluding the sale of intoxicants altogether from among them.

I do not propose to discuss the comparative merits of these methods of procedure. One does not exclude the other. They may very well be combined. One may be best suited for one kind of population, the other for another kind. But either, to be effectual, must involve a large interference with the liberty of the individual to do as he likes in the matter of buying and selling alcohol. It is the justifiability of that interference that I wish briefly to consider.

We justify it on the simple ground of the recognised right on the part of society to prevent men from doing as they like, if in the exercise of their peculiar tastes, in doing as they like, they create a social nuisance. There is no right to freedom in the purchase and sale of a particular commodity, if the general result of allowing such freedom is to detract from freedom in the higher sense – from the general power of men to make the best of themselves. Now, with anyone who looks calmly at the facts there can be no doubt that the present habits of drinking in England do lay a heavy burden on the free development of man's powers for social good – a heavier burden probably than arises from all other preventible causes put together. It used to be the fashion to look on drunkenness as a vice which was the concern only of the person who fell into it, so long as it did not lead him to commit an assault on his neighbours. No thoughtful man any longer looks on it in this way. We know that, however decently carried on, the excessive drinking of one man means an injury to others in health, purse, and capability, to which no limits can be placed. Drunkenness in the head of a family means, as a rule, the impoverishment and degradation of all members of the family; and the presence of a drink shop at the corner of a street means, as a rule, the drunkenness of a certain number of heads of families in that street. Remove the drink shops and, as the experience of many happy communities sufficiently shows, you almost, perhaps in time altogether, remove the drunkenness. Here, then, is a wide-spread social evil, of which society may, if it will, by a restraining law, to a great extent, rid itself to the infinite enhancement of the positive freedom enjoyed by its members. All that is required for the attainment of so blessed a result is so much effort and self-sacrifice on the part of the majority of citizens as is necessary for the enactment and enforcement of the restraining law. The majority of citizens may still be far from prepared for such an effort. That is a point on which I express no opinion. To attempt a restraining law in advance of the social sentiment necessary to give real effect to it, is always a mistake. But to argue that an effectual law in restraint of the drink traffic would be a wrongful interference with individual liberty, is to ignore the essential condition under which alone every particular liberty can rightly be allowed to the individual – the condition, namely, that the allowance of that liberty is not, as a rule, and on the whole, an impediment to social good.

The more reasonable opponents of the restraint for which I plead, would probably argue not so much that it was necessarily wrong in principle, as that it was one of those short cuts to a good end which ultimately defeat their own object. They would take the same line that has been taken by the opponents of state-interference in all its forms. 'Leave the people to themselves,' they would say. 'As their standard of self-respect rises, as they become better housed and better educated, they will gradually shake off the evil habit. The cure so effected may not be so rapid as that brought by a repressive law, but it will be more lasting. Better that it should come more slowly through the spontaneous action of individuals, than more quickly through compulsion.'

But here again we reply that it is dangerous to wait. The slower remedy might be preferable if we were sure that it was a remedy at all, but we have no such assurance. There is strong reason to think the contrary. Every year that the evil is left to itself, it becomes greater. The vested interest in the encouragement of the vice becomes larger, and the persons affected by it more numerous. If any abatement of it has already taken place, we may fairly argue that this is because it has not been altogether left to itself; for the licensing law, as it is, is much more stringent and more stringently administered than it was ten years ago. A drunken population naturally perpetuates and increases itself. Many families, it is true, keep emerging from the conditions which render them specially liable to the evil habit, but on the other hand descent through drunkenness from respectability to squalor is constantly going on. The families of drunkards do not seem to be smaller than those of sober men, though they are shorter-lived; and that the children of a drunkard should escape from drunkenness is what we call almost a miracle. Better education, better housing, more healthy rules of labour, no doubt lessen the temptations to drink for those who have the benefit of these advantages, but meanwhile drunkenness is constantly recruiting the ranks of those who cannot be really educated, who will not be better housed, who make their employments dangerous and unhealthy. An effectual liquor law in short is the necessary complement for our Factory Acts, our Education Acts, our Public Health Acts. Without it the full measure of their usefulness will never be attained. They were all opposed in their turn by the same arguments that are now used against a restraint of the facilities for drinking. Sometimes it was the argument that the State had no business to interfere with the liberties of the individual. Sometimes it was the dilatory plea that the better nature of man would in time assert itself, and that meanwhile it would be lowered by compulsion. Happily a sense of the facts and necessities of the case got the better of the delusive cry of liberty. Act after Act was passed preventing master and workman, parent and child, housebuilder and householder, from doing as they pleased, with the result of a great addition to the real freedom of society. The spirit of self-reliance and independence was not weakened by those acts. Rather it received a new development. The dead weight of ignorance and unhealthy surroundings, with which it would otherwise have had to struggle, being partially removed by law, it was more free to exert itself for higher objects. When we ask for a stringent liquor-law, which should even go to the length of allowing the householders of a district to exclude the drink traffic altogether, we are only asking for a continuation of the same work – a continuation necessary to its complete success. It is a poor sophistry to tell us that it is moral cowardice to seek to remove by law a temptation which every one ought to be able to resist for himself. It is not the part of a considerate self-reliance to remain in presence of a temptation merely for the sake of being tempted. When all temptations are removed which law can remove there will still be room enough – nay, much more room – for the play of our moral energies. The temptation to excessive drinking is one which upon sufficient evidence we hold that the law can at least greatly diminish. If it can, it ought to do so. This then, along with the effectual liberation of the soil, is the next great conquest which our democracy, on behalf of its own true freedom, has to make. The danger of legislation, either in the interests of a privileged class or for the promotion of particular religious opinions, we may fairly assume to be over. The popular jealousy of law, once justifiable enough, is therefore out of date. The citizens of England now make its law. We ask them by law to put a restraint on themselves in the matter of strong drink. We ask them further to limit – or even altogether to give up – the not very precious liberty of buying and selling alcohol, in order that they may become more free to exercise the faculties and improve the talents which God has given them.

William Morris

(1834–1896)

How I became a Socialist is an account of Morris's personal political odyssey, written two years before his death for the Socialist Democratic Federation newspaper *Justice* (16 June 1894), which he had helped to subsidise. As a document it also serves to convey the fissiparous nature of late nineteenth-century socialism. By the 1870s the British socialist tradition embodied in Owenism was a largely spent force and the new socialism owed much of its impetus to competing European ideologies.

Morris had briefly tried working within the constraints of the existing political system. In the mid–1870s, at the time of the Bulgarian atrocities and their aftermath, which had seemed to threaten European war, Morris had embraced the Liberal side and campaigned enthusiastically against Disraeli's bellicose policies. He was swiftly disillusioned, however, by what he saw as the ineffectual nature of the Liberal leadership, and further disenchanted with Liberal policy toward Ireland, which he diagnosed as essentially imperialistic. Besides, he felt that liberalism was still dominated by Whiggish rather than radical thought, still inclined to base its piecemeal remedies upon an acceptance of the existing political and economic framework. This last factor was to form his major difference of opinion with the Fabians, who voiced the fear that Morris's insistence on class warfare and the need for revolution made his writings profitable for confirmed socialists but unnecessarily alarmist for potential converts. Though personally antipathetic to anarchism, Morris championed local rather than central government, and extra-parliamentary activity and organisation in direct opposition to Fabians like Shaw who 'look upon Parliament as *the* means and it seems to me . . . fall into the error of moving heaven and earth to fill the ballot boxes with Socialist votes which will not represent Socialist *men*' (quoted in R. P. Arnot, *William Morris, the Man and the Myth* (1964), p. 83). Morris's interest lay in seeing the socialist spirit triumphant rather than using political machination to achieve socialist measures. Engels commented repeatedly on this political naiveté, referring to Morris and his friend Bax as 'nos deux bébés en politique' and to Morris himself as 'a settled sentimental socialist' and 'hopelessly muddle-headed' (quoted in P. Faulkner, *Against the Age: An Introduction to William Morris* (1980), p. 144).

As to the seriousness of Morris's commitment to socialism as an ideology there could be no doubt. He sold much of his library, including precious *incunabula*, to finance the Social Democratic Federation which he joined in January 1883. The end of 1884 saw Morris, accompanied by nine other leading members, who included Edward Aveling and his wife, Marx's daughter Eleanor, leave the Federation as a result of the attempts by Hyndman, the Federation's first chairman, 'to substitute arbitrary rule therein for fraternal co-operation'. The manner of their secession made the Socialist League which they then founded an unstable affair, soon to be threatened by internal dissension when the anarchist element gained control. Morris strove to heal these breaches in the contemporary socialist movement. He continued his financial support for the League's paper, *Commonweal*, even when it was under anarchist control, while continuing to support *Justice* with his literary contributions. The concluding paragraphs of the essay offer a concise summary of Morris's distinctive contribution to socialist thought in exploring the place of art and the artist in a socialist society. By this stage in his life Morris was realist enough to recognise that art had no inherent ability to mould men's vision of an ideal society. Despite the personal pleasure he derived from his own work he recognised that, not only were the artefacts he produced out of the working man's reach financially but, conditioned by the assumptions of a capitalist society, the poor framed their desires in terms of material reward rather than cultural aspiration. The function of the artist must therefore be both revolutionary, in evolving a relevant and yet visionary art, and educative, in setting forth 'the true ideal of a full and reasonable life'.

The second text reproduced here, *Dawn of a New Epoch*, was given as a lecture in 1886 and published in 1888. It reveals many of those influences to which Morris paid tribute in his autobiographical essay. He starts by defining his consciousness of change in terms clearly derived from Marx's historical analysis of the emergence of class warfare, detectable particularly in his use of such terms as 'means of production', 'labour-power', the 'reserve army of labour' (pp. 205–7). In the course of the lecture we encounter Carlyle's doctrine of the absolute value of work, transformed via Ruskin's contribution to the moral distinction between productive and unproductive work, into an assertion of the dignity of productive labour – a dignity which, under socialist conditions, might become the true reward of labour. Proudhon's maxim, 'all property is theft', receives lengthy elaboration by Morris, whose socialism finds no place for Mill's retention of private property, nor for Carlyle or Ruskin's admiration for the captains of industry. Yet Morris remains every bit as jealous as Mill for the freedom of the individual so that he instinctively shies away from contemplating the mechanisms necessary to effect the revolution he proposes. He argues instead for a change of spirit which will in its wake bring about the death of the acquisitive commercialism lying behind man's competitive and bellicose instincts and foster free fellowship, whether between workers or between international communities.

True to his concern with overthrowing class barriers, Morris lectured and wrote for a more broadly constituted audience than any of the authors in this volume. Moreover he wrote under great pressure. In 1889, for instance, he attended some sixty-three meetings and made speeches at most of them. This was in addition to time spent on his business interests which ranged from the production of painted glass to carpeting and upholstery, and on his role as guardian of the English cultural heritage, acting as secretary to the Society for the Protection of Ancient Buildings and adviser to the South Kensington Museum and the Royal School of Art and Needlework. Morris's reliance upon the tricks and cadences of the spoken word rather than the subtler constructions of written prose are everywhere apparent. His direct, personal form of address aims at an intimacy which will persuade his audience of his concern and integrity. Shaw was to recall that his very sincerity and dislike of anything that smacked of charlatanism prevented Morris from becoming an easy or individualistic orator (*Morris as I knew him* (1936)). The repeated use of 'now' as a connective lends the impression of a man thinking on his feet, proceeding inch by inch with his argument, summarising before continuing to his next point and determined to carry his audience with him. Unashamedly he repeats assertions of arguments to ensure that they have been fully grasped (e.g. twice on p. 214). Moreover the internal structure of his sentences and his often rhythmic use of couplets and of near synonyms (e.g. 'forcibly and artificially', 'justice and fair dealing') employ the redundancies of the spoken word rather than the honed articulation of the study. Although his sentences sometimes lack the subordinating links or even the punctuation we would expect, they are always clear: clear, that is, in conveying exactly what Morris intends to say. This last qualification may seem unnecessarily mystifying, but despite the simplicity of his vocabulary, the directness of his statements, the listener or reader knows he has been stirred but may be excused for asking himself to what account precisely. Morris's prose brandishes the great abstract nouns, 'justice', 'goodness', 'duty', 'wisdom' but rarely leads us to feel that these commonly acknowledged ideas have been any more narrowly defined, or the path to their attainment made any more obvious. When, on the other hand his language assumes a more metaphorical slant, the effect is not necessarily illuminating. At home with the metaphor of pictures (p. 202) or chairs (p. 213), when he ranges more widely a certain abandon takes over. What, for instance, does the image 'the silent sap of the years is being laid aside for open assault' (p. 202) convey? The connection of the silent sap with the 'nascent order' of the previous sentence is obscure, and the passive voice leaves it unclear as to who is doing the laying aside. 'Silent sap', we are left suspecting, appealed more for its alliterative qualities than its symbolic power. A further example of the appeal of declamatory alliteration to the detriment of meaning is offered by Morris's comparison of Homer and Huxley near the end of *How I Became a Socialist*. The choice of Thomas Henry Huxley, the famous champion of Darwinian evolutionary theory, may seem an easy way of establishing the appeal of imaginative literature against the world of 'scientific analysis', but its very specificity is damaging to Morris's argument as a whole. Since he describes himself as a man by 'disposition careless of metaphysics and religion', the challenge Huxley's works offered to Christianity does not seem a useful point of reference. Nor is it any more helpful to contemplate Huxley as a type of man at the forefront of scientific theory, since within a paragraph Morris takes trouble to distinguish himself from mere 'railers against progress', and elsewhere refers to technical advances as potentially useful if they free men to do the work they most enjoy. Rather, Morris seems once again to have been drawn by a series of ever-more apocalyptic contrasts between past and future towards attempting to establish two absolutes, the imaginative and the scientific world, in a way that his more sober arguments would not support and his examples render suspect. It is such moments of excitable hyperbole that lend justification to Raymond Williams's description of Morris's style as a 'generalised kind of swearing'.

11. *How I became a Socialist* (1894)

The Collected Works of William Morris, ed. May Morris (24 vols., 1910–15), vol. XXIII, pp. 121–40

I am asked by the Editor to give some sort of a history of the above conversion, and I feel that it may be of some use to do so, if my readers will look upon me as a type of a certain group of people, but not so easy to do clearly, briefly and truly. Let me, however, try. But first, I will say what I mean by being a Socialist, since I am told that the word no longer expresses definitely and with certainty what it did ten years ago. Well, what I mean by Socialism is a condition of society in which there should be neither rich nor poor, neither master nor master's man, neither idle nor overworked, neither brain-sick brain workers, nor heart-sick hand workers, in a word, in which all men would be living in equality of condition, and would manage their affairs unwastefully, and with the full consciousness that harm to one would mean harm to all – the realization at last of the meaning of the word COMMONWEALTH.

Now this view of Socialism which I hold to-day, and hope to die holding, is what I began with; I had no transitional period, unless you may call such a brief period of political radicalism during which I saw my ideal clear enough, but had no hope of any realization of it. That came to an end some months before I joined the (then) Democratic Federation, and the meaning of my joining that body was that I had conceived a hope of the realization of my ideal. If you ask me how much of a hope, or what I thought we Socialists then living and working would accomplish towards it, or when there would be effected any change in the face of society, I must say, I do not know. I can only say that I did not measure my hope, nor the joy that it brought me at the time. For the rest, when I took that step I was blankly ignorant of economics; I had never so much as opened

Adam Smith, or heard of Ricardo, or of Karl Marx.[1] Oddly enough, I *had* read some of Mill, to wit, those posthumous papers of his (published, was it in the *Westminster Review* or the *Fortnightly*?) in which he attacks Socialism in its Fourierist guise.[2] In those papers he put the arguments, as far as they go, clearly and honestly, and the result, so far as I was concerned, was to convince me that Socialism was a necessary change, and that it was possible to bring it about in our own days. Those papers put the finishing touch to my conversion to Socialism. Well, having joined a Socialist body(for the Federation soon became definitely Socialist), I put some conscience into trying to learn the economical side of Socialism, and even tackled Marx, though I must confess that, whereas I thoroughly enjoyed the historical part of *Capital*, I suffered agonies of confusion of the brain over reading the pure economics of that great work. Anyhow, I read what I could, and will hope that some information stuck to me from my reading; but more, I must think, from continuous conversation with such friends as Bax[3] and Hyndman[4] and Scheu,[5] and the brisk course of propaganda meetings which were going on at the time, and in which I took my share. Such finish to what of education in practical Socialism as I am capable of I received afterwards from some of my Anarchist friends, from whom I learned, quite against their intention, that Anarchism was impossible, much as I learned from Mill against *his* intention that Socialism was necessary.

But in this telling how I fell into *practical* Socialism I have begun, as I perceived, in the middle, for in my position of a well-to-do man, not suffering from the disabilities which oppress a working man at every step, I feel that I might never have been drawn into the practical side of the question if an ideal had not forced me to seek towards it. For politics as politics, i.e., not regarded as a necessary if cumbersome and disgustful means to an end, would never have attracted me, nor when I had become conscious of the wrongs of society as it now is, and the oppression of poor people, could I have ever believed in the possibility of a *partial* setting right of those wrongs. In other words, I could never have been such a fool as to believe in the happy and 'respectable' poor.

If, therefore, my ideal forced me to look for practical Socialism, what was it that forced me to conceive of an ideal? Now, here comes in what I said of my being (in this paper) a type of a certain group of mind.

Before the uprising of *modern* Socialism almost all intelligent people either were, or professed themselves to be, quite contented with the civilization of this century. Again, almost all of these really were thus contented, and saw nothing to do but to perfect the said civilization by getting rid of a few ridiculous survivals of the barbarous ages. To be short, this was the *Whig* frame of mind, natural to the modern prosperous middle-class men, who, in fact, as far as mechanical progress is concerned, have nothing to ask for, if only Socialism would leave them alone to enjoy their plentiful style.

But besides these contented ones there were others who were not really contented, but had a vague sentiment of repulsion to the triumph of civilization, but were coerced into silence by the measureless power of Whiggery. Lastly, there were a few who were in open rebellion against the said Whiggery – a few, say two, Carlyle and Ruskin. The latter, before my days of practical Socialism, was my master towards the ideal aforesaid,[6] and, looking backward, I cannot help saying, by the way, how deadly dull the world would have been twenty years ago but for Ruskin! It was through him that I learned to give form to my discontent, which I must say was not by any means vague.[7] Apart from the desire to produce beautiful things, the leading passion of my life has been and is hatred of modern civilization. What shall I say of it now, when the words are put into my mouth, my hope of its destruction – what shall I say of its supplanting by Socialism?

What shall I say concerning its mastery of and its waste of mechanical power, its commonwealth so poor, its enemies of the commonwealth so rich, its stupendous organization – for the misery of life! Its contempt of simple pleasures which everyone could enjoy but for its folly? Its eyeless vulgarity which has destroyed art, the one certain solace of labour? All this I felt then as now, but I did not know why it was so. The hope of the past times was gone, the struggles of mankind for many ages had produced nothing but this sordid, aimless, ugly confusion; the immediate future seemed to me likely to intensify all the present evils by sweeping away the last survivals of the days before the dull squalor of civilization had settled down in the world. This was a bad look-out indeed, and, if I may mention myself as a personality and not as a mere type, especially so to a man of my disposition, careless of metaphysics and religion, as well as of scientific analysis, but with a deep love of the earth and the life on it, and a passion for the history of the past of mankind. Think of it! Was it all to end in a counting-house on the top of a cinder-heap, with Podsnap's[8] drawing-room in the offing, and a Whig committee dealing out champagne to the rich and margarine to the poor in such convenient proportions as would make all men contented together, though the pleasure of the eyes was gone from the world, and the place of Homer was to be taken by Huxley? Yet, believe me, in my heart, when I really forced myself to look towards the future, that is what I saw in it, and, as far as I could tell, scarce anyone seemed to think it worth while to struggle against such a consummation of civilization. So there I was in for a fine pessimistic end of life, if it had not somehow dawned on me that amidst all this filth of civilization the seeds of a great change, what we others call Social-Revolution, were beginning to germinate. The whole face of things was changed to me by that discovery, and all I had to do then in order to become a Socialist was to hook myself on to the practical movement, which, as before said, I have tried to do as well as I could.

To sum up, then the study of history and the love and practice of art forced me into a hatred of civilization which, if things were to stop as they are, would turn history into inconsequent nonsense, and make art a collection of the curiosities of the past, which would have no serious relation to the life of the present.

But the consciousness of revolution stirring amidst our hateful modern society prevented me, luckier than many others of artistic perceptions, from crystallizing into a mere railer against 'progress' on the one hand, and on the other from wasting time and energy in any of the numerous schemes by which the quasi-artistic of the middle classes hope to make art grow when it has no longer any root, and thus I became a practical Socialist.

A last word or two. Perhaps some of our friends will say, what have we to do with these matters of history and art? We want by means of Social-Democracy to win a decent livelihood, we want in some sort to live, and that at once. Surely any one who professes to think that the question of art and cultivation must go before that of the knife and fork (and there are some who do propose that) does not understand what art means, or how that its roots must have a soil of a thriving and unanxious life. Yet it must be remembered that civilization has reduced the workman to such a skinny and pitiful existence, that he scarcely knows how to frame a desire for any life much better than that which he now endures perforce. It is the province of art to set the true ideal of a full and reasonable life before him, a life to which the perception of creation of beauty, the enjoyment of real pleasure that is, shall be felt to be as necessary to man as his daily bread, and that no man, and no set of men, can be deprived of this except by mere opposition, which should be resisted to the utmost.

12. *Dawn of a New Epoch* (1886)

The Collected Works of William Morris, ed. May Morris (24 vols., 1910–15), vol. XXIII, pp. 277–81

Perhaps some of my readers may think that the above title is not a correct one: it may be said, a new epoch is always dawning, change is always going on, and it goes on so gradually that we do not know when we are out of an old epoch and into a new one. There is truth in that, at least to this extent, that no age can see itself: we must stand some way off before the confused picture with its rugged surface can resolve itself into its due order, and seem to be something with a definite purpose carried through all its details. Nevertheless, when we look back on history we do distinguish periods in the lapse of time that are not merely arbitrary ones, we note the early growth of the ideas which are to form the new order of things, we note their development into the transitional period, and finally the new epoch is revealed to us bearing in its full development, unseen as yet, the seeds of the newer order still which shall transform it in its turn into something else.

Moreover, there are periods in which even those alive in them become more or less conscious of the change which is always going on; the old ideas which were once so exciting to men's imaginations, now cease to move them, though they may be accepted as dull and necessary platitudes: the material circumstances of man's life which were once only struggled with in detail, and only according to a kind of law made manifest in their working, are in such times conscious of change, and are only accepted under protest until some means can be found to alter them. The old and dying order, once silent and all-powerful, tries to express itself violently, and becomes at once noisy and weak. The nascent order once too weak to be conscious of need of expression, or capable of it if it were, becomes conscious now and finds a voice. The silent sap of the years is being laid aside for open assault; the men are gathering under arms in the trenches, and the forlorn hope is ready, no longer trifling with little solacements of the time of weary waiting, but looking forward to mere death or the joy of victory.

Now I think, and some who read this will agree with me, that we are now living in one of these times of conscious change; we not only are, but we feel also ourselves to be living between the old and the new; we are expecting something to happen, as the phrase goes: at such times it behoves us to understand what is the old which is dying, what is the new which is coming into existence? That is a question practically important to us all, since these periods of conscious change are also in one way or other, times of serious combat, and each of us, if he does not look to it and learn to understand what is going on, may find himself fighting on the wrong side, the side with which he really does not sympathize.

What is the combat we are now entering upon – who is it to be fought between? Absolutism and Democracy, perhaps some will answer. Not quite, I think; that contest was practically settled by the great French Revolution; it is only its embers which are burning now: or at least that is so in the countries which are not belated, like Russia, for instance. Democracy, or at least what used to be considered Democracy, is now triumphant; and though it is true that there are countries where freedom of speech is repressed besides Russia, as *e.g.*, Germany and Ireland,[9] that only happens when the rulers of the triumphant Democracy are beginning to be afraid of the new order of things, now becoming conscious of itself, and are being driven into reaction in consequence. No, it is not Absolutism and Democracy as the French Revolution understood those two words that are the enemies now: the issue is deeper than it was; the two foes are now Mastership and Fellowship. This is a far more serious quarrel than the old one, and involves a much completer revolution. The grounds of conflict are really quite different. Democracy said and says, men shall not be the masters of others because hereditary privileges have made a race or a family so, and they happen to belong to such race; they shall individually grow into being the masters of others by the development of certain qualities under a system of authority which *artificially* protects the wealth of every man, if he has acquired it in accordance with this artificial system, from the interference of every other, or from all others combined.

The new order of things says, on the contrary, why have masters at all? let us be *fellows* working in the harmony of association for the common good, that is, for the greatest happiness and completest development of every human being in the community.

This ideal and hope of a new society founded on industrial peace and forethought, bearing with it its own ethics, aiming at a new and higher life for all men, has received the general name of Socialism, and it is my firm belief that it is destined to supersede the old order of things founded on industrial war, and to be the next step in the progress of humanity.

Now, since I must explain further what are the aims of Socialism, the ideal of the new epoch, I find that I must begin by explaining to you what is the constitution of the old order which it is destined to supplant. If I can make that clear to you, I shall have also made clear to you the first aim of Socialism: for I have said that the present and decaying order of things, like those which have gone before it, has to be propped up by a system of artificial authority; when the artificial authority has been swept away, harmonious association will be felt by all men to be a necessity of their happy and undegraded existence on the earth, and Socialism will become the condition under which we shall all live, and it will develop naturally, and probably with no violent conflict, whatever detailed system may be necessary: I say the struggle will not be over these details, which will surely vary according to the difference of unchangeable natural surroundings, but over the question, shall it be mastership or fellowship?

Let us see then what is the condition of society under the last development of mastership, the commercial system, which has taken the place of the Feudal system.

Like all other systems of society, it is founded on the necessity of man conquering his subsistence from Nature by labour, and also, like most other systems that we know of, it presupposes the unequal distribution of labour among different classes of society, and the unequal distribution of the results of that labour: it does not differ in that respect from the system which it supplanted; it has only altered the method whereby that unequal distribution should be arranged. There are still rich people and poor people amongst us, as there were in the Middle Ages; nay, there is no doubt that, relatively at least to the sum of wealth existing, the rich are richer and the poor are poorer now than they were then. However that may be, in any case now as then there are people who have much work and little wealth living beside other people who have much wealth and little work. The richest are still the idlest, and those who work hardest and perform the most painful tasks are the worst rewarded for their labour.

To me, and I should hope to my readers, this seems grossly unfair; and I may remind you here that the world has always had a sense of its injustice. For century after century, while society has strenuously bolstered up this injustice forcibly and artificially, it has professed belief in philosophies, codes of ethics, and religions which have inculcated justice and fair dealing between men: nay, some of them have gone so far as to bid us bear one another's burdens, and have put before men the duty, and in the long run the pleasure, of the strong working for the weak, the wise for the foolish, the helpful for the helpless; and yet these precepts of morality have been set aside in practice as persistently as they have been preached in theory; and naturally so, since they attack the very basis of class society. I as a Socialist am bound to preach them to you once more, assuring you that they are no mere foolish dreams bidding us to do what we now must acknowledge to be impossible, but reasonable rules of action, good for our defence against the tyranny of Nature. Anyhow, honest men have the choice before them of either putting these theories in practice or rejecting them altogether. If they will but face that dilemma, I think we shall soon have a new world of it; yet I fear they will find it hard to do so: the theory is old, and we have got used to it and its form of words: the practice is new, and would involve responsibilities we have not yet thought much of.

Now the great difference between our present system and that of the feudal period is that, as far as the conditions of life are concerned, all distinction of classes is abolished except that between rich and poor: society is thus simplified; the arbitrary distinction is gone, the real one remains and is far more stringent than the arbitrary one was. Once all society was rude, there was little real difference between the gentleman and the non-gentleman, and you had to dress them differently from one another in order to distinguish them. But now a well-to-do man is a refined and cultivated being, enjoying to the full his share of the conquest over Nature which the modern world has achieved, while the poor man is rude and degraded, and has no share in the wealth conquered by modern science from Nature: he is certainly no better as to material condition than the serf of the Middle Ages, perhaps he is worse: to my mind he is at least worse than the savage living in a good climate.

I do not think that any thoughtful man seriously denies this: let us try to see what brings it about; let us see it as clearly as we all see that the hereditary privilege of the noble caste, and the consequent serf slavery of the workers of the Middle Ages, brought about the peculiar conditions of that period.

Society is now divided between two classes, those who monopolize all the means of the production of wealth save one; and those who possess nothing except that one, the Power of Labour. That power of labour is useless to its possessors and cannot be exercised without the help of the other means of production; but those who have nothing but labour-power – *i.e.*, who have no means of making others work for them, must work for themselves in order to live; and they must therefore apply to the owners of the means of fructifying labour – *i.e.*, the land, machinery, &c., for leave to work that they may live. The possessing class (as for short we will call them) are quite prepared to grant this leave, and indeed they must grant it if they are to use the labour-power of the non-possessing class for their own advantage, which is their special privilege. But that privilege enables them to *compel* the non-possessing class to sell them their labour-power on terms which ensure the continuance of their monopoly. These terms are at the outset very simple. The possessing class, or masters, allow the men just so much of the wealth produced by their labour as will give them such a livelihood as is considered necessary at the time, and will permit them to breed and rear children to a working age: that is the simple condition of the 'bargain' which obtains when the labour-power required is low in quality, what is called unskilled labour, and when the workers are too weak or ignorant to combine so as to threaten the masters with some form of rebellion. When skilled labour is wanted, and the labourer has consequently cost more to produce, and is rarer to be found, the price of the article is higher: as also when the commodity labour takes to thinking and remembers that after all it is also *men*, and as aforesaid holds out threats to the masters; in that case they for their part generally think it prudent to give way, when the competition of the market allows them to do so, and so the standard of livelihood for the workers rises.

But to speak plainly the greater part of the workers, in spite of strikes and Trades' Unions, do get little more than a bare subsistence wage, and when they grow sick or old they would die outright if it were not for the refuge afforded them by the workhouse, which is purposely made as prison-like and wretched as possible, in order to prevent the lower-paid workers from taking refuge in it before the time of their *industrial* death.

Now comes the question as to how the masters are able to force the men to sell their commodity labour-power so dirt-cheap without treating them as the ancients treated their slaves – *i.e.*, with the whip. Well, of course you understand that the master having paid his workmen what they can live upon, and having paid for the wear and tear of machinery and other expenses of that kind, has for his share whatever remains over and above, *the whole of which he gets from the exercise of the labour-power possessed by the worker*: he is anxious therefore to make the most of this privilege, and competes with his fellow-manufacturers to the utmost in the market: so that the distribution of wares is organized on a gambling basis, and as a consequence many more hands are needed when trade is brisk than when it is slack, or even in an ordinary condition: under the stimulus also of the lust for acquiring this surplus value of labour, the great machines of our epoch were invented and are yearly improved, and they act on labour in a threefold way: first they get rid of many hands; next they lower the quality of the labour required, so that skilled work is wanted less and less; thirdly, the improvement in them forces the workers to work harder while they are at work, as notably in the cotton-spinning industry. Also in most trades women and children are employed, to whom it is not even pretended that a subsistence wage is given. Owing to all these causes, the reserve army of labour necessary to our present system of manufactures for the gambling-market, the introduction of labour-saving machines (labour saved for the master, mind you, not the man), and the intensifying of the labour while it lasts, the employment of the auxiliary labour of women and children: owing to all this there are in ordinary years even, not merely in specially bad years like the current one, more workers than there is work for them to do. The workers therefore undersell one another in disposing of their one commodity, labour-power, and are *forced* to do so, or they would not be allowed to work, and therefore would have to starve or go to the prison called the workhouse. This is why the masters at the present day are able to dispense with the exercise of obvious violence which in bygone times they used towards their slaves.

This then is the first distinction between the two great classes of modern Society: the upper class possesses wealth, the lower lacks wealth; but there is another distinction to which I will now draw your attention: the class which lacks wealth is the class that produces it, the class that possesses it does not produce it, it consumes it only. If by any chance the so-called lower class were to perish or leave the community, production of wealth would come to a standstill, until the wealth-owners had learned how to produce, until they had descended from their position, and had taken the place of their former slaves. If, on the contrary, the wealth-owners were to disappear, production of wealth would at the worst be only hindered for a while, and probably would go on pretty much as it does now.

But you may say, though it is certain that some of the wealth-owners, as landlords, holders of funds, and the like, do nothing, yet there are many of them who work hard. Well, that is true, and perhaps nothing so clearly shows the extreme folly of the present system than this fact that there are so many able and industrious men employed by it, in working hard at – nothing: nothing or worse. They work, but they do not produce.

It is true that some useful occupations are in the hands of the privileged classes, physics, education, and the fine arts, *e.g.* The men who work at these occupations are certainly working usefully; and all that we can say against them is that they are sometimes paid too high in proportion to the pay of other useful persons, which high pay is given them in recognition of their being the parasites of the possessing classes. But even as to numbers these are not a very large part of the possessors of wealth, and, as to the wealth they hold, it is quite insignificant compared with that held by those who do nothing useful.

Of these last, some, as we all agree, do not pretend to do anything except amuse themselves, and probably these are the least harmful of the useless classes. Then there are others who follow occupations which would have no place in a reasonable condition of society, as, *e.g.*, lawyers, judges, jailers, and soldiers of the higher grades, and most Government officials. Finally comes the much greater group of those who are engaged in gambling or fighting for their individual shares of the tribute which their class compels the working-class to yield to it: these are the group that one calls broadly business men, the conductors of our commerce, if you please to call them so.

To extract a good proportion of this tribute, and to keep as much as possible of it when extracted for oneself, is the main business of life for these men, that is, for most well-to-do and rich people; it is called, quite inaccurately, 'money-making'; and those who are most successful in this occupation are, in spite of all hypocritical pretences to the contrary, the persons most respected by the public.

A word or two as to the tribute extracted from the workers as aforesaid. It is no trifle, but amounts to at least two-thirds of all that the worker produces; but you must understand that it is not all taken directly from the workman by his immediate employer, but by the employing class. Besides the tribute or profit of the direct employer, which is in all cases as much as he can get amidst his competition or war with other employers, the worker has also to pay taxes in various forms, and the greater part of the wealth so extorted is at the best merely wasted: and remember, whoever *seems* to pay the taxes, labour in the long run is the only real taxpayer. Then he has to pay house-rent, and very much heavier rent in proportion to his earnings than well-to-do people have. He has also to pay the commission of the middle-men who distribute the goods which he has made, in a way so wasteful that now all thinking people cry out against it, though they are quite helpless against it in our present society. Finally, he has often to pay an extra tax in the shape of a contribution to a benefit society or trades' union, which is really a tax on the precariousness of his employment caused by the gambling of his masters in the market. In short, besides the profit or the result of unpaid labour which he yields to his immediate master he has to give back a large part of his wages to the class of which his master is a part.

The privilege of the possessing class therefore consists in their living on this tribute, they themselves either not working or working unproductively – *i.e.*, living on the labour of others; not otherwise than as the master of ancient days lived on the labour of his slave, or as the baron lived on the labour of his serf. If the capital of the rich man consists of land, he is able to force a tenant to improve his land for him and pay him tribute in the form of rack-rent; and at the end of the transaction has his land again, generally improved, so that he can begin again and go on for ever, he and his heirs, doing nothing, a mere burden on the community for ever, while others are working for him. If he has houses on his land he has rent for them also, often receiving the value of the building many times over, and in the end house and land once more. Not seldom a piece of barren ground or swamp, worth nothing in itself, becomes a source of huge fortune to him from the development of a town or a district, and he pockets the results of the labour of thousands upon thousands of men, and calls it his property: or the earth beneath the surface is found to be rich in coal or minerals, and again he must be paid vast sums for allowing others to labour them into marketable wares, to which labour he contributes nothing.

Or again, if his capital consists of cash, he goes into the labour market and buys the labour-power of men, women, and children, and uses it for the production of wares which shall bring him in a profit, buying it of course at the lowest price that he can, availing himself of their necessities to keep their livelihood down to the lowest point which they will bear: which indeed he *must* do, or he himself will be overcome in the war with his fellow-capitalists. Neither in this case does he do any useful work, and he need not do any semblance of it, since he may buy the brain-power of managers at a somewhat higher rate than he buys the hand-power of the ordinary workman. But even when he does seem to be doing something, and receives the pompous title of 'organizer of labour,' he is not really organizing *labour*, but the battle with his immediate enemies, the other capitalists, who are in the same line of business with himself.

Furthermore, though it is true, as I have said, that the working-class are the only producers, yet only a part of them are allowed to produce usefully; for the men of the non-producing classes having often much more wealth than they can *use* are forced to *waste* it in mere luxuries and follies, that on the one hand harm themselves, and on the other withdraw a very large part of the workers from useful work, thereby compelling those who do produce usefully to work the harder and more grievously: in short, the essential accompaniment of the system is waste.

How could it be otherwise, since it is a system of war? I have mentioned incidentally that all the employers of labour are at war with each other, and you will probably see that, according to my account of the relations between the two great classes, they also are at war. Each can only gain at the other's loss: the employing class is forced to make the most of its privilege, the possession of the means for the exercise of labour, and whatever it gets to itself can only be got at the expense of the working-class; and that class in its turn can only raise its standard of livelihood at the expense of the possessing class; it is *forced* to yield as little tribute to it as it can help; there is therefore constant war always going on between these two classes, whether they are conscious of it or not.

To recapitulate: In our modern society there are two classes, a useful and a useless class; the useless class is called the upper, and useful the lower class. The useless or upper class, having the monopoly of all the means of the production of wealth save the power of labour, can and does compel the useful or lower class to work for its own disadvantage, and for the advantage of the upper class; nor will the latter allow the useful class to work on any other terms. This arrangement necessarily means an increasing contest, first of the classes one against the other, and next of the individuals of each class among themselves.

Most thinking people admit the truth of what I have just stated, but many of them believe that the system, though obviously unjust and wasteful, is necessary (though perhaps they cannot give their reasons for their belief), and so they can see nothing for it but palliating the worst evils of the system: but, since the various palliatives in fashion at one time or another have failed each in its turn, I call upon them, firstly, to consider whether the system itself might not be changed, and secondly, to look round and note the signs of approaching change.

Let us remember first that even savages live, though they have poor tools, no machinery, and no co-operation, in their work: but as soon as a man begins to use good tools and work with some kind of co-operation he becomes able to produce more than enough for his own bare necessaries. All industrial society is founded on that fact, even from the time when workmen were mere chattel slaves. What a strange society then is this of ours, wherein while one set of people cannot use their wealth, they have so much, but are obliged to waste it, another set are scarcely if at all better than those hapless savages who have neither tools nor co-operation! Surely if this cannot be set right, civilized mankind must write itself down a civilized fool.

Here is the workman now, thoroughly organized for production, working for production with complete co-operation, and through marvellous machines; surely if a slave in Aristotle's time could do more than keep himself alive, the present workman can do much more – as we all very well know that he can. Why therefore should he be otherwise than in a comfortable condition? Simply because of the class system, which with one hand plunders, and with the other wastes the wealth won by the workman's labour. If the workman had the full results of his labour he would in all cases be comfortably off, if he were working in an unwasteful way. But in order to work unwastefully he must work for his own livelihood, and not to enable another man to live without producing: if he has to sustain another man in idleness who is capable of working for himself, he is treated unfairly; and, believe me, he will only do so as long as he is compelled to submit by ignorance and brute force. Well, then, he has a right to claim the wealth produced by his labour, and in consequence to insist that all shall produce who are able to do so; but also undoubtedly his labour must be organized, or he will soon find himself relapsing into the condition of a savage. But in order that his labour may be organized properly he must have only one enemy to contend with – Nature to wit, who as it were eggs him on to the conflict against herself, and is grateful to him for overcoming her; a friend in the guise of an enemy. There must be no contention of man with man, but *association* instead; so only can labour be really organized, harmoniously organized. But harmony cannot co-exist with contention for individual gain: men must work for the common gain if the world is to be raised out of its present misery; therefore that claim of the workman (that is of every able man) must be subject to the fact that he is but a part of a harmonious whole: he is worthless without the co-operation of his fellows, who help him according to their capacities: he ought to feel, and will feel when he has his right senses, that he is working for his own interest when he is working for that of the community.

So working, his work must always be profitable, therefore no obstacle must be thrown in the way of his work: the means whereby his labour-power can be exercised must be free to him. The privilege of the proprietary class must come to an end. Remember that at present the custom is that a person so privileged is in the position of a man (with a policeman or so to help) guarding the gate of a field which will supply livelihood to whomsoever can work in it: crowds of people who don't want to die come to that gate; but there stands law and order, and says 'pay me five shillings before you go in'; and he or she that hasn't the five shillings has to stay outside, and die – or live in the workhouse. Well, that must be done away with; the field must be free to everybody that can use it. To throw aside even this transparent metaphor, those means of the fructification of labour, the land, machinery, capital, means of transit, &c., which are now monopolized by those who cannot use them, but who abuse them to force unpaid labour out of others, must be free to those who can use them; that is to say, the workers properly organized for production; but you must remember that this will wrong no man, because as all will do some service to the community – *i.e.*, as there will be no non-producing class, the organized workers will be the whole community, there will be no one left out.

Society will thus be recast, and labour will be free from all compulsion except the compulsion of Nature, which gives us nothing for nothing. It would be futile to attempt to give you details of the way in which this would be carried out; since the very essence of it is freedom and the abolition of all arbitrary or artificial authority; but I will ask you to understand one thing: you will no doubt want to know what is to become of private property under such a system, which at first sight would not seem to forbid the accumulation of wealth, and along with that accumulation the formation of new classes of rich and poor.

Now private property as at present understood implies the holding of wealth by an individual as against all others, whether the holder can use it or not: he may, and not seldom he does, accumulate capital, or the stored-up labour of past generations, and neither use it himself nor allow others to use it: he may, and often he does, engross the first necessity of labour, land, and neither use it himself or allow any one else to use it; and though it is clear that in each case he is injuring the community, the law is sternly on his side. In any case a rich man accumulates property, not for his own use, but in order that he may evade with impunity the law of Nature which bids man labour for his livelihood, and also that he may enable his children to do the same, that he and they may belong to the upper or useless class: it is not wealth that he accumulates, well-being, well-doing, bodily and mental; he soon comes to the end of his real needs in that respect, even when they are most exacting: it is power over others, what our forefathers called *riches*, that he collects; power (as we have seen) to force other people to live for his advantage poorer lives than they should live. Understand that that *must* be the result of the possession of *riches*.

Now this power to compel others to live poorly Socialism would abolish entirely, and in that sense would make an end of private property: nor would it need to make laws to prevent accumulation artificially when once people had found out that they could employ themselves, and that thereby every man could enjoy the results of his own labour: for Socialism bases the rights of the individual to possess wealth on his being able to use that wealth for his own personal needs, and, labour being properly organized, every person, male or female, not in nonage or otherwise incapacitated from working, would have full opportunity to produce wealth and thereby to satisfy his own personal needs; if those needs went in any direction beyond those of an average man, he would have to make personal sacrifices in order to satisfy them; he would have, for instance, to work longer hours, or to forego some luxury that he did not care for in order to obtain something which he very much desired: so doing he would at the worst injure no one: and you will clearly see that there is no other choice for him between so doing and his forcing some one else to forego *his* special desires; and this latter proceeding by the way, when it is done without the sanction of the most powerful part of society, is called *theft*; though on the big scale and duly sanctioned by artificial laws, it is, as we have seen, the ground-work of our present system. Once more, that system refuses permission to people to produce unless under artificial restrictions; under Socialism, every one who could produce would be free to produce, so that the price of an article would be just the cost of its production, and what we now call profit would no longer exist: thus, for instance, if a person wanted chairs, he would accumulate them till he had as many as he could use, and then he would stop, since he would not have been able to buy them for less than their cost of production and could not sell them for more: in other words, they would be nothing else than chairs; under the present system they may be means of compulsion and destruction as formidable as loaded rifles.

No one therefore would dispute with a man the possession of what he had acquired without injury to others, and what he could use without injuring them, and it would so remove temptations toward the abuse of possession, that probably no laws would be necessary to prevent it.

A few words now as to the differentiation of reward of labour, as I know my readers are sure to want an exposition of the Socialist views here as to those who direct labour or who have specially excellent faculties towards production. And, first, I will look on the super-excellent workman as an article presumably needed by the community; and then say that, as with other articles so with this, the community must pay the cost of his production: for instance, it will have to seek him out, to develop his special capacities, and satisfy any needs he may have (if any) beyond those of an average man, so long as the satisfaction of those needs is not hurtful to the community.

Furthermore, you cannot give him more than he can use, so he will not ask for more, and will not take it: it is true that his work may be more special than another's, but it is not more necessary if you have organized labour properly; the ploughman and the fisherman are as necessary to society as the scientist or the artist, I will not say more necessary: neither is the difficulty of producing the more special and excellent work at all proportionate to its speciality or excellence: the higher workman produces his work as easily perhaps as the lower does his work; if he does not do so, you must give him extra leisure, extra means for supplying the waste of power in him, but you can give him nothing more. The only reward that you *can* give the excellent workman is opportunity for developing and exercising his excellent capacity. I repeat, you *can* give him nothing more worth his having: all other rewards are either illusory or harmful. I must say in passing, that our present system of dealing with what is called a man of genius is utterly absurd: we cruelly starve him and repress his capacity when he is young; we foolishly pamper and flatter him and again repress his capacity when he is middle-aged or old: we get the least out of him, not the most.

These last words concern mere rarities in the way of workmen; but in this respect it is only a matter of degree; the point of the whole thing is this, that the director of labour is in his place because he is fit for it, not a mere accident; being fit for it, he does it easier than he would do other work, and needs no more compensation for the wear and tear of life than another man does, and not needing it will not claim it, since it would be no use to him; his special reward for his special labour is, I repeat, that he can do it easily, and so does not feel it a burden; nay, since he can do it *well* he likes doing it, since indeed the main pleasure of life is the exercise of energy in the development of our special capacities. Again, as regards the workmen who are under his direction, he needs no special dignity or authority; they know well enough that so long as he fulfils his function and really does direct them, if they do not heed him it will be at the cost of their labour being more irksome and harder. All this, in short, is what is meant by the organization of labour, which is, in other words, finding out what work such and such people are fittest for and leaving them free to do that: we won't take the trouble to do that now, with the result that people's best faculties are wasted, and that work is a heavy burden to them, which they naturally shirk as much as they can; it should be rather a pleasure to them: and I say straight out that, unless we find some means to make all work more or less pleasurable, we shall never escape from the great tyranny of the modern world.

Having mentioned the difference between the competitive and commercial ideas on the subject of the individual holding of wealth and the relative position of different groups of workmen, I will very briefly say something on what for want of a better word I must call the political position which we take up, or at least what we look forward to in the long run. The substitution of association for competition is the foundation of Socialism, and will run through all acts done under it, and this must act as between nations as well as between individuals: when profits can no more be made, there will be no necessity for holding together masses of men to draw together the greatest proportion of profit to their locality, or to the real or imaginary union of persons and corporations which is now called a nation. What we now call a nation is a body whose function it is to assert the special welfare of its incorporated members at the expense of all other similar bodies: the death of competition will deprive it of this function; since there will be no attack there need be no defence, and it seems to me that this function being taken away from the nation it can have no other, and therefore must cease to exist as a political entity. On this side of the movement opinion is growing steadily. It is clear that, quite apart from Socialism, the idea of local administration is pushing out that of centralized government: to take a remarkable case: in the French Revolution of 1793, the most advanced party was centralizing: in the latest French Revolution, that of the Commune of 1871, it was federalist. Or take Ireland: the success which is to-day attending the struggles of Ireland for independence is, I am quite sure, owing to the spread of this idea: it no longer seems a monstrous proposition to liberal-minded Englishmen that a country should administer its own affairs: the feeling that it is not only just, but also very convenient to all parties for it to do so, is extinguishing the prejudices fostered by centuries of oppressive and wasteful mastership. And I believe that Ireland will show that her claim for self-government is not made on behalf of national rivalry, but rather on behalf of genuine independence; the consideration, on the one hand, of the needs of her own population, and, on the other, goodwill towards that of other localities. Well, the spread of this idea will make our political work as Socialists the easier; men will at last come to see that the only way to avoid the tyranny and waste of bureaucracy is by the Federation of Independent Communities: their federation being for definite purposes: for furthering the organization of labour, by ascertaining the real demand for commodities, and so avoiding waste: for organizing the distribution of goods, the migration of persons – in short, the friendly intercommunication of people whose interests are common, although the circumstances of their natural surroundings made necessary differences of life and manners between them.

I have thus sketched something of the outline of Socialism, by showing that its aim is first to get rid of the monopoly of the means of fructifying labour, so that labour may be free to all, and its resulting wealth may not be engrossed by a few, and so cause the misery and degradation of the many: and, secondly, that it aims at organizing labour so that none of it may be wasted, using as a means thereto the free development of each man's capacity; and, thirdly, that it aims at getting rid of national rivalry, which in point of fact means a condition of perpetual war, sometimes of the money-bag, sometimes of the bullet, and substituting for this worn-out super-stition a system of free communities living in harmonious federation with each other, managing their own affairs by the free consent of their members; yet acknowledging some kind of centre whose function it would be to protect the principle whose practice the communities should carry out; till at last those principles would be recognized by every one always and intuitively, when the last vestiges of centralization would die out.

I am well aware that this complete Socialism, which is sometimes called Communism, cannot be realized all at once; society will be changed from its basis when we make the form of robbery called profit impossible by giving labour full and free access to the means of its fructification – *i.e.*, to raw material. The demand for this emancipation of labour is the basis on which all Socialists may unite. On more indefinite grounds they cannot meet other groups of politicians; they can only rejoice at seeing the ground cleared of controversies which are really dead, in order that the last controversy may be settled that we can at present foresee, and the question solved as to whether or no it is necessary, as some people think it is, that society should be composed of two groups of dishonest persons, slaves submitting to be slaves yet for ever trying to cheat their masters, and masters conscious of their having no support for their dishonesty of eating the common stock without adding to it save the mere organization of brute force, which they have to assert for ever in all details of life against the natural desire of man to be free.

It may be hoped that we of this generation may be able to prove that it is unnecessary; but it will, doubt it not, take many generations yet to prove that it is necessary for such degradation to last as long as humanity does; and when that is finally proved we shall at least have one hope left – that humanity will not last long.

George Bernard Shaw

(1856–1950)

Shaw attended his first Fabian Society meeting on 10 May 1884. His meeting the previous year with Henry George, the American apostle of the single tax on the value of land, had given direction and impetus to Shaw's crash course of promiscuous reading and self-education. Convinced of the importance of the economic basis to social reform, Shaw read Ricardo, Smith, Mill and Marx in swift succession and joined the Economic Circle, composed of professional economists and London University lecturers. In deciding to join these groups Shaw was aligning himself with 'a body of educated middle-class intelligentsia, my own class in fact' rather than opting for the proletarian emphasis dominant in the socialist activities espoused by Morris.

The choice of Fabianism had wider ideological implications. The *Fabian Essays* of 1889 from which this essay is taken, represented a coherent statement of a collectivist political programme. The group had, however, initially come together in 1884 as one of the various free-thinking ethical societies prolifer-ating in London, and, like others, drew its membership from many sources. Shaw's own development from the 'libertarianism' of such writers as Godwin, Shelley, Mill and Bradlaugh can be compared to the disillusion-ment of Annie Besant and Beatrice Potter (later Webb) with the evolu-tionary individualism of Herbert Spencer; but Hubert Bland's roots were in a paternalistic Tory reformism, Thomas Bolas's in the 'municipal socialism' of the Radical politician, Joseph Chamberlain. As the Society's reputation grew, it attracted followers of T. H. Green, and was sufficiently clearly identified by 1901 that a speech calling for 'national efficiency' delivered by the former Liberal leader, Lord Rosebery, could be caricatured as 'Sidney Webb and Water', after the Society's most prolific writer and leading organiser.

Such influence among established political leaders reflected the distinctive aim of the Fabians. Named after Quintus Fabius Maximus, known as *Fabius Cunctator*, the 'delayer', a Roman dictator and general whose studied evasion of pitched battles in the war with Hannibal enabled the Roman army to recoup its strength, the Society took 'permeation' as their watchword. Prepared to work at first within the Liberal and Conservative parties before lending their support to the emergent Labour party, the Fabians favoured lectures, research and publishing as the tools of revolution. Between May 1888 and April 1889 alone they delivered seven hundred lectures; all the pieces collected by Shaw as editor of the first group of *Fabian Essays* had earlier been presented as lectures.

This intensive educational programme reflected the Fabian conviction that systematic endeavour should prove capable of awakening man to the evolutionary process, and thus elicit his conscious and responsible co-operation in effecting the change as swiftly and smoothly as possible. Like other historicist thinkers represented in this book, such as Green, Marx and Engels, Fabians held a belief in inexorable historical progress alongside a recognition that the awakening of human consciousness to its implications played a vital part in creating a better society. Like Marx, its leading figures appealed to 'scientific' principles rather than to Green's theodicy, and, against Green's vision of a decentralised liberal community, looked to a Saint-Simonian form of state where the efficient 'administration of things' had replaced the 'government of men'. Like Green, however, they disavowed the idea of an apocalyptic upheaval, and a unique historical role for the working class. Fabianism's slogan, 'the inevitability of gradualness', represented a faith in the cumulative impact of innovations in social policy, rationally formulated by impartial administrative and scientific élites.

The Fabian emphasis upon the mechanics of change dictates the content and direction of Shaw's lecture. Shaw deploys the historical survey with which we have become familiar by the end of this volume as an evolutionary introduction to social democracy, which is presented as the natural, morally unambiguous successor to an increasingly chaotic and inequitable capitalism. It is characteristic that he strives to maintain a balance between the need to voice intolerable wrongs and to allay the fears of revolutionary fanaticism which adhered to the word 'socialism'. This is particularly apparent in the somewhat unstructured statement of the leading theme in his economics, that social injustice originates in the 'rent' or 'unearned increment' extracted through the monopolistic possession of property or talent (pp. 226ff) – a theory derived from Ricardo, Mill, Henry George and, in part, Marx. Against populist calls for a once-and-for-all appropriation on behalf of the community, he presents the picture of a gradual and inexorable transfer through municipal initiative 'that will satisfy the moral sense of the ordinary citizen as effectively as that of the skilled economist' (p. 235).

It could be argued that it was in his role as orator and preacher of Fabianism that Shaw gained the experience necessary to a dramatist intent upon achieving mass conversion among his theatrical audiences. Certainly the Preface to this collection of essays devotes twice as much space to describing the circumstances and composition of these essays as it does to the declaration of aims with which it concludes. Shaw stresses that the essays, revised but not recast, were prepared as lectures of an hour's duration, not as text-book teaching. In his own essay he makes a virtue of necessity by repeatedly drawing attention to the brevity with which he is forced to outline his position. In the name of brevity, aphoristic definitions are invented (p. 229) and grand sweeping panoramas of English history are conjured up without fear of pedantic qualification. As Shaw begins his survey of British history since the Middle Ages, a swift, rollicking rhythm is established, as short, clipped sentences of monotonously regular introductory construction, deal out hammer blows which deaden the listener's powers of analysis and contradiction. When Shaw introduces the villain of the historical drama, Capitalism, stylistic change reinforces his point. As auditors we become accustomed to the cumulative catalogues and settle back comfortably to listen to the stream of complimentary epithets heaped upon the heads of 'merchant princes' (p. 223), when we are suddenly shocked out of our complacency by the paradox of 'pillars of society' displaying 'murderous rapacity' and the chronologically dislocating simile which concludes the third paragraph. Furthermore in the ensuing paragraph, whilst sentences still begin with their subjects in a manner reminiscent of the second and third paragraphs, the remainder of the sentence becomes noticeably more sprawling and shapeless as feudal society collapses. The brief sentence 'then came chaos' inaugurates a train of imagery which enables Shaw to introduce 'modern political economy' as the gross, misshapen offspring of human reason labouring under self-delusion. Shaw's personal vision of a new creation, proffered three paragraphs from the end of the essay, may strike some as no less horrific. The sheer temerity of Shaw's technique at this concluding stage of his lecture cannot fail to make an impression. Having toyed with the idea of a free-thinker as future Dean of Westminster, Shaw impudently continues 'This, then, is the humdrum programme of the practical Social Democrat to-day'. This is perhaps the most striking example of the way in which Shaw repeatedly works within the essay. He employs the vocabulary of the patient, lucid expositor ('I will explain', 'in fact', 'really', 'It will be seen that'), suggesting a maturity of approach which distances him from 'young Socialists of catastrophic views' and that has been achieved through a wealth of study and experience, to clothe views of a highly idiosyncratic nature and to allow opinions to masquerade as well-proven facts. The modes of reason and logic are juxtaposed with the vocabulary of moral outrage. Carefully assembled dates and statistics jostle alongside phrases such as 'one in a million'. Glimpses of an almost Swiftian savagery of vision emerge as Shaw pictures men treated like 'human vermin'. Readers fresh from Shaw's plays and expecting dramatic polemic may at first be startled by the sheer accumulation of factual detail within the overall structure (some of the lists of government legislation have been cut for the sake of brevity), but for Shaw and his colleagues these were not mere statistics. Rather, each marked a significant stage in the long march to socialism with its rational management of human affairs based on scientific knowledge.

This fairly early essay already bears the seeds of Shaw's later thinking. His thoughts and conjectures as to the future relation between the skills of managers and artisans were to culminate in his passionate advocacy of an equal incomes policy. Admiration for sustained effort and effective organisation increasingly inclined him to distrust liberalism's association with *laissez-faire* and the protection of the individual to the detriment of the state's interests; and the pessimism of the concluding paragraph about the cultural potential of humanity as presently constituted, suggests an affinity with the mood of Carlyle's later writings. Both end by elevating heroes in a manner which has led their critics to accuse them of fascism, because conviction in the justice of their cause, together with despair at its progress, led them to embrace means which appeared to foreshorten the initial time-scale. Shaw's later disillusionment with Fabianism may have implied a rejection of its democratic character, so strongly insisted upon in this essay; yet the Fabian cast of mind in general, reminiscent as it was of an unsentimental Benthamite concern with efficiency and social engineering, had its dark side. Despite Shaw's denunciation of imperialism (p. 240), he and his fellow-Fabians took up during the Boer War (1899–1902) a distinctly ambiguous attitude towards the use of imperial arms in the furtherance of 'civilisation'. The social psychology of Graham Wallas's *Human Nature in Politics* (1907), which identified the non-rational motives for human action, reminds us not only of Shaw's pessimism noted above, but also of a wider European intellectual disillusionment with the power of Reason, which formed a breeding ground for élitist and authoritarian politics. And the Webbs' notorious *The Soviet Union: A New Civilisation* (1935) revealed them, not as sentimental fellow-travellers of a workers' state, but admirers of the rational planning and puritanical discipline of Stalin's Russia. It is hard to avoid concluding that Shaw's later disagreements with Fabianism had less to do with ideological differences, and rather more, as Sydney and Beatrice Webb drew the Society into respectability and mainstream parliamentary politics, with his own basic instincts to *épater les bourgeois* and outrage the world with uncomfortable paradoxes.

Beyond this role as a voice crying in the wilderness, there is a further factor linking Shaw to Carlyle and Ruskin. Like them, he divides the world, not into rich and poor, exploiter and exploited, but into workers and idlers. Nothing was to be served by transforming a poor worker into an idle rentier. His objection to maintaining the poor, even as an interim measure, on state subsidies (e.g. p. 232), derived not from the sense of patronage, nor from an implied evasion of more fundamental problems, but from the belief that idleness is demoralizing. Lenin's witticism about Shaw as 'a good man fallen amongst Fabians' is illuminating in suggesting that Shaw's opposition to capitalism was primarily ethical. Like that of Carlyle and Ruskin, his radicalism lay in the conviction that nothing could be effected without a change of heart.

13. 'The Transition to Social Democracy' (1889)
Fabian Essays in Socialism (1889), pp. 173–84, 187–201

When the British Association honoured me by an invitation to take part in its proceedings, I proposed to do so by reading a paper entitled '*Finishing* the Transition to Social Democracy'[1]. The word 'finishing' has been, on consideration, dropped. In modern use it has gathered a certain sudden and sinister sense which I desire carefully to dissociate from the process to be described. I suggested it in the first instance only to convey in the shortest way that we are in the middle of the transition instead of shrinking from the beginning of it; and that I propose to deal with the part of it that lies before us rather than that which we have already accomplished. Therefore, though I shall begin at the beginning, I shall make no apology for traversing centuries by leaps and bounds at the risk of sacrificing the dignity of history to the necessity for coming to the point as soon as possible.

Briefly, then, let us commence by glancing at the Middle Ages. There you find, theoretically, a much more orderly England than the England of to-day. Agriculture is organised on an intelligible and consistent system in the feudal manor or commune: handicraft is ordered by the gilds of the towns. Every man has his class, and every class its duties. Payments and privileges are fixed by law and custom, sanctioned by the moral sense of the community, and revised by the light of that moral sense whenever the operation of supply and demand disturbs their adjustment. Liberty and Equality are unheard of; but so is Free Competition. The law does not suffer a laborer's wife to wear a silver girdle: neither does it force her to work sixteen hours a day for the value of a modern shilling. Nobody entertains the idea that the individual has any right to trade as he pleases without reference to the rest. When the townsfolk, for instance, form a market, they quite understand that they have not taken that trouble in order to enable speculators to make money. If they catch a man buying goods solely in order to sell them a few hours later at a higher price, they treat that man as a rascal; and he never, as far as I have been able to ascertain, ventures to plead that it is socially beneficient, and indeed a pious duty, to buy in the cheapest market and sell in the dearest. If he did, they would probably burn him alive, not altogether inexcusably. As to Protection, it comes naturally to them.

This Social Order, relics of which are still to be found in all directions, did not collapse because it was unjust or absurd. It was burst by the growth of the social organism. Its machinery was too primitive, and its administration too naïve, too personal, too meddlesome to cope with anything more complex than a group of industrially independent communes, centralized very loosely, if at all, for purely political purposes. Industrial relations with other countries were beyond its comprehension. Its grasp of the obligations of interparochial morality was none of the surest: of international morality it had no notion. A Frenchman or a Scotchman was a natural enemy: a Muscovite was a foreign devil: the relationship of a negro to the human race was far more distant than that of a gorilla is now admitted to be. Thus, when the discovery of the New World began that economic revolution which changed every manufacturing town into a mere booth in the world's fair, and quite altered the immediate objects and views of producers, English adventurers took to the sea in a frame of mind peculiarly favourable to commercial success. They were unaffectedly pious, and had the force of character which is only possible to men who are founded on convictions. At the same time, they regarded piracy as a brave and patriotic pursuit, and the slave trade as a perfectly honest branch of commerce, adventurous enough to be consistent with the honor of a gentleman, and lucrative enough to make it well worth the risk. When they stole the cargo of a foreign ship, or made a heavy profit on a batch of slaves, they regarded their success as a direct proof of divine protection. The owners of accumulated wealth hastened to 'venture' their capital with these men. Persons of all richer degrees, from Queen Elizabeth downward, took shares in the voyages of the merchant adventurers. The returns justified their boldness; and the foundation of the industrial greatness and the industrial shame of the eighteenth and nineteenth centuries was laid: modern Capitalism thus arising in enterprises for which men are now, by civilized nations, hung or shot as human vermin. And it is curious to see still, in the commercial adventurers of our own time, the same incongruous combination of piety and rectitude with the most unscrupulous and revolting villainy. We all know the merchant princes whose enterprise, whose steady perseverance, whose high personal honor, blameless family relations, large charities, and liberal endowment of public institutions mark them out as very pillars of society; and who are nevertheless grinding their wealth out of the labor of woman and childen with such murderous rapacity that they have to hand over the poorest of their victims to sweaters whose sole special function is the evasion of the Factory Acts. They have, in fact, no more sense of social solidarity with the wage-workers than Drake had with the Spaniards or negroes.

With the rise of foreign trade and Capitalism, industry so far outgrew the control, not merely of the individual, but of the village, the gild, the municipality, and even the central government, that it seemed as if all attempt at regulation must be abandoned. Every law made for the better ordering of business either did not work at all, or worked only as a monopoly enforced by exasperating official meddling, directly injuring the general interest, and reacting disastrously on the particular interest it was intended to protect. The laws, too, had ceased to be even honestly intended, owing to the seizure of political power by the capitalist classes, which had been prodigiously enriched by the operation of economic laws which were not then understood. Matters reached a position in which legislation and regulation were so mischievous and corrupt, that anarchy became the ideal of all progressive thinkers and practical men. The intellectual revolt formally inaugurated by the Reformation was reinforced in the eighteenth century by the great industrial revolution which began with the utilization of steam and the invention of the spinning jenny. Then came chaos. The feudal system became an absurdity when its basis of communism with inequality of condition had changed into private property with free contract and competition rents. The gild system had no machinery for dealing with division of labour, the factory system, or international trade: it recognized in competitive individualism only something to be repressed as diabolical. But competitive individualism simply took possession of the gilds, and turned them into refectories for aldermen, and notable additions to the grievances and laughing stocks of posterity.

The desperate effort of the human intellect to unravel this tangle of industrial anarchy brought modern political economy into existence. It took shape in France, where the confusion was thrice confounded; and proved itself a more practical department of philosophy than the metaphysics of the schoolmen, the Utopian socialism of More, or the sociology of Hobbes. It could trace its ancestry to Aristotle; but just then the human intellect was rather tired of Aristotle, whose economics, besides, were those of slave holding republics. Political economy soon declared for industrial anarchy; for private property; for individual recklessness of everything except individual accumulation of riches; and for the abolition of all the functions of the State except those of putting down violent conduct and invasions of private property. It might have echoed Jack Cade's exclamation, 'But then we are in order, when we are most out of order'.[a]

Although this was what political economy decreed, it must not be inferred that the greater economists were any more advocates of mere licence than Prince Kropotkin, or Mr Herbert Spencer, or Mr Benjamin Tucker of Boston, or any other modern Anarchist.[2] They did not admit that the alternative to State regulation was anarchy: they held that Nature had provided an all-powerful automatic regulator in Competition: and that by its operation self-interest would evolve order out of chaos if only it were allowed its own way.

[a] Henry VI Pt. 2, IV, ii, 189–90.

13. 'The Transition to Social Democracy'

They loved to believe that a right and just social order was not an artificial and painfully maintained legal edifice, but a spontaneous outcome of the free play of the forces of Nature. They were reactionaries against feudal domineering and medieval meddling and ecclesiastical intolerance; and they were able to shew how all three had ended in disgraceful failure, corruption and self-stultification. Indignant at the spectacle of the peasant struggling against the denial of those rights of private property which his feudal lord had successfully usurped, they strenuously affirmed the right of private property for all. And whilst they were dazzled by the prodigious impulse given to production by the industrial revolution under competitive private enterprise, they were at the same time, for want of statistics, so optimistically ignorant of the condition of the masses, that we find David Hume, in 1766, writing to Turgot that 'no man is so industrious but he may add some hours more in the week to his labor; and scarce anyone is so poor but he can retrench something of his expense'.[3] No student ever gathers from a study of the individualist economists that the English proletariat was seething in horror and degradation whilst the riches of the proprietors were increasing by leaps and bounds.

The historical ignorance of the economists did not, however, disable them for the abstract work of scientific political economy. All their most cherished institutions and doctrines succumbed one by one to their analysis of the laws of production and exchange. With one law alone – the law of rent – they destroyed the whole series of assumptions upon which private property is based. The apriorist notion that among free competitors wealth must go to the industrious, and poverty be the just and natural punishment of the lazy and improvident, proved as illusory as the apparent flatness of the earth. Here was a vast mass of wealth called economic rent, increasing with the population, and consisting of the difference between the product of the national industry as it actually was and as it would have been if every acre of land in the country had been no more fertile or favorably situated than the very worst acre from which a bare living could be extracted: all quite incapable of being assigned to this or that individual or class as the return to his or its separate exertions: all purely social or common wealth, for the private appropriation of which no permanently valid and intellectually honest excuse could be made. Ricardo was quite as explicit and far more thorough on the subject than Mr Henry George.[4] He pointed out – I quote his own words – that 'the whole surplus produce of the soil, after deducting from it only such moderate profits as are sufficient to encourage accumulation, must finally rest with the landlord'.

It was only by adopting a preposterous theory of value that Ricardo was able to maintain that the laborer, selling himself for wages to the proprietor, would always command his cost of production, *i.e.*, his daily subsistence. Even that slender consolation vanished later on before the renewed investigation of value made by Jevons, who demonstrated that the value of a commodity is a function of the quantity available, and may fall to zero when the supply outruns the demand so far as to make the final increment of the supply useless. A fact which the unemployed had discovered, without the aid of the differential calculus, before Jevons was born. Private property, in fact, left no room for new comers. Malthus pointed this out, and urged that there should be no newcomers – that the population should remain stationary. But the population took exactly as much notice of this modest demand for stagnation as the incoming tide took of King Canute's ankles. Indeed the demand was the less reasonable since the power of production per head was increasing faster than the population (as it still is), the increase of poverty being produced simply by the increase and private appropriation of rent. After Ricardo had completed the individualist synthesis of production and exchange, a dialectical war broke out. Proudhon[5] had only to skim through a Ricardian treatise to understand just enough of it to be able to shew that political economy was a *reductio ad absurdum* of private property instead of a justification of it. Ferdinand Lassalle,[6] with Ricardo in one hand and Hegel in the other, turned all the heavy guns of the philosophers and economists on private property with such effect that no one dared to challenge his characteristic boasts of the irresistible equipment of Social Democracy in point of culture. Karl Marx, without even giving up the Ricardian value theory, seized on the blue books which contained the true history of the leaps and bounds of England's prosperity, and convicted private property of wholesale spoliation, murder and compulsory prostitution; of plague, pestilence, and famine; battle, murder, and sudden death. This was hardly what had been expected from an institution so highly spoken of. Many critics said that the attack was not fair: no one ventured to pretend that the charges were not true. The facts were not only admitted; they had been legislated upon. Social Democracy was working itself out practically as well as academically. Before I recite the steps of the transition, I will, as a matter of form, explain what Social Democracy is, though doubtless nearly all my hearers are already conversant with it.

What the achievement of Socialism involves economically, is the transfer of rent from the class which now appropriates it to the whole people. Rent being that part of the produce which is individually unearned, this is the only equitable method of disposing of it. There is no means of getting rid of economic rent. So long as the fertility of land varies from acre to acre, and the number of persons passing by a shop window per hour varies from street to street, with the result that two farmers or two shopkeepers of exactly equal intelligence and industry will reap unequal returns from their year's work, so long will it be equitable to take from the richer farmer or shopkeeper the excess over his fellow's gain which he owes to the bounty of Nature or the advantage of situation, and divide that excess or rent equally between the two. If the pair of farms or shops be left in the hands of a private landlord, he will take the excess, and, instead of dividing it between his two tenants, live on it himself idly at their expense. The economic object of Socialism is not, of course, to equalize farmers and shopkeepers in couples, but to carry out the principle over the whole community by collecting all rents and throwing them into the national treasury. As the private proprietor has no reason for clinging to his property except the legal power to take the rent and spend it on himself – this legal power being in fact what really constitutes him a proprietor – its abrogation would mean his expropriation. The socialization of rent would mean the socialization of the sources of production by the expropriation of the present private proprietors, and the transfer of their property to the entire nation. This transfer, then, is the subject matter of the transition to Socialism, which began some forty-five years ago, as far as any phase of social evolution can be said to begin at all.

It will be at once seen that the valid objections to Socialism consist wholly of practical difficulties. On the ground of abstract justice, Socialism is not only unobjectionable, but sacredly imperative. I am afraid that in the ordinary middle-class opinion Socialism is flagrantly dishonest, but could be established off-hand to-morrow with the help of a guillotine, if there were no police, and the people were wicked enough. In truth, it is as honest as it is inevitable; but all the mobs and guillotines in the world can no more establish it than police coercion can avert it. The first practical difficulty is raised by the idea of the entire people collectively owning land, capital, or anything else. Here is the rent arising out of the people's industry: here are the pockets of the private proprietors. The problem is to drop that rent, not into those private pockets, but into the people's pocket. Yes; but where is the people's pocket? Who is the people? what is the people? Tom we know, and Dick: also Harry; but solely and separately as individuals: as a trinity they have no existence. Who is their trustee, their guardian, their man of business, their manager, their secretary, even their stakeholder? The Socialist is stopped dead at the threshold of practical action by this difficulty until he bethinks himself of the State as the representative and trustee of the people. Now if you will just form a hasty picture of the governments which called themselves States in Ricardo's day, consisting of rich proprietors legislating either by divine right or by the exclusive suffrage of the poorer proprietors, and filling the executives with the creatures of their patronage and favoritism; if you look beneath their oratorical parliamentary discussions, conducted with all the splendor and decorum of an expensive sham fight; if you consider their class interests, their shameless corruption, and the waste and mismanagement which disgraced all their bungling attempts at practical business of any kind, you will understand why Ricardo, clearly as he saw the economic consequences of private appropriation of rent, never dreamt of State appropriation as a possible alternative. The Socialist of that time did not greatly care: he was only a benevolent utopian who planned model communities, and occasionally carried them out, with negatively instructive and positively disastrous results. When his successors learned economics from Ricardo, they saw the difficulty quite as plainly as Ricardo's vulgarizers, the Whig doctrinaires who accepted the incompetence and corruption of States as permanent inherent State qualities, like the acidity of lemons. Not that the Socialists were not doctrinaires too; but outside economics they were pupils of Hegel, whilst the Whigs were pupils of Bentham and Austin. Bentham's was not the school in which men learned to solve problems to which history alone could give the key, or to form conceptions which belonged to the evolutional order. Hegel, on the other hand, expressly taught the conception of the perfect State; and his pupils saw that nothing in the nature of things made it impossible, or even specially difficult, to make the existing State, if not absolutely perfect, at least practically trustworthy. They contemplated the insolent and inefficient government official of their day without rushing to the conclusion that the State uniform had a magic property of extinguishing all business capacity, integrity, and common civility in the wearer. When State officials obtained their posts by favoritism and patronage, efficiency on their part was an accident, and politeness a condescension. When they retained their posts without any effective responsibility to the public, they naturally defrauded the public by making their posts sinecures, and insulted the public when, by personal inquiry, it made itself troublesome. But every successfully conducted private business establishment in the kingdom was an example of the ease with which public ones could be reformed as soon as there was the effective will to find out the way. Make the passing of a sufficient examination an indispensable preliminary to entering the executive; make the executive responsible to the government and the government responsible to the people; and State departments will be provided with all the guarantees for integrity and efficiency that private money-hunting pretends to. Thus the old bugbear of State imbecility did not terrify the Socialist: it only made him a Democrat. But to call himself so simply, would have had the effect of classing him with the ordinary destructive politician who is a Democrat without ulterior views for the sake of formal Democracy – one whose notion of Radicalism is the pulling up of aristocratic institutions by the roots – who is, briefly, a sort of Universal Abolitionist. Consequently, we have the distinctive term Social Democrat, indicating the man or woman who desires through Democracy to gather the whole people into the State, so that the State may be trusted with the rent of the country, and finally with the land, the capital, and the organization of the national industry – with all the sources of production, in short, which are now abandoned to the cupidity of irresponsible private individuals.

The benefits of such a change as this are so obvious to all except the existing private proprietors and their parasites, that it is very necessary to insist on the impossibility of effecting it suddenly. The young Socialist is apt to be catastrophic in his views – to plan the revolutionary programme as an affair of twenty-four lively hours, with Individualism in full swing on Monday morning, a tidal wave of the insurgent proletariat on Monday afternoon, and Socialism in complete working order on Tuesday. A man who believes that such a happy despatch is possible, will naturally think it absurd and even inhuman to stick at bloodshed in bringing it about. He can prove that the continuance of the present system for a year costs more suffering than could be crammed into any Monday afternoon, however sanguinary. This is the phase of conviction in which are delivered those Socialist speeches which make what the newspapers call 'good copy', and which are the only ones they as yet report. Such speeches are encouraged by the hasty opposition they evoke from thoughtless persons, who begin by tacitly admitting that a sudden change is feasible, and go on to protest that it would be wicked. The experienced Social Democrat converts his too ardent follower by first admitting that if the change could be made catastrophically it would be well worth making, and then proceeding to point out that as it would involve a readjustment of productive industry to meet the demand created by an entirely new distribution of purchasing power, it would also involve, in the application of labor and industrial machinery, alterations which no afternoon's work could effect. You cannot convince any man that it is impossible to tear down a government in a day; but everybody is convinced already that you cannot convert first and third class carriages into second class; rookeries and palaces into comfortable dwellings; and jewellers and dressmakers into bakers and builders, by merely singing the 'Marseillaise'. No judicious person, however deeply persuaded that the work of the court dressmaker has no true social utility, would greatly care to quarter her idly on the genuinely productive workers pending the preparation of a place for her in their ranks. For though she is to all intents and purposes quartered on them at present, yet she at least escapes the demoralization of idleness. Until her new place is ready, it is better that her patrons should find dressmaking for her hands to do, than that Satan should find mischief. Demolishing a Bastille with seven prisoners in it is one thing: demolishing one with fourteen million prisoners is quite another. I need not enlarge on the point: the necessity for cautious and gradual change must be obvious to everyone here, and could be made obvious to everyone elsewhere if only the catastrophists were courageously and sensibly dealt with in discussion.

What then does a gradual transition to Social Democracy mean specifically? It means the gradual extension of the franchise; and the transfer of rent and interest to the State, not in one lump sum, but by instalments. Looked at in this way, it will at once be seen that we are already far on the road, and are being urged further by many politicians who do not dream that they are touched with Socialism – nay, who would earnestly repudiate the touch as a taint. Let us see how far we have gone. ... [Shaw proceeds to review the legal and social advances made since 1832 towards the establishment of a Social Democracy.]

... First, then, as to the consummation of Democracy. Since 1885 every man who pays four shillings a week rent can only be hindered from voting by anomalous conditions of registration which are likely to be swept away very shortly. This is all but manhood suffrage; and it will soon complete itself as adult suffrage. However, I may leave adult suffrage out of the question, because the outlawry of women, monstrous as it is, is not a question of class privilege, but of sex privilege. To complete the foundation of the democratic State, then, we need manhood suffrage, abolition of all poverty disqualifications, abolition of the House of Lords, public payment of candidature expenses, public payment of representatives, and annual elections. These changes are now inevitable, however unacceptable they may appear to those of us who are Conservatives. They have been for half a century the commonplaces of Radicalism. We have next to consider that the State is not merely an abstraction: it is a machine to do certain work; and if that work be increased and altered in its character, the machinery must be multiplied and altered too. Now, the extension of the franchise does increase and alter the work very considerably; but it has no direct effect on the machinery. At present the State machine has practically broken down under the strain of spreading democracy, the work being mainly local, and the machinery mainly central. Without efficient local machinery the replacing of private enterprise by State enterprise is out of the question; and we shall presently see that such replacement is one of the inevitable consequences of Democracy. A Democratic State cannot become a *Social*-Democratic State unless it has in every centre of population a local governing body as thoroughly democratic in its constitution as the central Parliament. This matter is also well in train. In 1888 a Government avowedly reactionary passed a Local Government Bill which effected a distinct advance towards the democratic municipality. It was furthermore a Bill with no single aspect of finality anywhere about it. Local Self-Government remains prominent within the sphere of practical politics. When it is achieved, the democratic State will have the machinery for Socialism.

And now, how is the raw material of Socialism – otherwise the Proletarian man – to be brought to the Democratic State machinery? Here again the path is easily found. Politicians who have no suspicion that they are Socialists, are advocating further instalments of Socialism with a recklessness of indirect results which scandalizes the conscious Social Democrat. The phenomenon of economic rent has assumed prodigious proportions in our great cities. The injustice of its private appropriation is glaring, flagrant, almost ridiculous. In the long suburban roads about London, where rows of exactly similar houses stretch for miles countrywards, the rent changes at every few thousand yards by exactly the amount saved or incurred annually in travelling to and from the householder's place of business. The seeker after lodgings, hesitating between Bloomsbury and Tottenham, finds every advantage of situation skimmed off by the landlord with scientific precision. As lease after lease falls in, houses, shops, good-wills of businesses which are the fruits of the labor of lifetimes, fall into the maw of the ground landlord. Confiscation of capital, spoliation of households, annihilation of incentive, everything that the most ignorant and credulous fundholder ever charged against the Socialist, rages openly in London, which begins to ask itself whether it exists and toils only for the typical duke and his celebrated jockey and his famous racehorse. Lord Hobhouse[7] and his unimpeachably respectable committee for the taxation of ground values are already in the field claiming the value of the site of London for London collectively; and their agitation receives additional momentum from every lease that falls in. Their case is unassailable; and the evil they attack is one that presses on the ratepaying and leaseholding classes as well as upon humbler sufferers. This economic pressure is reinforced formidably by political opinion in the workmens' associations. Here the moderate members are content to demand a progressive Income Tax, which is virtually Lord Hobhouse's proposal; and the extremists are all for Land Nationalization, which is again Lord Hobhouse's principle. The cry for such taxation cannot permanently be resisted. and it is very worthy of remark that there is a new note in the cry. Formerly taxes were proposed with a specific object – as to pay for a war, for education, or the like. Now the proposal is to tax the landlords in order to get some of *our* money back from them – take it from them first and find a use for it afterwards. Ever since Mr Henry George's book reached the English Radicals, there has been a growing disposition to impose a tax of twenty shillings in the pound on obviously unearned incomes: that is, to dump four hundred and fifty millions a year down on the Exchequer counter; and then retire with three cheers for the restoration of the land to the people.

The results of such a proceeding, if it actually came off, would considerably take its advocates aback. The streets would presently be filled with starving workers of all grades, domestic servants, coach builders, decorators, jewellers, lace-makers, fashionable professional men, and numberless others whose livelihood is at present gained by ministering to the wants of these and of the proprietary class. 'This', they would cry, 'is what your theories have brought us to! Back with the good old times, when we received our wages, which were at least better than nothing.' Evidently the Chancellor of the Exchequer would have three courses open to him. (1.) He could give the money back again to the landlords and capitalists with an apology. (2.) He could attempt to start State industries with it for the employment of the people. (3.) Or he could simply distribute it among the unemployed. The last is not to be thought of: anything is better than *panem et circenses.*[a] The second (starting State industries) would be

---

[a] Literally 'bread and circuses'. According to Juvenal (*Satire* X, 80), the only interests of the common people of Rome after their disenfranchisement.

far too vast an undertaking to get on foot soon enough to meet the urgent difficulty. The first (the return with an apology) would be a *reductio ad absurdum* of the whole affair – a confession that the private proprietor, for all his idleness and his voracity, is indeed performing an indispensable economic function – the function of capitalizing, however wastefully and viciously, the wealth which surpasses his necessarily limited power of immediate personal consumption. And here we have checkmate to mere Henry Georgism, or State appropriation of rent without Socialism. It is easy to shew that the State is entitled to the whole income of the Duke of Westminster,[8] and to argue therefrom that he should straightway be taxed twenty shillings in the pound. But in practical earnest the State has no right to take five farthings of capital from the Duke or anybody else until it is ready to invest them in productive enterprise. The consequences of withdrawing capital from private hands merely to lock it up unproductively in the treasury would be so swift and ruinous, that no statesmen, however fortified with the destructive resources of abstract economics, could persist in it. It will be found in the future as in the past that governments will raise money only because they want it for specific purposes, and not on *a priori* demonstrations that they have a right to it. But it must be added that when they *do* want it for a specific purpose, then, also in the future as in the past, they will raise it without the slightest regard to *a priori* demonstrations that they have no right to it.

Here then we have got to a dead lock. In spite of democrats and land nationalizers, rent cannot be touched unless some pressure from quite another quarter forces productive enterprise on the State. Such pressure is already forthcoming. The quick starvation of the unemployed, the slow starvation of the employed who have no relatively scarce special skill, the unbearable anxiety or dangerous recklessness of those who are employed to-day and unemployed to-morrow, the rise in urban rents, the screwing down of wages by pauper immigration and home multiplication, the hand-in-hand advance of education and discontent, are all working up to explosion point. It is useless to prove by statistics that most of the people are better off than before, true as that probably is, thanks to instalments of Social Democracy. Yet even that is questionable; for it is idle to claim authority for statistics of things that have never been recorded. Chaos has no statistics: it has only statisticians; and the ablest of them prefaces his remarks on the increased consumption of rice by the admission that 'no one can contemplate the present condition of the masses without desiring something like a revolution for the better'.

The masses themselves are being converted so rapidly to that view of the situation, that we have Pan-Anglican Synods, bewildered by a revival of Christianity, pleading that though Socialism is eminently Christian, yet 'the Church must act safely as well as sublimely'. During the agitation made by the unemployed last winter (1887–8), the Chief Commissioner of Police in London started at his own shadow, and mistook Mr John Burns for the French Revolution, to the great delight of that genial and courageous champion of his class.[9] The existence of the pressure is further shewn by the number and variety of safety valves proposed to relieve it – monetization of silver, import duties, 'leaseholds enfranchisement', extensión of joint stock capitalism masquerading as co-operation, and other irrelevancies. My own sudden promotion from the street corner to this platform is in its way a sign of the times. But whilst we are pointing the moral and adorning the tale according to our various opinions, an actual struggle is beginning between the unemployed who demand work and the local authorities appointed to deal with the poor. In the winter, the unemployed collect round red flags, and listen to speeches for want of anything else to do. They welcome Socialism, insurrectionism, currency craze – anything that passes the time and seems to express the fact that they are hungry. The local authorities, equally innocent of studied economic views, deny that there is any misery; send leaders of deputations to the Local Government Board, who promptly send them back to the guardians; try bullying; try stoneyards; try bludgeoning; and finally sit down helplessly and wish it were summer again or the unemployed at the bottom of the sea. Meanwhile the charity fund, which is much less elastic than the wages fund, overflows at the Mansion House[a] only to run dry at the permanent institutions. So unstable a state of things cannot last. The bludgeoning, and the shocking clamor for bloodshed from the anti-popular newspapers, will create a revulsion among the humane section of the middle class. The section which is blinded by class prejudice to all sense of social responsibility, dreads personal violence from the working class with a superstitious terror that defies enlightenment or control. Municipal employment must be offered at last. This cannot be done in one place alone: the rush from other parts of the country would swamp an isolated experiment. Wherever the pressure is, the relief must be given on the spot. And since public decency, as well as consideration for its higher officials, will prevent the County Council from instituting a working day of sixteen hours at a wage of a penny an hour or less, it will soon have on

[a] The Lord Mayor of London's official residence.

its hands not only the unemployed, but also the white slaves of the sweater, who will escape from their dens and appeal to the municipality for work the moment they become aware that municipal employment is better than private sweating. Nay, the sweater himself, a mere slave driver paid 'by the piece', will in many instances be as anxious as his victims to escape from his hideous trade. But the municipal organization of the industry of these people will require capital. Where is the municipality to get it? Raising the rates is out of the question: the ordinary tradesmen and householders are already rated and rented to the limit of endurance: further burdens would almost bring them into the street with a red flag. Dreadful dilemma! in which the County Council, between the devil and the deep sea, will hear Lord Hobhouse singing a song of deliverance, telling a golden tale of ground values to be municipalized by taxation. The land nationalizers will swell the chorus: the Radical progressive income taxers singing together, and the ratepaying tenants shouting for joy. The capital difficulty thus solved – for we need not seriously anticipate that the landlords will actually fight, as our President[10] once threatened – the question of acquiring land will arise. The nationalizers will declare for its annexation by the municipality without compensation; but that will be rejected as spoliation, worthy only of revolutionary Socialists. The no-compensation cry is indeed a piece of unpractical catastrophic insurrectionism; for whilst compensation would be unnecessary and absurd if every proprietor were expropriated simultaneously, and the proprietary system at once replaced by full blown Socialism, yet when it is necessary to proceed by degrees, the denial of compensation would have the effect of singling out individual proprietors for expropriation whilst the others remained unmolested, and depriving them of their private means long before there was suitable municipal employment ready for them. The land, as it is required, will therefore be honestly purchased; and the purchase money, or the interest thereon, will be procured, like the capital, by taxing rent. Of course this will be at bottom an act of expropriation just as much as the collection of Income Tax to-day is an act of expropriation. As such, it will be denounced by the landlords as merely a committing of the newest sin the oldest kind of way. In effect, they will be compelled at each purchase to buy out one of their body and present his land to the municipality, thereby distributing the loss fairly over their whole class, instead of placing it on one man who is no more responsible than the rest. But they will be compelled to do this in a manner that will satisfy the moral sense of the ordinary citizen as effectively as that of the skilled economist.

We now foresee our municipality equipped with land and capital for industrial purposes. At first they will naturally extend the industries they already carry on, road making, gas works, tramways, building, and the like. It is probable that they will for the most part regard their action as a mere device to meet a passing emergency. The Manchester School will urge its Protectionist theories as to the exemption of private enterprise from the competition of public enterprise, in one supreme effort to practise for the last time on popular ignorance of the science which it has consistently striven to debase and stultify. For a while the proprietary party will succeed in hampering and restricting municipal enterprise; in attaching the stigma of pauperism to its service; in keeping the lot of its laborers as nearly as possible down to private competition level in point of hard work and low wages. But its power will be broken by the disappearance of that general necessity for keeping down the rates which now hardens local authority to humane appeals. The luxury of being generous at someone else's expense will be irresistible. The ground landlord will be the municipal milch cow; and the ordinary ratepayers will feel the advantage of sleeping in peace, relieved at once from the fear of increased burdens and of having their windows broken and their premises looted by hungry mobs, nuclei of all the socialism and scoundrelism of the city. They will have just as much remorse in making the landlord pay as the landlord has had in making them pay – just as much and no more. And, as the municipality becomes more democratic, it will find landlordism losing power, not only relatively to democracy, but absolutely.

The ordinary ratepayer, however, will not remain unaffected for long. At the very outset of the new extension of municipal industries, the question of wage will arise. A minimum wage must be fixed; and though at first, to avoid an overwhelming rush of applicants for employment, it must be made too small to tempt any decently employed labourer to foresake his place and run to the municipality, still, it will not be the frankly infernal competition wage. It will be, like medieval wages, fixed with at least some reference to public opinion as to a becoming standard of comfort. Over and above this, the municipality will have to pay to its organizers, managers, and incidentally necessary skilled workers the full market price of their ability, minus only what the superior prestige and permanence of public employment may induce them to accept. But whilst these high salaries will make no more disturbance in the labor market than the establishment of a new joint stock company would, the minimum wage for laborers will affect that market perceptibly. The worst sort of sweaters will find that if they are to keep their 'hands', they must treat them at least as well as the municipality. The consequent advance in wage will swallow up the sweater's narrow margin of profit. Hence the sweater must raise the price per piece against the shops and wholesale houses for which he sweats. This again will diminish the profits of the wholesale dealers and shopkeepers, who will not be able to recover this loss by raising the price of their wares against the public, since, had any such step been possible, they would have taken it before. But fortunately for them, the market value of their ability as men of business is fixed by the same laws that govern the prices of commodities. Just as the sweater is worth his profit, so they are worth their profit; and just as the sweater will be able to exact from them his old remuneration in spite of the advance in wages, so they will be able to exact their old remuneration in spite of the advance in sweaters' terms. But from whom, : will be asked, if not from the public by raising the price of the war ? Evidently from the landlord upon whose land they are organizin; production. In other words, they will demand and obtain a reduction of rent. Thus the organizer of industry, the employer pure and simple, the *entrepreneur*, as he is often called in economic treatises nowadays, will not suffer. In the division of the product his share will remain constant; whilst the industrious wage worker's share will be increased, and the idle proprietor's share diminished. This will not adjust itself without friction and clamor; but such friction is constantly going on under the present system in the opposite direction, *i.e.*, by the raising of the proprietor's share at the expense of the worker's.

The contraction of landlords' incomes will necessarily diminish the revenue from taxation on such incomes. Let us suppose that the municipality, to maintain its revenue, puts on an additional penny in the pound. The effect will be to burn the landlord's candle at both ends – obviously not a process that can be continued to infinity. But long before taxation fails as a source of municipal capital, the municipalities will have begun to save capital out of the product of their own industries. In the market the competition of those industries with the private concerns will be irresistible. Unsaddled with a single idle person, and having, therefore, nothing to provide for after paying their employees except extension of capital, they will be able to offer wages that no business burdened with the unproductive consumption of an idle landlord or shareholder could afford, unless it yielded a heavy rent in consequence of some marked advantage of site. But even rents, when they are town rents, are at the mercy of a municipality in the long run. The masters of the streets and the traffic can nurse one site and neglect another. The rent of a shop depends on the number of persons passing its windows per hour. A skilfully timed series of experiments in paving, a new bridge, a tramway service, a barracks, or a small-pox hospital are only a few of the circumstances of which city rents are the creatures. The power of the municipality to control these circumstances is as obvious as the impotence of competing private individuals. Again, competing private individuals are compelled to sell their produce at a price equivalent to the full cost of production at the margin of cultivation. The municipality could compete against them by reducing prices to the average cost of production over the whole area of municipal cultivation. The more favorably situated private concerns could only meet this by ceasing to pay rent; the less favorably situated would succumb without remedy. It would be either stalemate or checkmate. Private property would either become barren, or it would yield to the actual cultivator of average ability no better an income than could be obtained more securely in municipal employment. To the mere proprietor it would yield nothing. Eventually the land and industry of the whole town would pass by the spontaneous action of economic forces into the hands of the municipality; and, so far, the problem of socializing industry would be solved.

Private property, by cheapening the laborer to the utmost in order to get the greater surplus out of him, lowers the margin of human cultivation, and so arises the 'rent of ability'. The most important form of that rent is the profit of industrial management. The gains of a great portrait painter or fashionable physician are much less significant, since these depend entirely on the existence of a very rich class of patrons subject to acute vanity and hypochondriasis. But the industrial organizer is independent of patrons; instead of merely attracting a larger share of the product of industry to himself, he increases the product by his management. The market price of such ability depends upon the relation of the supply to the demand: the more there is of it the cheaper it is: the less, the dearer. Any cause that increases the supply lowers the price. Now it is evident that since a manager must be a man of education and address, it is useless to look ordinarily to the laboring class for a supply of managerial skill. Not one laborer in a million succeeds in raising himself on the shoulders of his fellows by extraordinary gifts, or extraordinary luck, or both. The managers must be drawn from the classes which enjoy education and social culture; and their price, rapidly as it is falling with the spread of eduction and the consequent growth of the 'intellectual proletariat', is still high. It is true that a very able and highly trained manager can now be obtained for about £800 a year, provided his post does not compel him to spend two-thirds of his income on what is called 'keeping up his position', instead of on his own gratification. Still, when it is considered that laborers receive less than £50 a year, and that the demand for laborers is necessarily vast in proportion to the demand for able managers – nay, that there is an inverse ratio between them, since the manager's talent is valuable in proportion to the quantity of labor he can organize – it will be admitted that £800 a year represents an immense rent of ability. But if the education and culture which are a practically indispensable part of the equipment of competitors for such posts were enjoyed by millions instead of thousands, that rent would fall considerably. Now the tendency of private property is to keep the masses mere beasts of burden. The tendency of Social Democracy is to educate them – to make men of them. Social Democracy would not long be saddled with the rents of ability which have during the last century made our born captains of industry our masters and tyrants instead of our servants and leaders. It is even conceivable that rent of managerial ability might in course of time become negative, astonishing as that may seem to the many persons who are by this time so hopelessly confused amid existing anomalies, that the proposition that 'whosoever of you will be the chiefest, shall be servant of all' strikes them rather as a Utopian paradox than as the most obvious and inevitable of social arrangements. The fall in the rent of ability will, however, benefit not only the municipality, but also its remaining private competitors. Nevertheless, as the prestige of the municipality grows, and as men see more and more clearly that the future is to it, able organizers will take lower salaries for municipal than for private employment; whilst those who can beat even the municipality at organizing, or who, as professional men, can deal personally with the public without the intervention of industrial organization, will pay the rent of their places of business either directly to the municipality, or to the private landlord whose income the municipality will absorb by taxation. Finally, when rents of ability had reached their irreducible natural level, they could be dealt with by a progressive Income Tax in the very improbable case of their proving a serious social inconvenience.

It is not necessary to go further into the economic detail of the process of the extinction of private property. Much of that process as sketched here may be anticipated by sections of the proprietary class successively capitulating, as the net closes about their special interests, on such terms as they may be able to stand out for before their power is entirely broken.

We may also safely neglect for the moment the question of the development of the House of Commons into the central government which will be the organ for federating the municipalities, and nation-alizing inter-municipal rents by an adjustment of the municipal contributions to imperial taxation: in short, for discharging national as distinct from local business.[11] One can see that the Local Government Board of the future will be a tremendous affair; that foreign States will be deeply affected by the reaction of English progress; that international trade, always the really dominant factor in foreign policy, will have to be reconsidered from a new point of view when profit comes to be calculated in terms of net social welfare instead of individual pecuniary gain; that our present system of imperial aggression, in which, under pretext of exploration and colonization, the flag follows the filibuster and trade follows the flag, with the missionary bringing up the rear, must collapse when the control of our military forces passes from the capitalist class to the people; that the disappearance of a variety of classes with a variety of what are now ridiculously called 'public opinions' will be accompanied by the welding of society into one class with a public opinion of inconceiv-able weight; that this public opinion will make it for the first time possible effectively to control the population; that the economic independence of women, and the supplanting of the head of the household by the individual as the recognized unit of the State, will materially alter the status of children and the utility of the institution of the family; and that the inevitable reconstitution of the State Church on a democratic basis may, for example, open up the possi-bility of the election of an avowed Freethinker like Mr John Morley or Mr Bradlaugh[12] to the deanery of Westminster. All these things are mentioned only for the sake of a glimpse of the fertile fields of thought and action which await us when the settlement of our bread and butter question leaves us free to use and develop our higher faculties.

This, then, is the humdrum programme of the practical Social Democrat to-day. There is not one new item in it. All are applications of principles already admitted, and extensions of practices already in full activity. All have on them that stamp of the vestry which is so con-genial to the British mind. None of them compels the use of the words Socialism or Revolution: at no point do they involve guillotining, declaring the Rights of Man, swearing on the altar of the country, or anything else that is supposed to be essentially un-English. And they are all sure to come – landmarks on our course already visible to far-sighted politicians even of the party which dreads them.

13. 'The Transition to Social Democracy'

Let me, in conclusion, disavow all admiration for this inevitable, but sordid, slow, reluctant, cowardly path to justice. I venture to claim your respect for those enthusiasts who still refuse to believe that millions of their fellow creatures must be left to sweat and suffer in hopeless toil and degradation, whilst parliaments and vestries grudgingly muddle and grope towards paltry instalments of betterment. The right is so clear, the wrong so intolerable, the gospel so convincing, that it seems to them that it *must* be possible to enlist the whole body of workers – soldiers, policeman, and all – under the banner of brotherhood and equality; and at one great stroke to set Justice on her rightful throne. Unfortunately, such an army of light is no more to be gathered from the human product of nineteenth century civilization than grapes are to be gathered from thistles. But if we feel glad of that impossibility; if we feel relieved that the change is to be slow enough to avert personal risk to ourselves; if we feel anything less than acute disappointment and bitter humiliation at the discovery that there is yet between us and the promised land a wilderness in which many must perish miserably of want and despair: then I submit to you that your institutions have corrupted us to the most dastardly degree of selfishness. The Socialists need not be ashamed of beginning as they did by proposing militant organization of the working classes and general insurrection. The proposal proved impracticable; and it has now been abandoned – not without some outspoken regrets – by English Socialists. But it still remains as the only finally possible alternative to the Social Democratic programme which I have sketched to-day.

Notes

J. F. BRAY (1809–1897)

1 'The social system' acquired the status of a semi-technical phrase in Owenite literature, as in John Gray's work *The Social System* (1830). Eighteenth-century social theorists, modelling themselves on the natural sciences, had increasingly tended to use the word 'system' as part of their vocabulary, writers on economics, particularly, making analogies between Harvey's theories on the circulation of blood and the process whereby money and commodities circulated in society. We have been unable to identify the first use of the concept 'social system', but it is more than likely that it derived from Saint-Simon or his followers, whose writings abound with the word 'system' used in a variety of different contexts.

2 Bray uses as his example here *The Rights of Industry* (1831), esp. pp. 17–20, published by the Society for the Diffusion of Useful Knowledge. Founded by Henry Brougham, the utilitarian Whig politician, the Society played an active part in campaigning to instruct the working classes into the 'realities' of economic life and away from radical social and political demands. Its output was thus a leading target of working-class activists. Bray elsewhere attributed authorship of this anonymous work to Brougham himself, but subsequent research has identified the writer as Charles Knight (1791–1873), at various times author, editor and publisher for the mass reading public.

CARLYLE (1795–1881)

1 The Poor Law Amendment Act of 1834 compelled able-bodied paupers to earn their relief in the workhouse. For the principles of political economy upon which this Act was based, see the Introductory essay (p. 10). Carlyle provided the following evidence in a footnote: 'The Return of Paupers for England and Wales, at Ladyday 1842 is, Indoor 221,687, Outdoor 1,207,402, Total 1,429,089' *Official Report*.

2 James Morison (1770–1840) – not Morrison as Carlyle calls him – was an immensely successful 'Hygeist' as he himself termed it. His universal panacea, a quack product chiefly composed of gamboge, was dispensed from The British College of Health which he founded in 1828.

3 The radical programme published in 1838 and known as 'The People's Charter' demanded six reforms: Manhood suffrage, payment of MPs, abolition of the property qualifications for MPs, equal constituencies,

annual elections and the ballot. The last was quietly dropped and a
five-point charter appeared by 1848.

4 Introducing his Chronicle source at the beginning of bk II, Carlyle drew
repeated comparisons between Jocelin and Samuel Johnson's anecdotal
biographer, James Boswell. He found 'the thin watery gossip of our
Jocelin' 'much preferable to pedantry and inane grey haze' in providing
an accessible account of twelfth-century monastic life.

5 These two contentious tithes had been mentioned in bk II, ch. 5. The
holders of the town-fields were obliged to gather 4,000 eels annually
from Lakenheath marshes, but were unable to do so when the supply
dried up. The reap-silver was a sum paid by a tenant to his superior as
commutation of service at harvest time. The poor were forced to pay
with their belongings which aroused a protest from women (female
chartists who resented the intrusion in their homes). The frequent use of
such terms and Latin phrases suggest Carlyle's attempt to convey the
authenticity of his source.

6 Carlyle derives his mythical picture of Hell from Milton's *Paradise Lost*,
bk I, ll:229–37, where the burning lake on which Satan lies prostrate is
compared to the boiling interior of volcanic Mount Etna in Sicily.

7 The Opium War of 1840–2 had brought China into the news and this
was reported to be a favourite expression of the Emperor's.

8 Newton's mechanistic universe presupposed a Great Spirit or Mechanic
responsible for its creation. Carlyle was opposed to the teaching of
natural theology (William Paley's book of this name, published in 1802,
became the standard textbook of the rationalist school) and espoused the
romantic view that God was immanent in His creation.

9 The will of the Earl of Bridgewater (d. 1829), an eccentric clergyman, left
a bequest of £8,000 in trust to the president of the Royal Society for
work *On the Power, Wisdom and Goodness of God, as Manifested in the
Creation; Illustrating Such Work by All Reasonable Arguments*. Eight
works of natural theology were commissioned and became known as *The
Bridgewater Treatises*.

10 In bk III, ch.1. Carlyle had referred to 'that great Hat seven-feet high,
which now perambulates London Streets'. This advertisement, formed
of lath-and-plaster became for Carlyle a symbol of time misspent upon
sham and self-advertisement rather than upon improving the quality of
the product.

11 Carlyle alludes to William Pulteney Alison (1790–1859), *Observations on
the Management of the Poor in Scotland and its Effects on the Health of the
Great Towns* (1840). In Scotland only the disabled could claim relief and
Dr Alison's pamphlet was devoted to demonstrating how the poor of
Scotland endured even worse sufferings than their English equivalents.

12 An allusion to the Spartan habit of allowing weakly children to die by
exposure in pursuit of a society organised to form a powerful military
machine.

13 The Marquis of Chandos moved the amendment to the Great Reform
Bill of 1832 enfranchising all £50 leaseholders and tenants.

14 A phrase taken from bk III, ch.3, 'The Gospel of Dilettantism', to

summarise Carlyle's indictment of the aristocracy as an idle game-preserving class who neglected their real duty to govern.

15 A list of ancient taxes. *Scaccarium*-tallies were an attempt by the Treasury to raise a ransom for Richard I by stripping St Edmund's shrine of gold. 'Ship-moneys' were a tax levied in war-time on maritime towns, cities and counties of England to provide the King with ships. 'Coat-and-conduct moneys' were the sum raised to provide uniforms and to pay for the expense of conducting to the coast each man furnished by a hundred to serve in the King's army.

16 The Court of Chancery under the Lord High Chancellor dealt with matters of equity, providing redress for grievances which had no remedy in the courts of common law. The excessive technicalities and the number of lawyers its working required had made it a by-word for the law's delay. Charles Dickens's *Bleak House* (1852), in which he echoes Carlyle's descriptions, is the most famous indictment of a system ended in 1873 when Chancery's competitive functions were abolished.

17 An area of London notorious for rioting. The silk-weavers who congregated here had been hard hit by the introduction of machinery.

18 Bills designed to limit the working day and regulate for the safety of factory workers.

19 Sir James Graham's Factory Bill, then under discussion, incorporated a proposal for the compulsory education of factory children. Dissenting opposition to the clause which placed Anglican clergy at the head of the governing body of the necessary schools, forced the withdrawal of the education clauses before the Act was passed in 1843.

20 During the Napoleonic War period the government's largest annual revenue was £105,600,000 in 1814. Of this, £71,700,000 was devoted to war expenditure.

21 The name, reminiscent of the French Revolutionary calendar, used by the Chartists in campaigning for a month's general strike.

22 Jean Paul Friedrich Richter (1763–1825), a German humorist, was much admired by Carlyle who wrote two essays about him (1827, 1830). Carlyle adopted Richter's technique of appearing in fictional garb in his own work. This quotation is repeated from a passage of *Sievenkäs* quoted in Carlyle's second essay.

23 Cf. Matthew Arnold's poem upon the same theme, 'To Marguerite – Continued', in which he counter-claims 'A God, a God their severance ruled!'.

24 For Carlyle the gig (a two-wheeled carriage drawn by one horse) became the ludicrous symbol of respectability after reading the following alleged exchange in a murder trial of the time. 'Q. What sort of person was Mr Weare? A. Mr Weare was respectable. Q. What do you mean by respectability? A. He kept a gig.'

FRIEDRICH ENGELS (1820–95) and KARL MARX (1818–83)

1 Engels here encompasses the leading politicians of the day from 'left' to 'right'. Richard Cobden (1804–65), founder of the Anti-Corn-Law

Notes

League (1838) and leading radical; Lord John Russell (1792–1878), leader of the Whig opposition in 1844, later twice Prime Minister; Sir Robert Peel (1788–1850), Prime Minister 1840–6, architect of the new pragmatic Conservatism; Arthur Wellesley, 1st Duke of Wellington (1769–1852), victor of Waterloo, Prime Minister 1828–31, and symbol of old Toryism.

2 The references here are to the repeal in 1828 of the Test Act (1673), which discriminated against Nonconformity; the Catholic Relief Act of 1829 which entitled Catholics to sit in parliament; and the 1832 Reform Act.

3 The *Life of Jesus* by David Strauss (1808–74) was first published in weekly instalments by Hetherington Publishers during 1842, and later in the translation by George Eliot.

4 These four philanthropists were noted for their attempts to unite the landed interest and the Church with the working classes against middle-class liberalism. Antony Ashley Cooper, 7th Earl of Shaftesbury (1801–85); W. B. Ferrand (n.d.), truculent associate of Benjamin Disraeli's 'Young England' group; John Walter (1776–1847), proprietor of *The Times*; Richard Oastler (1789–1861), leader of the extra-parliamentary agitation in the 1830s for factory reform.

5 Pantheism – literally, God in everything. Pantheism denied the orthodox Christian belief in a separation between the 'material' and 'non-material' worlds which had been bridged uniquely by the birth of Christ when God was made man. Pantheism held, rather, that God is a permanent spiritual presence immanent in Nature and history. Engels does less than full justice here to the variety of pantheistic beliefs: some pantheists might argue that the writers whom Engels mentions in effect reduced the idea of God to an abstract principle of unity and change.

6 Friedrich Wilhelm Joseph von Schelling (1775–1854) was, in the early years of the century, the most famous and original of Kant's German disciples. He influenced Wordsworth and Coleridge, and his work was translated by Carlyle. In later years, the optimistic rationalism of his youth gave way to a more pessimistic theodicy, and in 1841 the Prussian authorities brought him to Berlin University to counter the influence of the radical Young Hegelians, of whom Strauss was one. For Hegel, see note 9 below.

7 Of the Young Hegelians, Ludwig Andreas von Feuerbach (1804–72) exercised the greatest influence over Marx and Engels. The reference is to 'Vorläufige Thesen zur Reformation der Philosophie' in *Anekdota zur neuesten deutsche Philosophie und Publicistik* (1843) produced by Bruno Bauer (1809–82), Arnold Ruge, Feuerbach and others.

8 Baruch Spinoza (1632–77), the Jewish Dutch philosopher, presented in his *Tractatus Theologico-Politicus* (1670) a materialist account characterised by metaphysical determinism. Although his system allowed no place for God outside the sphere of deterministic laws, he was an advocate of free speech, freedom of worship, and a republican form of government.

9 Georg Wilhelm Friedrich Hegel (1770–1831). Hegel's 'logical problem' was his attempt to establish that all the diverse products of the human mind, contending intellectual systems, beliefs, and modes of thought, were not in inherent conflict, but, looked at from a higher philosophical

standpoint, integral parts of a complex totality of true knowledge. History, he believed, revealed the tussle between these different systems as Mind, or Spirit, struggles to achieve its end of full self-consciousness.

10 Marx is here following the classical school's view that the central characteristic of an object which becomes a commodity is not the specific use to which it can be put, but that it can be exchanged for others in a ratio determined by the labour involved in creating it.

11 Marx here refers to the basic assumption of Political Economy, that individuals engage in different tasks under the division of labour out of personal self-interest. He was well aware that 'social contact' emerges in work, but points out that the basis of production is not mutual co-operation for common benefit, but using the labour and products of others as a means to one's own personal ends.

12 The reference here is unclear, but it appears to be an insertion made into the text by Engels after Marx's death, at the expense of a gentleman who had ventured to dispute Marx's use of quotation in the first German edition of *Capital*. The gentleman in question appears to be Mr Sedley Taylor (1834–1920), a musicologist of Trinity College, Cambridge (after whom a street in Cambridge was subsequently named), who, according to a later preface to *Capital* by Engels, 'dabbles in the mildest sort of co-operative affairs'.

13 Marx's paragraph, here, provides a model of socialist distribution akin to those of Bray or Proudhon.

14 Epicurus (341–270 BC), founded the hedonistic, materialist philosophy of epicureanism. He believed that, though the gods existed, they were wholly indifferent to human life, residing in the μετακόσμια (*Intermundia*), the realm between distinct material worlds.

15 Marx inserts here a long footnote accusing the classical writers of failing to distinguish between 'labour' and 'labour-power' in the determination of exchange value. The 'labour' involved in producing commodities is qualitatively as different as the objects themselves, he argues; hence, the basis of exchange must be an element common to all forms of labour. This he calls 'labour-power'. It was central to Marx's whole philosophy and economic analysis that, when the employer hired a man, he hired, not his specific creative capacities, but only 'labour-power' – his ability to turn the machines.

16 In the course of a long footnote, Marx takes the opportunity 'of shortly answering':

an objection taken by a German paper in America, to my work, 'Zur Kritik der Pol. Oekonomie, 1859.' In the estimation of that paper, my view that each special mode of production and the social relations corresponding to it, in short, that the economic structure of society, is the real basis on which the juridical and political superstructure is raised, and to which definite social forms of thought correspond; that the mode of production determines the character of the social, political, and intellectual life generally, all this is very true for our own times, in which material interests preponderate, but not for the middle ages, in which Catholicism, nor for Athens and Rome, where politics, reigned supreme. In the first place it strikes one as an odd thing for any one to suppose that these well-worn phrases about the middle ages and the ancient world are unknown to anyone else. This much, however, is clear, that the middle ages could not live on Catholicism, nor the ancient world on politics. On the contrary, it is the mode in which they gained a livelihood that explains why here politics, and there Catholicism, played the chief part. For the rest, it requires but a slight acquaintance with the history of the Roman republic, for example, to be aware that its secret history is the history of its landed property. On the other hand, Don Quixote long ago paid the penalty for wrongly imagining that knight errantry was compatible with all economic forms of society.

The passage referred to in the *Critique* is generally regarded as the basic formulation of Marx's materialist interpretation of history.

17 Physiocratic theory argued that 'rent' represented the 'surplus' over inputs of labour, capital and raw materials added directly by 'Nature' in the final agricultural output.

18 Marx references here *Observations on Certain Verbal Disputes in Political Economy* (1821), p. 16.

19 The reference here is to S. Bailey, *A Critical Dissertation on the Nature, Measure and Causes of Value* (1825), p. 165.

JOHN STUART MILL (1806–1873)

1 J. R. McCulloch (M'Culloch) (1789–1864), was for a brief time the first Professor of Political Economy at University College, London. A prolific writer with a penchant for statistical accumulation and analysis, his *Principles of Political Economy* (1825) was a leading text-book of economic orthodoxy before Mill's time.

2 For Smith and Malthus on these subjects, see our Introductory essay. The first edition of Malthus's *Essay on Population* had implied that absolute poverty was the inevitable lot of the labouring classes. Subsequent editions introduced the qualifications that 'subsistence level' was not an absolute standard, but in part a subjective valuation based upon cultural and historical experience, and also that education and 'moral improvement' could in the long run ease the population problem. Though undermining the thrust of Malthus's thesis, such qualifications were difficult to incorporate within the body of economic theorising.

3 In the first edition, the passage 'It may be a necessary stage ... trying and exciting occasion' had read:

> The northern and middle states of America are a specimen of this stage of civilization in very favourable circumstances; having, apparently, got rid of all social injustices and inequalities that affect persons of Caucasian race and of the male sex, while the proportion of population to capital and land is such as to ensure abundance to every able-bodied member of the community who does not forfeit it by misconduct. They have the six points of Chartism and they have no poverty: and all that these advantages do for them is that the life of the whole of one sex

is devoted to dollar-hunting, and of the other to breeding dollar-hunters.

4 In the 1848–9 editions of the *Principles*, the tenor of these following passages had been heavily critical of communist and socialist ideas. A major revision for the third (1852) edition substantially changed the whole tone, and set the pattern for subsequent versions. The original version comprised three sections, section 4 on Saint-Simon, section 5 on Fourier, and section 6 entitled 'The Institution of Property Requires, not Subversion, but Improvement'. In the revised version, material from section 6 was integrated into the discussion of the two socialist thinkers (e.g. p. 124, ll. 1–26, 'The Principle of Private Property ... Inseparable From It'), together with the general sentiment of the section heading (as in the last sentence, pp. 129–30). Eliminating the distinct section 6 had, however, the effect of toning down the distinction between 'improving' and 'subverting' property, and, together with other changes noted in notes 8 and 9 below, presented a more favourable picture of communism and socialism.

There is some dispute about the reasons for these changes. Many writers detect the hand of Harriet Taylor; and it does appear that, after her death in 1857, Mill took a less rosy view of socialist ideas. Certainly little enthusiasm is revealed in the 'Chapters on Socialism', posthumously published in the *Fortnightly Review*, 1879, and drawn from the manuscript of a book he was working upon at his death. Mill's Preface to the 1852 edition suggests, however, a slightly different explanation – that the 'year of revolution', 1848, had projected socialist ideas on to the European political stage and revealed them in a favourable light compared with the subsequent period of reaction. Mill's initially benign response would subsequently have been mitigated by their failure to develop in ways acceptable to him.

5 For Robert Owen (1771–1858) and his followers, see our headnote to J. F. Bray. Owen had been a successful self-made manufacturer and auto-didact, noted in the second decade of the century for his attempts to persuade fellow-industrialists into adopting the humanitarian factory management of his New Lanark mill. Failure to do so, and the ostracism he incurred by his denunciation of organised religion in 1817, turned his energies towards popular propaganda, the establishment of socialist communities and mass trade union organisation.

6 Louis Blanc (1811–82), the leading French advocate of a reformist democratic socialism. As a junior member of the republican Provisional Government in 1848, he inspired the establishment of state workshops to deal with unemployment. Étienne Cabet (1788–1856) founded in 1831 the radical journal *Populaire*. Under Owenite influence, he published the utopian work, *Voyage en Icarie* (1840) and, after the failure of the 1848 revolution, became engaged in establishing Icarian communities in America.

7 Count Henri-Claude de Saint Simon (1760–1825) and Charles Fourier (1772–1837) formed their ideas in France during the revolutionary wars and, as Mill implies, were generally regarded as the intellectual founders

of socialism. After their deaths, their schools of disciples became increasingly idiosyncratic and sectarian in nature, but their ideas also secured a wider audience. Marx and Engels were influenced by Saint-Simon's conception of a 'social science', his theory of history as a succession of social systems held together by dominant ideologies and ruling groups but eventually collapsing under the impact of socio-economic change, and his view that the future would see a society where the 'administration of things' had replaced the 'government of men'. Carlyle, by contrast, developed his thesis that the modern age required a new non-sectarian religious ethos, and new élites drawn from the intelligentsia and the 'captains of industry' to re-establish 'organic' social unity after the 'critical' phase of human history inaugurated by the French Revolution.

Mill's brief comments of Saint-Simon have been omitted from our text (p. 127), since his objections to the élitism and *étatisme* of the Saint-Simonian system are rehearsed elsewhere in our extracts. It is characteristic of Mill's approach that, in dealing with these two writers, he ignores the mystical, often surreal, elements in their thought. Fourier, for instance, believed in the astrological determination of natural phenomena, and the imminence of a predestined 'Age of Harmony' in which, among other things, urban and industrial life would disappear, and disagreeable lions and wolves would be miraculously transformed into benign anti-lions and anti-wolves.

8   In 1852, Mill significantly modified his discussion of communist principles. All editions of the *Principles* argue that communism might provide a stricter social discipline in relation to the overpopulation problem (p. 122), but after 1852 the nature of work in a communist society is treated differently. Whereas Mill originally argued that, because individuals will only see a small improvement to the public good from exerting themselves, 'the standard of industrial duty would therefore be fixed extremely low', he subsequently attacked the existing system of wage-labour as providing, by itself, insufficient 'incitement' to work (p. 121) and claimed that it 'must be considered for the present an undecided question' whether 'the energy of labour' would fall under communism (p. 122). Originally, too, the proposition that communism cannot provide a fair allocation of work (p. 122) was treated as decisive, but a new paragraph was added in 1852 beginning 'But these difficulties, though real, are not necessarily insuperable'. Mill always believed that communism's greatest problem was its threat to individuality and social diversity. Whereas our version states that 'It is yet to be ascertained . . .' whether the problem is insuperable (p. 126), the 1848 edition had asserted dogmatically:

> Lastly, the identity of education and pursuits would tend to impress on all the same unvarying type of character; to the destruction of that multiform development of human nature, those manifold unlikenesses, that diversity of tastes and talents, and variety of intellectual points of view, which not only form a great part of the interest of human life, but by bringing intellects into stimulating collision, and by presenting to each innumerable notions that he could not have

conceived of himself, are the mainspring of mental and moral progression.

We should note also that in the 1852 edition there occurs a passage (p. 123, l.28) which was subsequently withdrawn: 'The impossibility of foreseeing and prescribing the exact mode in which its difficulties should be dealt with, does not prove that it [communism] may not be the best and the ultimate form of human society'.

9 Building upon their general thesis that human character is the product of the environment, 'nurture' not 'nature' nor self-improvement, Owenites tended to attack the family as an instrument of socialisation into a corrupt society, and on both libertarian and egalitarian grounds to advocate a new relationship between the genders. The most significant Owenite work on these lines was that of the Irish landlord and Ricardian Socialist, William Thompson (1775–1833), *Appeal of one half the Human Race ...* (1825). Mill's own views on the issue were presented in *The Emancipation of Women* (1869).

10 Although Mill's account of Fourierism remained substantially the same in all editions, his general evaluation changed between 1849 and 1852. In the early versions, he emphasised the ethical instruction that socialist ideas purveyed, while being sceptical of their practicality. Thus, the following passage appeared in the first edition:

> Far, however, from looking upon the various classes of Socialists with any approach to disrespect, I honour the intentions of almost all who are publicly known in that character, the acquirements and talents of several, and I regard them, taken collectively, as one of the most valuable elements of human improvement now existing; both from the impulse they give to the reconsiderations and discussion of all the most important questions, and from the ideas they have contributed to many; ideas from which the most advanced supporters of the existing order of society have still much to learn.

But this view was accompanied by the dismissive comment on Fourierist schemes that 'nothing less would be requisite for the complete success of the scheme, than the organisation from a single centre, of the whole industry of a nation, or even of the world'. The later editions all modified this by calling for practical experiments in socialist organisation, which alone could test its viability (pp. 129–30).

11 Sections 5 and 6 here were continually revised through all editions. The former contained much information (omitted in our text) about experimental schemes of industrial partnership in France. Each new edition updated the information on their progress. Section 6 of the 1848–9 editions was entitled 'Probable Future Development of this Principle', where Mill clearly states 'To this principle, in whatever form embodied, it seems to me that futurity has to look for obtaining the benefits of co-operation, ...' in preference to Owenite and other communist co-operative ventures. In 1852 this was replaced by the section entitled 'Examples of the Association of Labourers among Themselves', which subsequently grew in size to overshadow the previous section on industrial partnership, and began:

Notes

The form of association, however, which if mankind continue to improve, must be expected in the end to predominate, is not that which can exist between a capitalist as chief, and workpeople without a voice in the management, but the association of the labourers themselves on terms of equality, collectively owning the capital with which they carry on their operations, and working under managers elected and removeable by themselves.

This change of emphasis was, of course, very much in line with Mill's modifications to his earlier discussions of socialist and communist theory.

JOHN RUSKIN (1819–1900)

1 *Unto This Last* derives its title and its 'revolutionary' ideas of an absolute justice alien to the conventions of the market place from Matthew 20:1–16. In this parable the owner of a vineyard hires a series of unemployed men, agreeing to pay a penny for a day's labour to the first comers and 'whatsoever is right' to subsequent hired hands. When those who had worked longest discovered that they were to be paid the same sum as those hired near the end of the day they complained and received this answer: 'Friend, I do thee no wrong: didst not thou agree with me for a penny? / Take that thine is, and go thy way: I will give unto this last even as unto thee'.

The many lengthy footnotes which Ruskin added between the essay's appearance in periodical and book form have been excised.

2 Ruskin's references, which give book, chapter and section, are to J. S. Mill, *Principles of Political Economy* (2 vols., 1848).

3 Ruskin objects to Mill's distinction between unproductive and productive labour as offering a false dichotomy because it ignores too many other determining factors.

4 Ruskin's note reads, 'Filigree; that is to say, generally, ornament dependent on complexity, not on art'.

5 Ruskin's example, taken from the second scene of the Introduction to Shakespeare's *Taming of the Shrew*, is chosen to illustrate his contention that the agreeableness of an object, taken as a means of quantifying its economic value, is determined both by the number and the kind of people who like it.

6 Ruskin's references are to D. Ricardo, *Principles of Political Economy and Taxation* (1817). Ruskin deliberately distorts Ricardo's argument, so that he may subject him to ridicule, by omitting the crucial phrase 'whatever might be the quantity of production ...' from the end of the second sentence of his quotation.

7 The name of a seventeenth-century Venetian church built as a thanks-offering for the cessation of the plague. (Cf. *Stones of Venice, Works* vol. x, p. 443.)

8 A note by Ruskin referred the reader to George Herbert, *The Church Porch*, stanza 28:

> Wealth is the conjurer's devil,
> Whom when he thinks he hath, the devil hath him.

Gold thou mayst safely touch; but if it stick
Unto thy hands, it woundeth to the quick.

9 *Habet* (he has it) was the shout that went up from the crowd when a gladiator had been fatally wounded. *Quo plurimum posset*: the original quotation runs, *quo plurimum populus Romanus posset* (wherein the Roman people have their power). Ruskin is alluding to the story told in Livy's *Annales* of the occasion in 362 BC when an abyss had opened in the forum. The soothsayers declared that the Roman republic could only be saved by throwing Rome's greatest treasure into the chasm. Instantly Mettius Curtius leaped in fully armed and on horseback, declaring that Rome possessed no greater treasure than its brave and honourable citizens.

10 Ruskin's derivation quietly ignores the classical tradition that Zeus of Nysa, the youthful Greek god of wine, took his name from Mt Nysa, where his father, Zeus, had entrusted him to the nymphs for safe upbringing.

11 The first line of Pope's couplet runs, 'Yet sure, of qualities deserving praise'. *Moral Essays*, Epistle iii, 'To Allen, Lord Bathurst: of the use of riches'.

12 The term used by R. Whately, Drummond Professor of Political Economy at Oxford (1829–31), in his *Lectures on Political Economy* (1831). He wished to abandon the name 'Political Science' because it had connotations of state or household management which he considered too broad for the narrow science of exchange value. Cf. Ruskin's assertion below, para. 84.

13 This convoluted passage is based upon Zechariah 5:1–11, in which Zechariah is shown a vision of God's avenging justice uncovering and punishing deceit.

14 II Samuel 23:15–17. 'And David longed, and said, Oh that one would give me a drink of the water of the well of Bethlehem, which is by the gate! / And the three mighty men brake through the host of the Philistines, and drew water out of the well of Bethlehem, that was by the gate, and took it, and brought it to David: nevertheless he would not drink thereof, but poured it out unto the Lord. / And he said, Be it far from me, O Lord, that I should do this; is not this the blood of the men that went in jeopardy of their lives? therefore he would not drink it. These things did these three mighty men.'

15 Zechariah 11:4–17, speaks of God's anger with the idle and self-seeking shepherds of his people. The parabolic narrative, clearly referring to a particular episode of Jewish history, makes it difficult to interpret the source and therefore to follow Ruskin's implication here.

16 *caput mortuum*: an alchemical term describing the residue from chemicals when all their volatile matter had escaped. Ruskin's attachment to Platonic idealism made him interested in the way that the principles behind the false science of alchemy could be seen to be related to more enduring truths. (See *Works*, vol. XXIII, p. 161; vol. XXVII, p. 283.)

17 Prince Rupert's drops are large blobs of molten glass which, when dropped into cold water, congeal to form toughened globules. These

globules, popularised by the seventeenth century Cavalier and amateur scientist, Prince Rupert of the Rhine, collapse into granules, not into sharp fragments, under sufficient force.

18 In a manner reminiscent of the comparative biblical criticism of this period, Ruskin draws upon a variety of mythologies to illustrate what he perceives as a universal truth. His restless, associative mind, however, is not content to pursue one line of argument at a time, but is attracted by the possible ramifications of each succeeding image. These allusions have the common purpose of supporting his thesis that true profit can only be gauged by the effective use to which it is put. Profit seen merely as acquisition or accumulation of goods for their own sake binds men to an endless treadmill of work from which no final satisfaction can ever be obtained. Ruskin starts by interpreting the classical legend of Ixion, whose greed first led him to murder his father-in-law rather than hand over the promised bridal gifts. Conversely the wedding guests, intent on securing the promised dowry, could also be seen as lured by their own greed into the fiery pit Ixion had prepared for them. This way of seeing the story reminds Ruskin of an analogous passage in Bunyan's *Pilgrim's Progress* where wayfarers are invited by Demas to see a silver mine in 'the Hill called *Lucre*', 'but going too near the brink of the pit, the ground being deceitful under them, broke, and they were slain'. Ruskin then returns to succeeding events in Ixion's life. Forgiven by Jupiter for the wrong he had done his father-in-law, Ixion had still learnt neither to curb his insatiable desire, nor to do as he would be done by. He rewarded Jupiter's pity by attempting to seduce the god's wife, Juno. Ixion thus becomes a type of folly as well as of vice.

Blinded by his lust Ixion embraces Nephele, a cloud shaped by Jupiter to resemble Juno. Real satisfaction of his desire is therefore denied him and the product or 'profit' of this union is merely the reproduction of lust embodied in the Centaurs, half man and half horse, who in turn lose their domain when lust drives them to attempt to carry off the women of the neighbouring kingdom. This story affords Ruskin the chance of providing two biblical allusions to confirm the moral tenor of the tale. Hosea 12:1 depicts the tribe of Ephraim as a type of falsehood and violence, whilst Proverbs 23:5 refers to the deceptive allure of wealth. The monstrous Centaurs then remind Ruskin of Dante's Geryon (*Inferno* xvii, l. 7) also formed with a man's head and an animal's body. Geryon is found dwelling amidst financial defrauders and usurers and carries the poet, in his vision, down to the eighth circle of hell, where those who had practised malicious fraud from a combination of financial and sexual motives have their abode. This combination of human cunning and animal lust returns Ruskin to Ixion's tale and his final punishment of being bound by Jupiter to a perpetually turning wheel in Hades. The image of a fixed wheel whose revelations achieve no progress brings Ruskin back to his starting place, namely the distinction between productive and unproductive capital, though not without a side-glance at further applications of the image of the wheel.

19 Mill assumes a pre-existing capital necessary to pay the wages of current

production. In turn future wages are produced out of the profit on current production, allowing the market demand to influence the allocation of the wages fund on successful goods. In Ruskin's view, Mill's theory erects a morally dangerous distinction between goods, wages, labour and product, obscuring the organic nature of the process which involves the consumer in the moral choices.

20 In essay II: 'The Veins of Wealth', paras. 40–1.

21 An allusion to the *Cornhill Magazine*'s reluctance to accept further essays.

22 For Ruskin's answer to the question of relative rates of pay for artisans and for artists or scientists see *Fors Clavigera* (*Works*, xxviii, 645), where he states that the intellectual labourer should ask no more than any other workman.

23 Cf. Anglican catechism where the catechumen defines his duty to his neighbour in terms of doing his duty 'in that state of life unto which it shall please God to call me'.

24 Ruskin's etymological speculation here as elsewhere in the essay is philologically suspect. His examples are chosen to prove that at all times commerce has been a constant state of flux by relating verbs of trade to those of motion. Thus, πωλέω (I sell): πέλω (I have become); πρᾶσις (a sale): περάω (to pass across); *venire* (to come): *vendre* (to sell); venal: *venio* (I come).

25 'How great blessing lies in asphodel' (i.e. in the common things of life). Hesiod, *Works and Days*, 41.

26 See Introductory essay p. 24 for Ruskin's comment on the plain style he had aimed at here, though he also remarked that he could still detect traces 'of my old bad trick of putting my words in braces, like game, neck to neck, and leaving the reader to untie them'.

MATTHEW ARNOLD (1822–88)

1 James Macdonell, a journalist, had used this phrase in the *Daily Telegraph*, 8 September 1866, when attacking Arnold for comparing his fellow countrymen unfavourably with the French and Germans. This epithet presumably stuck, since we find G. M. Hopkins writing to Robert Bridges in 1883, 'I do not like your calling Matthew Arnold Mr. Kidglove Cocksure'. *Letters of Gerard Manley Hopkins*, ed. C. C. Abbot (rev. ed 1956), i. 172.

2 Heinrich Friedrich Karl, Baron vom Stein (1751–1831), a Prussian diplomat and minister of state, was the inspiration behind a number of reforms such as the abolition of serfdom in Prussia (1810), and the abolition of distinctions in land tenure. The unsettled political situation in Europe at that period resulted in Stein being forced to flee his country before putting his ideas into effect. Arnold proceeds, in the remainder of this letter, to telescope into a single act the work initiated by Stein but not completed until 1850.

3 The first number of 'My Countrymen' had been published in the *Cornhill Magazine* in February 1866. The title referred to Fitzjames Stephen's critical article 'Mr. Matthew Arnold and His Countrymen', *Saturday*

Review, 3 December 1864, which attacked Arnold's views on the state of England as voiced in 'The Functions of Criticism at the Present Time'. In May 1868 Arnold thought of publishing his writings on social and political questions in a single volume, but in the event *Culture and Anarchy* appeared separately in 1869. Arnold then resumed the Arminius letters in the *Pall Mall Gazette* between 1869 and 1870. When he gathered the Arminius letters into the volume *Friendship's Garland* in 1871, 'My Countrymen' was bound at the end despite its date of composition.

4 The Liberal MP John Bright spoke of Stein's reforms at a banquet in Dublin on 30 October 1866. A letter to *The Times* on 3 November, attempted to dismiss the Prussian reforms as no more than the tithe commutation effected in Britain a quarter of a century before, and a *Times* leader (2 November) denounced Bright for his alleged 'levelling tendencies'.

5 Originally Arnold had used 'Philistine' to denote the average Englishman, a John Bull figure. The link between Philistinism and the middle classes had been forged in 'My Countrymen' (see above n. 3).

6 *The Times*, 6 November 1866.

7 On 17 July 1866, the Marquis of Clanricarde, a major Irish landowner, alluding to the Common's Bill on Irish land tenure, claimed that it laid out a system of confiscation comparable to that envisaged by a Wolfe Tone or a French army of invasion.

8 A Prussian edict of 1749.

9 The Home Secretary, Sir George Cornewall Lewis, wished to include a question about 'religious profession' in the census. Edward Baines, a prominent Dissenting MP, objected on the grounds that the government was attempting to intrude upon a matter of conscience. The government yielded to the strength of Nonconformist feeling upon the subject. Arnold's own frequently voiced distaste for what he saw as the divisive parochialism of Dissent surfaces here in his choice of name and sects. The Particular Baptists were strict Calvinists and therefore exclusive in the practice of their faith, whilst the Muggletonians, founded in 1651 by the visionary tailor Ludowicke Muggleton and his cousin, were the dwindling remnants of a sect which had only ever attracted a small band of followers. The fictional character, Bottles, built up by Arnold in a series of references throughout *Friendship's Garland*, is an extreme product of Arnold's prejudice against the Liberal creed as practised by self-made, middle-class radicals. The practically orientated education this bottle manufacturer received at a dissenting academy is derided as being a mere disguise for lack of classical learning, yet his efforts to improve his son's chances by sending him to public school are condemned as a snobbish desire to acquire a gentlemanly manner. Furthermore, Bottles, it is suggested here, thinks nothing of betraying his own class and conscience by transferring his allegiance from Dissent to the Established Church.

10 The eighth section of Bagehot's *The English Constitution*, published in the *Fortnightly Review* 6 (Dec. 1866), 807–26, was entitled 'Its supposed Checks and Balances'.

11 The radical Bright had suggested an educational test as qualification for

enfranchisement in the parliamentary debate over the Elective Franchise Bill on 30 May 1866.

12 In 'Shooting Niagara and After?', *Macmillan's Magazine* 16 (Aug. 1867), 328, Carlyle had written 'The English Nobleman has still left in him something considerable of chivalry and magnanimity'. In the ensuing paragraphs Arnold argues that aristocratic characteristics such as resistance to ideas of any sort and *hauteur* make the aristocracy the least useful section of the community to look to for the defence of reason against the forces of anarchy.

13 Robert Lowe (1811–92) the leading figure of the 'Adullamites', a group of Liberal MPs who defeated Gladstone's attempt to introduce a moderate franchise reform bill.

14 An organisation agitating for franchise reform, whose planned meeting in Hyde Park, when prohibited, resulted in the riots which had spurred Arnold to write *Culture and Anarchy*.

15 This paragraph employs the distinction developed in ch. 4 'Hebraism and Hellenism', where the Hebrew is defined as one who cannot rest till he has 'at last got out of the law a network of prescriptions to enwrap his whole life', whilst the 'uppermost idea with Hellenism is to see things as they really are'.

16 A Bill presented to Parliament in 1866 which proposed that when a man died intestate his widow and younger children should receive a fixed share rather than the entire property passing to his nearest male heir. Arnold objected to this measure because it seemed so paltry. He wished instead to see a positive re-evaluation of society in the face of which feudal habits and class divisions would quietly fade away as incompatible with truth and reason.

17 A paraphrase of a *Times* leader of 7 July 1868.

18 Frederic Bastiat (1801–50), French economist and supporter of free trade who was famed for the distinction he developed between 'usefulness' and 'value'. He had also produced a study of the English Corn Law repeal movement.

19 *Porro Unum est Necessarium*, taken from the Vulgate rendering of Luke 10: 41–2, is the title of ch. 5 of *Culture and Anarchy*. In this Arnold deplores the Hebraising habit of clinging to a limited concept of absolute revealed truth in contradistinction to the Hellenising habit of allowing intelligence free play in response to contemporary needs.

20 A reference to *The Times*, 10 July 1868 in which an article on pauperism quoted the statistics for 1 January 1868.

21 Again Arnold paraphrases rather than giving an accurate transcription of arguments appearing in *The Times* of 11 December 1867 and 29 January 1868. These entries claim that dispensing charity to alleviate suffering will prevent the work force moving to places where jobs are to be found.

22 Robert Buchanan (1841–1901), poet and essayist, had reviewed Arnold's work unfavourably. The prose passage Arnold quotes is from Buchanan's *David Gray, and Other Essays, Chiefly on Poetry* (1868). The ensuing line of poetry forms the epigraph to this book.

Notes

THOMAS HILL GREEN (1836–82)

1 The Ground Game Act (1880), commonly termed the 'Hares and Rabbits' Act, established the rights of tenant farmers to game on their property and to claim compensation for damage to it arising out of the hunting needs of landlords.

2 The Compensation for Disturbance Bill, to which Green here refers, was defeated in the House of Lords in 1880. It sought to recompense Irish tenants, compelled to leave their holdings by the current economic depression, for improvements made to their property. In 1882 the Irish Land Act so significantly increased tenant rights that the system came to be called one of 'dual ownership' in the land. 'Rack-rent', in legal parlance, is a rent equivalent to, or just short of, the annual value of a property. Rack-renting was the system under which landlords raised rents as tenants undertook investments in their holdings, and hence appropriated from the farmer any profits thereby earned. The Agricultural Holdings Act (1875) embodied the principle of compensation for improvements to property.

3 Green refers here to the laws of primogeniture and entail, effectively abolished in 1925. By limiting inheritance to the eldest child, and constraining his right to free disposal of his inheritance, they were held to restrict the allocation of land according to market criteria and hence prevent its most productive use.

4 The Licensing Act of 1872 superseded most earlier legislation on the sale of alcohol, tightening up the allocation and withdrawal of licenses, hours of opening, and the law on adulteration. Green supported the leading temperance pressure group, the United Kingdom Alliance, whose pet proposal for 'local option' would have permitted ratepayers completely to ban the sale of alcohol in their area.

5 Green's panoramic review in this paragraph does little justice to the details of individual legislation nor the complexity of issues involved. His references appear to be to: the Municipal Corporations Act (1835), which substantially increased the electorate for local urban government and increased financial liability; the Commission on charities which, in the 1830s, undertook a systematic investigation of the uses to which trustees of charitable endowments were putting their funds (a system regularised in 1853 with the creation of the Charity Commissioners); and various pieces of Church legislation in the 1830s. Among them were the Irish Church Temporalities Act (1833); the Established Church Act (1836), which reformed cathedral chapters and limited the earnings of the higher clergy; and the Pluralities Act (1838), which regulated the conditions under which clergy could hold more than one benefice.

6 W. E. Gladstone (1818–96), an adherent of orthodox Political Economy, was Chancellor of the Exchequer in 1852–5, 1859–66, 1873–4, 1880–2. The essence of 'Gladstonian finance' was the curtailment of public expenditure, repayment of the National Debt to reduce government dependence on short-term loans, and the reduction of both income tax and duties on

commodities. Due to the substantial growth of national income in the 1850s and 1860s, a large part of this programme was achieved. The 'taxes on knowledge' were newspaper stamp duties and taxes on paper. The former were abolished in 1855, the latter in 1861. Their removal led to the advent of the 'penny press'.

7   Anthony John Mundella (1825–97), a wealthy manufacturer, radical and MP for Sheffield (1868–97), was a noted campaigner for the extension of education, trade union rights, and factory legislation. Later a Liberal minister, he had been a major inspiration for the Factory Act of 1875, to which Green refers.

8   William Edward Forster (1818–86). As minister responsible for education between 1868 and 1874, he had pushed through the Elementary Eduction Act (1870) against strong opposition. This empowered the election, in areas where voluntary schools could not meet educational needs, of school boards entitled to draw on rates to support an alternative school system. The measure entailed transferring to the Boards the right to decide on three controversial questions: whether education should be compulsory; the charging of school fees; and the religious content of the curriculum. Most subsequent legislation was concerned with making statutory provisions on these questions.

WILLIAM MORRIS (1834–96)

1   Morris read *Capital* in its French translation. Despite his alleged difficulties with it he made frequent reference to the historical chapters in his lectures and his copy needed rebinding in 1884.

2   Morris had presumably read J. S. Mill's posthumously published 'Chapters on Socialism', *Fortnightly Review*, 25 (1879), 215–37, 373–82, 513–30. Fourier's opposition to the commercial exploitation of labour, individual property and parasitism would have found favour with Morris as would his search for a system which would provide the possibility of obtaining pleasure in labour.

3   Ernest Belfort Bax (1854–1926), musician, music critic, journalist, socialist, philosopher, historian and barrister. Bax had visited Germany in 1875 as a music student. Whilst there he became interested in German history and philosophy and later (1880–2) became the German correspondent for London's *Standard*. He was also to influence and befriend the young Shaw. In 1893 Morris and Bax collaborated to produce *Socialism: its growth and outcome*.

4   Henry Mayers Hyndman (1842–1921) was from a wealthy aristocratic background. He was inspired by the Paris Commune (1871) to write the first socialist manifesto in English since the collapse of Owenism: *England for All* (1881). Hyndman's socialism was Marxist in complexion, though his contact with Marx was limited by Marx's annoyance at Hyndman's reluctance to acknowledge his debt and by Engels' antipathy. Hyndman's origins and personality prevented him from achieving any identity with the workers whose cause he pleaded or lasting co-operation with his social and intellectual peers in the movement. Shaw wrote of

him that he 'seemed to have been born in a frock coat and top hat. In old age he looked like God in Blake's illustrations to Job'. (*Ruskin's Politics*, p. 20).

5 Andreas Scheu (n.d.) was a Viennese furniture maker. As a member of the Democratic Federation he worked to build a Scottish socialist movement.

6 Morris had read *Past and Present* whilst an undergraduate at Oxford.

7 Morris's admiration for Ruskin was a continuous factor in his socialism. Ruskin's stress on the importance of providing men with creative labour and his view of art as the expression of men's pleasure in their labour found sympathy with Morris. In February 1892 Morris had written his own Preface to 'On the Nature of Gothic' from Ruskin's *Stones of Venice* (1851–3) and issued it as one of the Kelmscott Press's first publications.

8 A character in Dickens's *Our Mutual Friend* (1865), whose income was derived parasitically from inheritance, marriage and 'Marine Insurance' and whose world was blinkered both geographically and morally by his chauvinistic pride and refusal to admit the existence of disagreeable factors in life. Podsnappery became a byword for middle-class complacency.

9 Morris later appended the note, 'And the brick and mortar country, London, it seems (Feb. 1888)'. Morris had written to the *Pall Mall Gazette* proposing a Law and Liberty League to defend the right to free speech, and, on 13 November 1887, took an active part in the Bloody Sunday events around Trafalgar Square. The Metropolitan Police Commissioner, Sir Charles Warren, had imposed a ban on all public meetings in Trafalgar Square. John Burns (1858–1943), an executive member of the Democratic Federation, and the radical MP, R. B. Cunninghame Graham (1852–1936), led an assault on the police cordon. Burns and Cunninghame Graham were both imprisoned for six weeks for their part in the proceedings and Morris was at the gates of Pentonville prison to greet them on their release.

GEORGE BERNARD SHAW (1856–1950)

1 Shaw notes that the essay was first presented on 7 September 1888 to the Economics Section of the British Association for the Advancement of Science in Bath. The 'British ASS' was founded in 1831, covering all sciences except medicine, and meeting annually in different cities throughout Great Britain, and later the Commonwealth.

2 Prince Kropotkin, Peter Alexeivich (1842–1921) was a Russian geographer and revolutionary anarchist. He was arrested in Russia in 1874, and, escaping two years later, fled to western Europe. He visited London in 1881–2, and settled there in 1886. Kropotkin believed that there was a historical tendency towards a system of 'mutual aid', a concept derived from Proudhon (see below), which would render the state superfluous. Herbert Spencer (1820–1903) was a radical individualist, whose sociological theories were derived from evolutionary biology and supported a *laissez-faire* view of the state (e.g. *The Man Versus the State* (1884)).

Benjamin Tucker (1854–1939) was an American follower of Proudhon, editor of *Liberty*, a journal to which Shaw contributed, and author of such works as *State Socialism and Anarchism* (1888).

3 Anne-Robert-Jacques Turgot (1827–81) was a leading figure of the French Enlightenment, a Deist, historical economist, and minister of finance under Louis XVI. In office, he attempted to effect some of the physiocratic policies, but was removed by the King succumbing to pressure from the landowning classes. David Hume (1711–76), the Scottish sceptic, empiricist philosopher and historian, was a friend of, among others, Adam Smith. His *Political Discourses* (1752) contained some of the earliest arguments against mercantilism.

4 For Henry George and Jevons (below), see Introductory Essay, pp. 12, 14.

5 Pierre-Joseph Proudhon (1809–65), the first socialist intellectual of genuinely working-class origins. He coined the word 'anarchism', and also the famous aphorism 'property is theft' in his *What is Property?* (1840). His philosophy of 'mutualism' – voluntaristic co-operation among workers for mutual self-help – was influential well into the twentieth century, as was his pet project for credit unions, financial collectives offering cheap or free credit to farmers and labourers for economic improvements.

6 Ferdinand Lassalle (1825–64) was the most prominent mid-century German socialist. A consummate showman and belligerent propagandist, in 1862 he used the deadlock between Bismarck and German Liberalism to assert an autonomous role for the labour movement, but his initiative was cut short by his death in a duel in 1864. To Lassalle are attributed the phrases 'iron laws' and 'nightwatchman state' in the context of liberal economic and political theory. Although he was a self-proclaimed adherent of Marx, Marx in fact opposed him, partly because Lassalle's belief that universal suffrage would hasten the creation of national state socialism in Germany entailed a major distortion of Marx's views.

7 Sir Arthur, 1st Baron Hobhouse (1819–1904). A judge of strong liberal persuasions, he had been a member of the Royal Commission in the late 1860s on the operation of land legislation. In the 1880s, he was active in a number of areas of reform politics in London, and in 1888 became one of the first aldermen of the new London County Council.

8 The Duke of Westminster was reputedly the largest landowner in Britain. His large holdings in London made him a prime target for urban improvers like Shaw.

9 For John Burns' part in the Bloody Sunday affair of 1886, see Morris note 10. Shaw, who had been present at the demonstration, spoke out against a further march, and, when accused by Cunninghame Graham of having been the first to run away, remarked that this flattered him with showing more good sense than he had in fact manifested.

10 Shaw's footnote reads 'Lord Bramwell, President of the Economics Section of the British Association in 1888'.

11 Shaw had little time for the contemporary parliamentary system, and

came to favour a bicameral legislature consisting of Political and Social houses. This, he maintained, would keep governments better informed of public opinion, while freeing decision-making from the ignorance of the multitude. An advocate of strong local-government powers, Shaw wrote *The Commonsense of Municipal Trading* (1904) partly on the basis of his own unremitting hard work as an unpaid elected vestryman for St Pancras (1897–1904).

12 John Morley (1838–1923), radical intellectual and Secretary of State for Ireland in 1886. Charles Bradlaugh (1833–91), editor of the *National Reformer*, refused to give his oath of allegiance on the Bible when elected to the House of Commons in 1880, and precipitated a constitutional crisis which lasted until 1886.

Select booklist

PRIMARY SOURCES

In the cases of our more voluminous authors it seems helpful to provide an indication of annotated editions of their works, together with useful selections.

Arnold, M. *Culture and Anarchy* ed. J. Dover Wilson (1935).
    The Complete Prose Works of Matthew Arnold ed. R. H. Super (10 vols., Ann Arbor, Mich., 1960–74), vols. V, IX.
Bray, J. *Labour's Wrongs and Labour's Remedy* (Leeds, 1839, reprinted 1931).
Carlyle, T. *Past and Present* ed. R. Altick (Boston, Mass. 1965).
    A Carlyle Reader ed. G. B. Tennyson (Cambridge, 1984).
    Thomas Carlyle: Selected Writings ed. A. Shelston (1971).
    The Works of Thomas Carlyle: Centenary Edition, ed. H. D. Traill (30 vols., 1896–9).
Engels, F. *Engels: Selected Writings* ed. W. O. Henderson (1967) (*see also* under Marx).
Green, T. H. *Thomas Hill Green: The Works*, ed. R. L. Nettleship (3 vols., 1885–8).
Marx, K. *Marx on Economics* ed. R. Freedman (1962).
Marx, K. and F. Engels *Marx and Engels: Collected Works* (Moscow, 1975–).
    Marx and Engels: Selected Works (1968).
Mill, J. S. *Collected Works of John Stuart Mill*, vols. II, III, ed. J. M. Robson (Toronto and London, 1963–).
    Essays on Politics and Culture, ed. G. Himmelfarb (New York, 1962).
    Mill's Essays on Literature and Society, ed. J. B. Schneewind (New York, 1965).
    Principles of Political Economy, ed. D. Winch (1970), bks IV, V.
Morris, W. *The Collected Works of William Morris*, ed. May Morris (24 vols., 1910–15) vol. XXIII.
    William Morris: Selected Writings and Designs ed. A. Briggs (1962).
    William Morris: Artist, Writer and Socialist (2 vols., 1936), vol. II.
Ruskin, J. *The Works of John Ruskin* ed. E. T. Cook and A. Wedderburn (39 vols., 1900–12), vols. XVI, XXVII–XXIX.
    Unto This Last ed. P. M. Yarker (1970).
    The Genius of John Ruskin: Selections from his Writings ed. J. D. Rosenburg (1963).
    Ruskin Today, ed. K. Clark (1965), ch. 5.
Shaw, G. B. *The Works of Bernard Shaw* (33 vols., 1930–8), vols. XX, XXX.
General selections also worth noting are:

Select booklist

Readings in the Development of Economic Analysis 1776–1848 ed. R. D. C. Black (Newton Abbot, 1971).
The Victorian Prophets, ed. P. Keating (Glasgow, 1979).

SECONDARY MATERIAL

General

Historical background

W. L. Burn, *The Age of Equipoise* (1964) and G. Kitson Clark *The Making of Victorian England* (1962), offer the most readable introductions to the period. E. J. Hobsbawm, *Industry and Empire: An Economic History of Britain since 1750* (1968), provides a general account of economic and social change, and S. G. Checkland, *The Rise of Industrial Society in England, 1815–1885* (1964), a more thorough treatment of the early Victorian era. See also, for brief introductions, the essays of B. Supple and C. Dyhouse in L. Lerner (ed.), *The Victorians* (1978). B. Inglis, *Poverty and the Industrial Revolution* (1971), though a little lightweight, provides a good overall survey. For studies of social and economic policy, consult D. Roberts, *Victorian Origins of the British Welfare State* (New Haven, Conn. 1960) and A. J. Taylor, *Laissez-Faire and State Intervention in Nineteenth-Century Britain* (1975).

Economic Thought

The classic study of changes in economic ideas is J. Schumpeter's, *History of Economic Analysis* (1954). Rather more digestible for the general reader would be R. Lekachman, *A History of Economic Ideas* (New York, 1959), or W. J. Barber, *A History of Economic Thought* (1967), which deals with the major thinkers from Smith onwards. A. O. Hirschman, *The Passions and the Interests* (Princeton, N.J. 1977), traces the intellectual development and legitimation of the concept of 'interests'. A. S. Skinner and T. Wilson (eds.), *Essays on Adam Smith* (Oxford 1976), a bicentennial celebration, offers a wide-ranging set of pieces. Though highly technical in parts, D. P. O'Brien, *The Classical Economists* (Oxford, 1975), evaluates the methodology and contrasting conclusions of the school. Most of the period of our edition is traced by D. Winch, *The Emergence of Economics as a Science 1750–1870* (1971), while early chapters of T. W. Hutchenson, *On Revolutions and Progress in Economic Knowledge* (Cambridge, 1978), offer a thought-provoking discussion of differing conceptions of economic reasoning. J. Viner, *The Long View and the Short: Studies in Economic Theory and Policy* (Glencoe, Ill., 1958), contains some classic essays on Smith, Bentham and J. S. Mill.

General and comparative studies

(Where it is not obvious, the specific authors covered in the work are indicated in parentheses at the end)
Ashton, R. *The German Idea: Four English Writers and the Reception of German Thought 1800–1860* (Cambridge, 1980) (Carlyle).

Select booklist

Barker, E. *Political Thought in England: From Spencer to the Present Day* (1915) (Green).

Beer, M. *A History of British Socialism* (2 vols. 1953).

Chandler, A. *A Dream of Order: The Medieval Idea in Nineteenth Century English Literature* (1970) (Carlyle, Ruskin, Morris).

De Laura, D. J. (ed.) *Victorian Prose, A Guide to Research* (New York, 1973).

Duncan, G. *Marx and Mill: Two Views of Social Conflict and Social Harmony* (Cambridge, 1973).

Freeden, M. *The New Liberalism: An Ideology of Social Reform* (Oxford, 1978) (Green, the Fabians).

Gray, A. *The Socialist Tradition: From Moses to Lenin* (1945).

Halevy, E. *The Growth of Philosophic Radicalism* (1952).

Himmelfarb, G. *Victorian Minds* (1968) (Mill).

Holloway, J. *The Victorian Sage: Studies in Argument* (1953). (Carlyle, Arnold).

Houghton, W. E. *The Victorian Frame of Mind 1830–1870* (New Haven, 1957).

Letwin, S. R. *The Pursuit of Certainty: David Hume, Jeremy Bentham, John Stuart Mill, Beatrice Webb* (Cambridge, 1965).

Levine, G. and Madden, W. (eds.) *The Art of Victorian Prose* (New York, 1968) (Carlyle, Mill, Arnold, Ruskin).

Lippincott, B. E. *Victorian Critics of Democracy* (1938; reprinted, 1964).

Neff. E. *Carlyle and Mill* (New York, 1926).

Pankhurst, R. K. *The Saint-Simonians, Mill and Carlyle* (1957).

Sussman, H. L. *Fact into Figure: Typology in Carlyle, Ruskin and the Pre-Raphaelite Brotherhood* (Columbus, Ohio, 1979).

Victorians and the Machine: The Literary Response to Technology (Cambridge, Mass., 1968).

Watson, G. *The English Ideology* (1973).

Williams, R. *Culture and Society 1780–1850* (1958).

Criticism of Individual Writers

This selection has been compiled as a guide to books and articles which have the authors' interest in political economy, or their style, as the dominant theme. Where possible, a reliable biographical source has also been cited.

Bray

There is no full-scale study of Bray. Further detail can be obtained from H. J. Carr, 'John Francis Bray', *Economica* 7 (1940) 397–415; J. Bellamy and J. Savile, *Dictionary of Labour Biography*, vol. III (1976), pp. 21–5; the introduction to J. F. Bray, *A Voyage from Utopia*, ed. M. F. Lloyd-Prichard (1957); and J. P. Henderson, 'An English Communist: Mr Bray and His Remarkable Work', *History of Political Economy* 17 (1985), 73–96. Marx's comments on Bray can be found in his *Poverty of Philosophy* (1954). On the Ricardian socialists generally, see E. K. Hunt, 'The Relation of the Ricardian Socialists to Ricardo and Marx', *Science and Society* 44 (1980), 177–98: J. E. King, 'Utopian or Scientific? A Reconsideration of the Ricardian Socialists', *History of*

Political Economy 15 (1983), 345–73; and N. W. Thompson, *The People's Science: The Popular Political Economy of Exploitation and Crisis 1816–1834* (Cambridge, 1984). Also useful for background is P. Hollis, *The Pauper Press: A Study in Working Class Radicalism of the 1830s* (Oxford, 1970). On the Owenite movement, see S. Pollard and J. Salt (eds.), *Robert Owen: Prophet of The Poor* (1971), and J. F. C. Harrison, *Owen and the Owenites in Britain and America* (1969).

Carlyle

G. C. Calder, *The Writing of 'Past and Present': A Study of Carlyle's Manuscripts*, Yale Studies in English, vol. 112 (New Haven, 1949), demonstrates how, though in part conceived as a 'tract for the times', the work still underwent the same painstaking revisions that characterised his other work. A. J. La Valley, *Carlyle and the Idea of the Modern* (New Haven, Conn. 1968) is a very informative, though quirky, general study which places Carlyle in the prophetic tradition. A political theorist, P. Rosenberg, attempts 'a synthetic recreation of a critique of Political Economy which is latent in the pages of *Past and Present*' in *The Seventh Hero: Thomas Carlyle and the Theory of Radical Activism* (Cambridge, Mass. 1974), ch. 8. G. R. Stange, 'Refractions of *Past and Present*', *Carlyle Past and Present: A Collection of New Essays*, eds. K. J. Fielding and R. L. Tarr (1976) includes an account of Engels' use of Carlyle, whilst J. Clubbe (ed.), *Carlyle and his Contemporaries: Essays in Honour of C. R. Sanders* (Durham, N.C., 1976) includes four pertinent articles: R. D. Altick, '*Past and Present*: Topicality as Technique' (a byproduct of his labours as editor); J. R. Edwards, 'Carlyle and the Fictions of Belief: *Sartor Resartus* to *Past and Present*' (useful on style and structure); K. J. Fielding, 'Carlyle and the Saint-Simonians (1830–1932): New Considerations'; and E. Spivey, 'Carlyle and the Logic-Choppers: J. S. Mill and Diderot'. The most recent biography is F. Kaplan, *Thomas Carlyle: A Biography* (Cambridge, 1983).

Engels and Marx

The fullest biography of Engels is W. O. Henderson, *The Life of Friedrich Engels* (2 vols., 1976), with good short studies by D. McLellan, *Engels* (Glasgow, 1977), and T. Carver, *Engels* (Oxford, 1981). The most recent general biography of Marx is D. McLellan, *Karl Marx: His Life and Thought* (1973). The precise intellectual relationship between the two is controversial. Apart from the above, consult N. Levine, *The Tragic Deception: Marx contra Engels* (Oxford and Santa Barbara, Ca. 1975), and G. Stedman Jones, 'Engels and the Genesis of Marxism', *New Left Review* 106 (1977), 79–104. In addition to works listed in the Economic Thought section above, detailed studies of the development of Marx's economic ideas may be found in M. Dobb, *Marx as an Economist* (1943), marred slightly by its age and association with the orthodox Communist party approach; A. Gamble and P. Walton, *From Alienation to Surplus Value* (1972); and B. Fine, *Marx's Capital* (1975). A structuralist account of the text is offered by L. Althusser and E. Balibar,

Select booklist

Reading Capital (1971). D. McLellan, *Marx Before Marxism* (1970), considers the period of intellectual development up to 1845. Whether Marx's mature social philosophy was still imbued with the humanistic philosophy of liberation derived from his youthful romanticism and Hegelianism, or replaced by a deterministic historical materialism, has been the main theme of modern Marxist scholarship. Written from the former viewpoint is S. Avineri, *The Social and Political Thought of Karl Marx* (Cambridge, 1968); from the latter viewpoint is G. Cohen, *Karl Marx's Theory of History, a Defence* (Oxford, 1978). Marxism and literary criticism have had an uneasy relationship. See, however, S. Marcus, *Engels, Manchester and the Working Class* (New York, 1974), for a literary approach to Engels's masterpiece; P. Demetz, *Marx, Engels and the Poets* (Chicago, 1967), on their status as literary critics; and S. S. Prawer, *Karl Marx and World Literature* (Oxford, 1976), on the way Marx deployed his reading of literature.

Mill

Still the most readable and wide-ranging introduction to Mill is J. M. Robson, *The Improvement of Mankind* (Toronto and London, 1968). A. Ryan, *J. S. Mill* (1974), is a good general study from a philosopher, while R. J. Halliday, *J. S. Mill* (1976), provides a thorough discussion of Mill's eclectic stance. Apart from the general works mentioned in our Economic Thought section, Mill's economic ideas are analysed in P. Schwartz, *The New Political Economy of J. S. Mill* (1968), and their impact discussed in N. B. deMarchi, 'The Success of Mill's *Principles*', *History of Political Economy* 6 (1974), 119–57. The fullest biography is that by M. St J. Packe, *The Life of John Stuart Mill* (1954).

Ruskin

Two earlier works by economists, J. A. Hobson, *John Ruskin, Social Reformer* (1898), and J. T. Fain, *Ruskin and the Economists* (1956) have been succeeded by a work more easily digestible by the layman: J. C. Sherburne, *John Ruskin or the Ambiguities of Abundance: a Study in Social and Economic Criticism* (Cambridge, Mass., 1972). *New Approaches to Ruskin: Thirteen Essays*, ed. R. Hewison (1981) contains two valuable essays on *Unto This Last*: A. Lee, 'Ruskin and Political Economy: *Unto This Last*'; and N. Shrimpton, 'Rust and Dust: Ruskin's Pivotal Work'. G. B. Shaw, *Ruskin's Politics* (1921) illuminates the author as much as his subject. D. Leon, *Ruskin the Great Victorian* (1949) continues to provide an interesting and detailed study whilst we await the second volume to T. Hilton, *John Ruskin: The Early Years, 1819–59* (New Haven, Conn. and London, 1985).

Arnold

Of particular interest is S. M. B. Coulling, 'The Evolution of Culture and Anarchy', *Studies in Philosophy* 60 (1963), 637–8; which should be read in conjunction with the editorial notes by R. H. Super to vol. v of *Complete*

Select booklist

Prose Works. P. J. McCarthy, *Matthew Arnold and the Three Classes* (New York and London, 1964) is helpful in reaching an understanding of Arnold's view of the state. An interesting comparison, slightly coloured by a prejudice in favour of Mill's position on liberty, is to be found in E. Alexander, *Matthew Arnold and John Stuart Mill* (1965). L. Trilling, *Matthew Arnold* (1939), continues to provide a helpful general study of his life and thought.

Green

A biographical essay was incorporated into vol. III of Green's collected works, and published separately in 1906: R. L. Nettleship, *A Memoir of T. H. Green.* The only full study of Green is the excellent work by M. Richter, *The Politics of Conscience: T. H. Green and his Age* (1964). A. J. M. Milne, *The Social Philosophy of English Idealism* (1962) provides a rather technical philosophical analysis of Green among others. I. M. Greengarten, *Thomas Hill Green and the Development of Liberal-Democratic Thought* (Toronto, 1981) is a short study of tensions in Green's conceptions of human nature, written from the standpoint of the Canadian Marxist school of C. B. Macpherson. C. Harvie, *The Lights of Liberalism: University Liberals and the Challenge of Democracy* (1976), and J. B. Schneewind, *Sidgwick's Ethics and Victorian Moral Philosophy* (Oxford, 1977), allow us to contrast Green's ideas with those of others among his contemporaries.

Morris

Much of the work on Morris is still bedevilled by partisan affection. The first volume of P. Meier, *William Morris: The Marxist Dreamer*, trans. F. Gubb (2 vols., Sussex and New Jersey, 1978), provides useful information on sources and influences, though the conclusions drawn are sometimes suspect. E. P. Thompson's early work, *William Morris: Romantic to Revolutionary* (1955, rev. ed 1977), was followed by a lecture, *The Communism of William Morris* (1959). Among more recent work, the following provide relevant commentary: J. Lindsay, *William Morris, His Life and Work* (1975), chs. 12–15 (a balanced account of his political involvement) and P. Faulkner, *Against the Age: An Introduction to William Morris* (1980).

Shaw

E. R. Bentley, *Bernard Shaw* (Norfolk, Conn., 1947), whose first chapter is devoted to Political Economy, inaugurated a line of books which recognised Shaw's political beliefs to be of central importance to his life and work. I. J. C. Brown, *Shaw In His Time* (1965), chs. 8 and 9; L. Hugo, *Bernard Shaw: Playwright and Preacher* (1971), ch. 1, and C. Wilson, *Bernard Shaw: A Re-assessment* (1969), ch. 3, are all in this tradition. From outside the discipline of literary criticism have appeared, T. A. Knowlton, *The Economic Theory of George Bernard Shaw* (Orono, Maine, 1936) and E. J. Hobsbawm, 'Bernard Shaw's Socialism', *Science and Society* II (1947), 305–26. R. Skidelsky, 'The Fabian Ethic', *The Genius of Shaw: A Symposium*, ed.

M. Holroyd (1979), provides a coffee-table account of the circle in which Shaw was involved. The standard general history of the Fabians is A. M. McBriar, *Fabian Socialism and English Politics 1884–1918* (Cambridge, 1962), while the more detailed study of the Society's origins, W. Wolfe, *From Radicalism to Socialism: Men and Ideas in the Formation of the Fabian Socialist Doctrines* (New Haven, Conn., and London, 1975), contains a good detailed account of Shaw's specific contributions.